THE FLEXIBILITY
OF THE
HOMERIC FORMULA

THE FLEXIBILITY
OF THE
HOMERIC FORMULA

J. B. HAINSWORTH

OXFORD
AT THE CLARENDON PRESS
1968

Oxford University Press, Ely House, London W. 1

GLASGOW NEW YORK TORONTO MELBOURNE WELLINGTON
CAPE TOWN SALISBURY IBADAN NAIROBI LUSAKA ADDIS ABABA
BOMBAY CALCUTTA MADRAS KARACHI LAHORE DACCA
KUALA LUMPUR HONG KONG TOKYO

PRINTED IN GREAT BRITAIN

PREFACE

THIS book has been written at a time when the doctrines of oral composition in the early Greek epic, which at least in the English-speaking world had achieved a nearly settled state, are again subject to controversy. My first intention had been no more than to correct an emphasis on certain structuralist standpoints which seemed mistaken. But it soon appeared that this must be prefaced by an appraisal of the reasoning that convinces me of the oral technique of Homer. The problem was to keep this in reasonable proportion without a retreat into dogmatism; and it may be that the desire to be brief has caused me to pass over published views that ought to have been discussed, though I hope their influence will be discernible. It has not been possible to take account of work published since 1966.

The substance of the book has been taken from material collected for a University of London thesis. In the metamorphosis of thesis into book the traces of the larval form are not easily eradicated; nor should they be, if the intrusions of the writer's labours are kept to defined and omissible sections. There are some questions even in literature which can only be answered by detailed study of the text. I know no other way by which mere impressions of 'more' and 'less' can be converted into the certainties which we need in order to describe the fundamental skills of Homer with more precision.

It would be impossible to mention all the friends and colleagues who, often without knowing it, spoke the word of encouragement when I most needed it, but I desire particularly to thank Professor R. P. Winnington-Ingram, Professor T. B. L. Webster, Sir Maurice Bowra, and Dr. A. Hoekstra. Without the practical encouragement of my wife the work could never have been finished. Lastly my thanks are due to the officials and readers of the Clarendon Press for their patience and courtesy.

J.B.H.

West Wickham, Kent
February 1968

CONTENTS

ABBREVIATIONS

ABBREVIATIONS of periodical publications are, I trust, standard, or at least self-explanatory. The following titles I quote often and curtail accordingly:

Bowra, *HP* C. M. Bowra, *Heroic Poetry*, London 1952.

Hoekstra, *MFP* A. Hoekstra, *Homeric Modifications of Formulaic Prototypes: Studies in the Development of Greek Epic Diction*, Amsterdam 1965.

Kirk, *SoH* G. S. Kirk, *The Songs of Homer*, Cambridge 1962.

Lord, *SoT* A. B. Lord, *The Singer of Tales*, Cambridge, Mass. 1960.

Page, *HHI* D. L. Page, *History and the Homeric Iliad*, Berkeley 1959.

Parry, *ET* M. Parry, *L'Épithète traditionnelle dans Homère*, Paris 1928.

I

COMPOSITION WITH FORMULAE

THE most prominent characteristic of the Homeric diction, the repeated lines and especially the repeated phrases, technically called 'formulae', is widely recognized to be indicative of a tradition of oral improvised poetry,[1] and it is towards the elucidation of this improvising skill, or of one aspect of it, that this study is devoted. I thus assume, since my scope does not permit me to argue, that improvisation, properly understood, was indeed a Homeric art. This opinion is of quite recent origin as Homeric scholarship goes, for the notion that metrically complex verse of Homer's quality could be improvised is obviously likely to arouse initial incredulity. Some of this resistance comes from the elasticity in normal usage of the sense of the term 'improvisation'. It is conceived too often in the narrowest sense and taken to mean the creation of phrases and sentences *ex nihilo*. This is too rigorous and would make the term useless in the study of epic literature. Here I use the term chiefly in contrast with recitation. Recitation implies not merely the learning of a poem or passage by heart but also the existence of a text, whether written or not, which would make it possible for the hearer both to know what words were coming and to convict the reciter of error for his deviations. In my view of the matter the content of an improvised performance might well be rehearsed, the outline of the story might be well known and defined, and many of the lines might have become quite stereotyped in the course of many performances, but it could never be possible to forecast the impro-

---

[1] The list of those who adhere to some form of this argument is now too long to be usefully quoted. The position is implicitly rejected, or not considered, by the adherents of the neo-analytical school, cf. G. Schoeck, *Ilias und Aithiopis*, Zürich 1961, 12 f., H. J. Mette, *Lustrum* i (1956) 14. L. A. Stella, *Il poema di Ulisse*, Florence 1955, uses the analogy of the ancient Near Eastern literatures. But those poems are less schematized than the Homeric and the nature of their own tradition far from certain. D. C. Young's rhetorical essay 'Was Homer an Illiterate Improviser?', *Minnesota Review* v (1965) 65–75, deserves wider publicity but is as extremist as the modern Parryists it castigates and hardly touches the essentials of Parry's position.

viser's words except in terms of strong probabilities, nor would it be sensible to count deviation from previous performances an error. An improvised performance might be good or bad, but the words employed could not be right or wrong.[1] Yet even with this concession it is clear that improvisation is a skill, and requires a technique.

As a central factor in Homeric studies the theory that the two epics derive immediately, or at a very short remove,[2] from an improvising technique of composition dates from the publication of papers in 1930 and 1932 by the American scholar, Milman Parry. These were boldly given the general heading of 'Studies in the Epic Technique of Oral Verse-making'.[3] As a base for this theory Parry had the result of his own researches into the behaviour of Homeric formulae and investigations which had made some contemporary preliterate poetry available for comparative study. Parry's internal analyses of Homeric diction were highly original, but the comparative material was an old, if until then ineffective, part of the Homeric Question.

The argument from the oral character of known heroic poems

---

[1] Cf. *SoT* 129, 137. Of course a poem that is improvised as a whole may contain recited components (or indeed vice versa). This may well be the case with Homer: it is a common assumption in discussions of the Catalogue: we may also reasonably call recitation the repeated lines that arise when messages are delivered or commands executed. But the 'typical scenes' (e.g. of arming and sacrificing) are a marginal and instructive case: I agree with J. I. Armstrong, 'The Arming Motif in the *Iliad*', *AJP* lxxix (1958) 337–54, that these are not ready-made packages. See further Hoekstra, *MFP* 18–20.

[2] The extant Homeric text cannot have begun its existence as a verbatim record of a normal oral performance, as such a recording would need modern apparatus. At best it may represent a dictated poem (which is not a normal performance) as suggested by A. B. Lord, 'Homer's Originality: Oral dictated Texts', *TAPA* lxxxiv (1953) 124–34 (now reprinted in *Language and Background of Homer*, ed. Kirk, Cambridge 1964, 68 ff.), and *SoT* 124 ff. G. P. Goold, *TAPA* xci (1960) 287 n. 36, has even named the amanuensis (Stasinus). I agree with Combellack, *CP* lvi (1961) 181, that this is not easy to imagine. Bowra at first thought of an oral poet who learned to write, *HP* 240–1, but has now modified his view, cf. *Companion to Homer*, ed. Wace and Stubbings, London 1962, 37. The function of the rhapsode remains crucial but unelucidated. J. A. Notopoulos, 'The Homeric Hymns as Oral Poetry', *AJP* lxxxiii (1962) 337–68, impressed by their reputation as interpolators, holds that rhapsodes were creative poets still. The contrary view, which seems least unsatisfactory, is urged by Kirk, 'Homer and Modern Oral Poetry: some Confusions', *CQ* x (1960) 271–81, (reprinted in *Language and Background of Homer*, 79 ff.), with astute use of Lord's Yugoslav materials. On the whole question see now A. Parry, 'Have we Homer's *Iliad*?', *Yale Classical Studies* xx (1966) 177–216.

[3] I. 'Homer and the Heroic Style', *HSCP* xli (1930) 73–147, and II. 'The Homeric Language as the Language of an Oral Poetry', *HSCP* xliii (1932) 1–50.

to the oral nature of the Homeric tradition is by analogy. But it is a mistake to suppose that this analogy is at the heart of the case for Homer's being an improviser. Historically the analogical argument was necessary before any conception of an oral Homer could be formed. Today it seems astonishing that a succession of scholars could have patiently analysed and classified the pecularities of the Homeric language and established beyond any doubt the influence of metre in the formation of the language without realizing why it was that metre could have such dominating influence. But analogy is not by itself a proof, useful though it may be as a signpost for the direction of argument, and without the strictest control the demonstration of resemblances may be no more than choosing a level of generality at which important differences vanish.[1] Logically, however, I do not believe that the analogy of modern oral epic is required at all in the Homeric argument. The facts of Homeric language and style, it seems to me, force the conclusion that the Homeric technique of composition is an oral technique. However, the shape of the argument is that the oral Homer is the only reasonable explanation of the facts of language and diction. The value of the comparative material is that it prepares the mind to recognize that this explanation is eminently reasonable. The truth of this cannot be seen better than in Parry's own case. In his French theses of 1928, *L'Épithète traditionnelle dans Homère* and *Les Formules et la métrique d'Homère*, Parry works like a typical Homeric scholar. He examines, analyses, and classifies, showing that a prominent part of the Homeric diction, the names of gods and heroes with their ornamental epithets, is elaborately schematized on certain principles. The conclusion is drawn that, since it was too elaborate to be the work of one mind, the schematized diction must be the product of a long tradition. But why should the tradition have this result? What sort of a tradition was it? There was no answer to these questions—they were scarcely even posed—until Parry became familiar with contemporary traditions.

The methodical observation of the language itself was not of

---

[1] Parry's words at *HSCP* xli (1930) 79, 'There is too little known about the making of the early poetry in hexameters for us to liken the Singers to the Serbian Guslars without more ado, or to make Homer a Singer like any other', have not always inspired the caution—or research—that they should. Most obviously the Homeric diction is much more highly schematised than that of the other poems in question, cf. Bowra, *HP* 236–40.

course original with Parry. Over sixty years earlier some German scholars had established that the choice of certain words and forms in Homer fluctuates with metre rather than with sense.[1] They would have established their case in the eyes of most contemporary scholars, but the trend of criticism in the 1870s was towards other things. The intimate connexion between language and metre did not become accepted until the effect was felt of the brilliant series of papers published by Kurt Witte in the years before 1914.[2] Witte firmly demonstrates two things: (1) the mixture of dialects that Homer displays does not correspond to any earlier or later strata in the poems. The use of the archaic and contemporary, Ionic and Aeolic, vernacular and poetic formations is governed by a single rule. Homer derives material from all these sources, without any distinctions of sense or effect, provided that the metrics of the formations are different: thus ἡμῖν but ἄμμι, -ου but -οιο, -σι but -εσσι, and -ειν but -μεναι. (2) The formations which are especially characteristic of Homer are regularly found only in certain parts of the verse. For example, the archaic genitive in -οιο is densest before the feminine caesura and at the verse-end, with the 5th foot a good third in popularity, but very rarely anywhere else: the infinitive in -έμεν is most common in the 4th foot.[3] The argument can be stated only in these quantitative terms, but the regularity of placing is so pronounced, and any other cause than the pressure of metre so improbable, that it can hardly be questioned. It is true that Witte went further to contend that *composita* were formed under metrical constraint for such positions as from caesura to diaeresis and diaeresis to verse-end, words like ἐΰ-σκοπος, -ξοος, -φρονα, -τριχα; ἀγκυλο-μήτης, -τοξος, -χείλης, etc. By itself the argument from word-formation is damaged by aesthetic complications. The *composita* may be thought attractive *per se*. Nor does the poet confine himself so decisively to one or two positions for using them, although his preferences are well marked.[4]

---

[1] J. E. Ellendt, *Drei homerische Abhandlungen*, i, Leipzig 1864; H. Düntzer, *Homerische Abhandlungen*, Leipzig 1872.

[2] Published in the first five numbers of *Glotta* (1909–14), and summarized in *R.E.* viii, coll. 2213 ff., s.v. Homer: 'Sprache'.

[3] Parry, *ET* 8, quotes some figures for -οιο from Boldt, *Programm Tauberbischofstein*, 1880–1, 5, viz. 1st foot 7×, 2nd foot 26×, 3rd foot 520×, 4th foot 17×, 5th foot 352×, and 6th foot 716×. Chantraine, *Gram. hom.* i. 490–1 lists the infinitives in -έμεν.

[4] Risch, *Wortbildung der homerischen Sprache*, 165 ff., lists the *composita* by type of

It is a merit of Witte's work that he permitted no historical preconceptions to influence his investigations. This was remarkable forbearance in the light of most Homerists' ambition to reconstruct the prehistory of the poems. However, it is a pity that he was not able to pose and answer the question: *why* is the epic use of language controlled by metre? No one, I believe, has answered this question outright, but this is hardly important now when Witte's work has been subsumed as part of Parry's theory of oral improvisation.

The part of Homeric diction that was the subject of Parry's studies was one that had intrigued scholars for many years, the numerous perpetual[1] epithets or adjectival phrases sported by gods, goddesses, heroes, and heroines, with little obvious relevance to the context in which they are used. The argument is fundamental to our comprehension of what improvised composition in the Greek epic tradition means, and I therefore propose to describe it at some length.[2] If, then, we take a number of these combinations of a personal name with an epithet or adjectival phrase and group them according to the amount of space that they occupy—it was this simple operation that Parry was the first to perform systematically—we speedily discover that some over-all shapes are strongly represented, others scarcely at all. Thus in the nominative case are:

I. Shape $\cup - \underset{\smile\smile}{} - \cup \cup - \underline{\cup}$:

βοὴν ἀγαθὸς Μενέλαος	βοῶπις πότνια Ἥρη
ἀρηΐφιλος Μενέλαος	θεὰ λευκώλενος Ἥρη,—etc.

formation. From a scrutiny of the lists it is clear that no reasonable shape is avoided. Witte's argument would be decisively strengthened if it were restated in terms of those *composita* 'of quasi-independent use' (*ET* 80–4), that is, generic epithets like δουρικλυτός or ἱπποδάμοιο, which have a fixed position but do not cohere with any particular noun. The shape of special epithets is, of course, conditioned by that of their nouns.

[1] Parry narrowed the field slightly, using the term 'ornamental', which he did not define sharply, cf. L. Bergson, *L'Épithète ornementale dans Éschyle, Sophocle et Euripide*, Lund 1956, 9–10. Much material is thereby excluded, cf. *ET* 47 n. 1, 111 n. 1, 119 n. 1.

[2] The following paragraphs to p. 13 abbreviate in my own terms and with my own emphasis the central argument of *ET*, especially chapters i and iii. For other versions see Hoekstra, *MFP* 9 ff., Kirk, *SoH* 59 ff., and M. W. M. Pope's stimulating paper, 'The Parry–Lord Theory of Homeric Composition', *Acta Classica* vi (1963) 1–21.

II. Shape ⌣⌣ – ⌣ ⌣ – ⌣:

πολύμητις 'Οδυσσεύς   λευκώλενος "Ηρη
πτολίπορθος 'Οδυσσεύς   κορυθαίολος "Εκτωρ—etc.

III. Shape – ⌣ ⌣ – ⌣:

δῖος Ἀχιλλεύς   φαίδιμος "Εκτωρ
ὠκὺς Ἀχιλλεύς   πότνια "Ηρη—etc.

On the other hand, phrases shaped ⌣ ⌣ – ⌣ ⌣ are extremely few, only four in both epics, μέγας Εὔρυτος, Ζέφυρος μέγας, Πρίαμος μέγας, Πρόθοος θοός, and we should be very hard-pressed to find any shaped ⌣ – – – ⌣ beyond Ἀπόλλων Φοῖβος and 'Οδυσσεὺς δῖος.

The situation that confronts us at this point is closely parallel to that discovered by Witte in his study of the compound epithets. The phrases of the popular shapes I, II, and III are of dimensions that slip immediately into parts of the verse bounded by the feminine caesura in the 3rd foot, the masculine caesura in the 4th foot, the bucolic diaeresis, and the verse-end. And with almost complete uniformity they are found in those positions. The only reasonable explanation of the popularity and location of these shapes is in terms of a response to the pressure exerted by the metre, for metre is the only factor with which they can be correlated.

One way by which the probability of a hypothesis can be increased is by showing that it can be used to clarify matters which were not considered in its formulation. Can we do this here? Looking at the longest shape (no. I) we can see that the poet is pushed not only into using ornamental epithets but also into using several at once, thus adding verbosity to irrelevance: βοῶπις πότνια "Ηρη, θεὰ λευκώλενος "Ηρη, to which add ποδάρκης δῖος Ἀχιλλεύς, μέγας κορυθαίολος "Εκτωρ. This is by no means his sole resource. For all of the needed shapes there are some names which are too short, such as Ζεύς, or too long, such as Ἀγαμέμνων or Διομήδης; and some essential personages have names that are intrinsically awkward in the hexameter, such as Ποσειδάων (⌣ – – –), or the three long syllables of 'Ερμείας.[1] A simple para-

_____

[1] The sole Ποσειδάων-formula is Ποσ. ἐνοσίχθων. Ἀλέξανδρος must be equally cramping, yet the alternant Πάρις does not enter into formulae: 'Ερμείας does not enter into verse-end formulae, but the *human* cretics Αἰνείας, Αὐγείας, Ἀγχίσης, borrow the title of Agamemnon, ἄναξ ἀνδρῶν, so do Εὐφήτης, Εὔμηλος (originally

phrase is sometimes used, e.g. πατὴρ ἀνδρῶν τε θεῶν τε (shape I) = Ζεύς, Ἀτρέος υἱός and Τυδέος υἱός (shape III) = Ἀγαμέμνων and Διομήδης. For divinities, but not for mortals, the poet can take a title or description and substantivize it, using it simply or with an additional epithet, e.g. Κυλλοποδίων or (περικλυτὸς) Ἀμφιγυήεις = Ἥφαιστος, (γαιήοχος) Ἐννοσίγαιος = Ποσειδάων. In the last (or at least rarest) resort he can make a change in the syntax of his sentence from the third to the second person and so introduce the vocative in place of the nominative case: thus Πατρόκλεες ἱππεῦ and Εὔμαιε συβῶτα, both with the verb προσέφης.

As yet the Homeric response to the pressure of metre may be only a matter of degree, for if Homer is full of ornamental epithets, the ornamental epithet, as Lucian satirically observed,[1] is irresistible to the desperate poetaster. However, the fact that we have begun to look at phrases instead of single words exposes a feature that goes well beyond this extension of Witte's original thesis. Some of the phrases listed above refer to the same personage, e.g. ἀρηΐφιλος and βοὴν ἀγαθὸς Μενέλαος, δῖος and ὠκὺς Ἀχιλλεύς. At first sight we should either take no notice of these duplications or applaud them as a virtue of style, for we expect our poets to be imaginative and we have been taught that variety is interesting and repetition dull. But these are *a priori* notions and alien to the method of argument. If a full list is collected, it will be seen that the duplicate formulae are not equivalent in metrics: the initial sounds are either vowel, consonant, or double consonant. Pairs of formulae with these slight but crucial differences are quite common, though it is clear that demand for the phrase with one initial consonant is heaviest. Precise metrical pairs, such as the two Hera-formulae of shape I are very unusual, at least in the nominative singular, and the duplicates are usually explicable as analogical creations or as special forms always embedded in more complex formulae.[2] Thus formulae may be

'Εὔ- doubtless), and, in the adaptation ἄναξ ἐνέρων, the immortal Ἀϊδωνεύς. The main trouble is the initial vowel of the name which rules out the O-stem adjectives.

[1] *Timon* 1, Ὦ Ζεῦ φίλιε καὶ ξένιε καὶ ἑταιρεῖε καὶ ἐφέστιε καὶ ἀστεροπητὰ καὶ ὅρκιε καὶ νεφεληγερέτα καὶ ἐρίγδουπε, καί εἴ τι σὲ ἄλλο οἱ ἐμβρόντητοι ποιηταὶ καλοῦσι, καὶ μάλιστα ὅταν ἀπορῶσι πρὸς τὰ μέτρα.

[2] Cf. *ET* 221 ff., where two classes of metrical equivalents are distinguished, (i) where the pressure of the verse has not yet brought about economy, and (ii) where analogy has caused over-production: so Bergson, *L'Épithète ornementale*, 24 ff. This is rigorous method. Kirk, *SoH* 64, reminds us that human skill is fallible and the creative urge not always responsive to systems.

sought out with much artifice, but only just enough are invented to meet the need. The poet is very economical of his creative or retentive effort.

Parry called a group of phrases, such as our groups I, II, and III a *formula-type*. This concept proved to be most important in the theory of Homeric improvisation that he eventually evolved. By definition a formula-type is constituted by the list of those expressions, both formulae and uniquely occurring phrases, which share a common metre, position, and syntax, and belong to the same semantic category, e.g. 'expressions for gods and heroes lying between the feminine caesura and the verse-end beginning with a consonant' (*ET* 67). At the moment I wish only to stress that the formula-types are found to possess two qualities which are the basis of Parry's whole theory, economy, with which we are already familiar, and extension. Extension consists simply in the large number of expressions that are collected into a given formula-type and the sharpness of contrast that this presents with the meagre totals in lists of phrases which have a shape not developed into a formula-type.

The formulae may also be arranged according to their essential sense instead of shape into what I shall call a *formula-system*,[1] e.g. the nominative series διογενὴς 'Οδυσεύς, 'Οδυσεὺς δουρικλυτός, πολύτλας δῖος 'Οδυσσεύς, πολύμητις 'Οδυσσεύς, δῖος 'Οδυσσεύς. The formula-system also exhibits the qualities of economy and extension.

The systems and types of formulae complement each other. It is easy to picture a grid with the members of systems arranged horizontally and the members of types vertically (cf. *ET* 50–1), and from such a grid it is clear that the systems and types of the more frequent nominative personal names are a remarkable insurance against any eventuality. The coverage has been reckoned at 88 per cent.[2] Too much importance should not be attached to the precise figure, for some of the gaps may be fortuitous. When 'Ολύμπιος εὐρύοπα Ζεύς and διογενὴς Πηλέος υἱός are found but

---

[1] Parry, e.g. *ET* 135, used 'système de formules' in this sense (and in looser senses). But the term 'formula-system' has become appropriated also to sets of expressions of the *same* shape in which one element is a constant and the other a variable.

[2] Kirk, *SoH* 64. Whether all the expressions are in fact pre-existent formulae is another matter. For some vigorous pruning see Pope, *Acta Classica* vi (1963) 10 ff.

once in the systems of very frequently occurring names it is easy to see that the absence of any comparably shaped expressions in the system of, say, Μελέαγρος is simply because the *Iliad* and *Odyssey* are not Calydonian epics. The probability of an underestimate of the poet's resources is thus always present. Indeed, so is the possibility of an overestimate, for we have produced no evidence as yet to show that a unique expression has any right to be thought traditional.

The organization of the diction into economical and extensive systems and types is peculiarly Homeric. Even Homeric imitators such as Apollonius and Virgil do not achieve it. It is important to understand that this is not a difference of degree. All poets, perhaps, have some formulae, but we are not about to argue that Homer's is a traditional diction because it is more formulaic than anyone else's. If we were to reason in this way, it is easy to see that there could be no agreement at what point a style became sufficiently formulaic to be called traditional. The difference between Homer and his classical successors is one of kind. Neither Apollonius nor Virgil shows any economy or extension in their limited collections of formulae. Their choice of words is made on entirely different principles.[1]

With such economy visible in the phraseology is it not pertinent to ask if the principle of economy is applicable to the epithets as well as the phrases, and if not, why not? At first sight it appears that the poet is far more prolix than he need be: πολύμητις, πόδας ὠκύς, and μεγάθυμος all have the same metre. Why maintain this superfluity if the sense is unimportant? The single term μεγάθυμος, the least specific of the three, would have satisfied all requirements in every case.[2] An obvious argument

---

[1] Since this paragraph is directly in conflict with G. E. Dimock's contentions ('From Homer to Novi Pazar and back', *Arion* ii (1963) 40–57, see p. 47), it will be well to point out that Dimock is speaking of Lord's theory of improvisation, not Parry's, and that for Homer Lord's theory cannot in my view supersede wholly that of Parry. See below pp. 18 ff.

[2] The single use with Achilles, Ψ 168, shows the suitability of μεγάθυμος. Parry assumed, *ET* 64, that μεγάθυμος fell within the law of economy because it began with the equivalent of two consonants, but this is not needed at Ψ 168, nor does the poet allow the fact to affect his use of μεγάθυμος in this type of formula. In my view μεγάθυμος Ἀχιλλεύς is a created expression not a traditional one, created, as G. Beck explains, *Die Stellung des 24. Buches der Ilias in der alten Epentradition*, 40 n. 2, to avoid the assonance πόδας ὠκὺς Ἀχιλλεὺς | ἐς πόδας ἐκ κεφαλῆς: a painful reminder that work upon epithets is done with concordances and that concordances quote only one line.

would be that economy is only one of several desiderata, and that, desirable as it is, there must be a point at which economy results in an intolerable monotony. However, no two scholars would agree when this point was reached. But there is no need to use this subjective argument. If the formulae are examined, it is apparent that the epithets fall into two classes. Some are used exclusively with one character, others qualify any of the whole range of heroic personal names indiscriminately. Parry called the first group *special epithets*, the second *generic epithets*, because they were used of any members of the whole class of heroes (or heroines or gods, as the case may be). The personages distinguished by their own special epithets are either divine or, with some few exceptions, are major characters in the story. We do not know the origins of these epithets, which are doubtless diverse, but within the context of the poet's technique it is a simple matter to assume that a hero of the stature of Achilles or Odysseus is *sui generis*, and so merits his own honorific. The gods likewise have their own defined characteristics and spheres of action. Not all the epithets of these distinguished personages are of the special class. The shorter formulae especially have to fall back on generic epithets, e.g. δῖος and ἐσθλὸς Ὀδυσσεύς, and δῖος Ἀχιλλεύς, but because the word for 'swift' is available, ὠκὺς Ἀχιλλεύς. The special epithets are mostly composita, and a simplex of suitable sense, which is what the shorter formula needs, may not be available to comply with the requirements.

The system of generic epithets is an indispensable part of the poet's technique. The list of those used of two heroes or more totals forty-seven in the nominative case.[1] By calling on an epithet of the appropriate shape the poet can fit almost any personal name into any formula-type. The systems of generic epithets usually furnish a term, provided that the morphology of Greek permits it, adapted both to the final sound of the preceding word and to the initial sound of the following word. It would thus be perfectly possible for the poet to invent an entirely novel character (I do not say that he did) and use his name with as much dexterity as that of the most traditional hero in the epic. So useful an apparatus is worth a closer glance, and again upon investigation the twin principles of economy and extension are apparent.

In the nominative case the system for filling the space between

---

[1] Listed at *ET* Tableau III facing p. 112.

diaeresis and verse-end is as follows: δῖος ∪ – ⏕, φαίδιμος – –, – ∪
ἀμύμων, – ∪ ∪ ἥρως. The first pair is furnished with vocalic alternants: ἐσθλός ∪ – ⏕ and ἄλκιμος – –.[1] Of course, if the name is
the first element of the phrase the poet cannot adapt the expression in this way, except in so far as the names of very minor
personages might be interchangeable in the story. Thus far the
working of the generic system is parallel to the changes of special
epithets, but an efficient system of generic epithets would also
cope with differences in the initial and final sounds of the personal names themselves. In the system discussed the final sound
of the name would matter only in the rhythms – ∪ and – ∪ ∪.
However, the need does not arise: masculine names do not ter-
minate in an open vowel in the nominative, so that ἀμύμων and
ἥρως do not have to be paired with another epithet. (In other
places they are paired with δαΐφρων and κρείων.) This will seem
a convenient accident until it is realized that the same rule
applies to adjectives as well as to nouns. How then can ∪ – ⏕
or – – names be fitted in if they have an initial consonant (– ∪
will, of course, combine with ἀμύμων)? Names such as Νέστωρ,
Πηλεύς, Τυδεύς, etc. (the list includes some venerable and indispensable figures) use ἱππότα, originally a vocative formation.
This is a licence. There is no corresponding term with an initial
consonant. The problem was apparently desperate in the case of
the ∪ – ⏕ name. There can be no adjective shaped – ∪ with an
open short final in the nominative singular masculine, and nothing
that will pass for one. This lack, and the lack of monosyllabic
adjectives, means that masculine names longer than ∪ – ⏕ cannot
enter into this system.[2]

The systems that accommodate such longer names offer a
further refinement. For a name scanned ∪ ∪ – ⏕ means that the
last syllable of the epithet provides the arsis of the 5th foot so as
to give an over-all shape ⏕ – ∪ ∪ – ⏕ or ∪ – ⏕ – ∪ ∪ – ⏕. Now
a name with a vocalic initial such as Ἀγαπήνωρ requires that
syllable to be long by nature: so we have the epithets κρείων and
γέρων ἥρως or ἄναξ ἀνδρῶν. These same epithets would serve in
principle also for a name such as Πολυποίτης with a consonantal

---

[1] ἐσθλός is used only of Ὀδυσσεύς among names, but occurs also with ἑταῖρος.
Page, HHI 269, pairs φαίδιμος with ὄβριμος. But of mortals only Ἕκτωρ has ὄβριμος
in nom. sing. I take it to be the weightier honorific (with Ἄρης 4×). ἄλκιμος, besides
Αἴας, qualifies υἱός and cases of ἀνήρ.

[2] Certain feminine names can use δῖα with elision: δῖ᾽ Ἀφροδίτη, δῖ᾽ Ἄντεια.

initial, but at the cost of a surallongement. The heavy rhythm is lightened if an epithet such as κρατερός or μενεπτόλεμος is used where the final syllable needs the following consonant to give positional lengthening. This subtlety operates only inside the expression. It was seemingly not worth while to seek out pairs of epithets for the sake of evading surallongement outside the expression, e.g. in the arsis of the fourth foot in the case of the ⏖ – ∪ ∪ – ⏑ type. In fact the chief anxiety of the poet here is to ensure that the 4th foot arsis actually is long. Most of the generic epithets designed to fall in the second half of the 4th foot have two consonants initially (θρασύς, κλυτός, κρατερός, κρείων, ξανθός) without any alternant having only a single consonant.[1]

Counting all grammatical cases the generic epithets number sixty-one, against forty characters distinguished by special epithets.[2] Taking the two sorts of epithet-phrases together we are in the presence of a technique of verse-making of remarkable efficiency.[3] This is not stressed in *ET*, where the immediate purpose is somewhat different, namely to make historical inferences about the epithets. The question is there put: can these systems be the work of one man? Later poets do not achieve a diction refined on these lines and to this extent, not even those poets such as Apollonius and Virgil who are confessedly imitators of the Homeric manner. Therefore the answer is returned that this part of the diction at least is traditional, the work of several generations of poets. This conclusion is unavoidable and there is no need to overstate it. My belief is that Parry was not justified even at this point in asserting that all signs of creativity are negligible[4] and in glossing over unique combinations of name and special epithet as the victims of inadequate representation.[5]

---

[1] Cf. *ET* 65, and my remarks below pp. 26 f.   [2] *ET* 111, 113.

[3] Parry's relative neglect of evolutionary matters obscures here an important point. Though the epithet-systems seem to me proved, it is necessary to state that *Iliad* and *Odyssey* present them with very variable degrees of vitality: δῖος is a central term, but φαίδιμος (and ὄβριμος) are clearly archaistic. The most novel-looking names in fact, e.g. the Suitors Ἀμφίνομος, Ἀντίνοος, Εὐρύμαχος, etc. do not enter the traditional systems at all.

[4] 'On pourrait peut-être lui en (i.e. des formules) concéder quelques-unes', *ET* 21, is as far as Parry will go towards allowing absolute originality in expression; cf. *ET* 103, 'Des traces d'une certaine originalité existent, *peut-être*: mais c'est une originalité qui ne fait que réarranger sans modifications importantes les mots et les expressions de la tradition', and *HSCP* xli (1930) 137–8.

[5] Parry's position, *ET* 55, is that low frequency proves nothing but infrequent need and therefore cannot counterbalance the evidence of membership in a

The conclusion of the argument should read that the sentence-patterns and some (or most) of the name–epithet expressions are traditional. That is the limit of the proof. Finally it will be well to remind ourselves also of the limits of the evidence. First, the personal names in the nominative case are a convenient group owing to their frequency. In the oblique cases there are many more gaps in the structure, and in the systems of common nouns extension and economy of an impressive extent can be proved for only a relatively small number of words.[1] To assert that the whole of Homer is formulaic and traditional is to rely on the untrustworthy aid of an analogy.[2] Unfortunately Parry was later eager to make this deduction, and his followers have been many. Second, we have considered only decorative epithets, thus leaving the argument as a theory of verse-making incomplete. How does the poet handle functional words?[3] Third, except to explain away what we take to be anomalies, we have paid little attention to the interaction of the formulae with each other or to the immediate sources of the poet's vocabulary.

The big advance made in 1930 was the result of an external stimulus, the analogy of modern oral poetry.[4] Parry dared to proclaim for the first time in his published work that the motive for the schematization of the diction was the desire to improvise the verses of an orally composed epic. The evidence of *ET* was neither changed nor enlarged, nor did it need to be. The formula-types and systems are clearly an instrument for verse-making perfected under strong metrical pressure, pressure so strong that only the case of improvisation could account for it. For in what

---

formula-type. But the poet's need is not further analysed: no one is surprised at a unique expression for an incidental personage, but a unique expression in a common shape for a major god or hero is contrary to expectation. If the tradition really provided, say, κλυτότοξος Ἀπόλλων and χρυσήνιος Ἄρης, why does the poet so neglect them?

[1] Parry worked out the system for some place-names and ethnics, and for 'ship', 'horses', 'mankind', and 'shield', *ET* 121 ff. Miss D. H. F. Gray, *CQ* xli (1947) 109 ff. (= *Language and Background of Homer*, 55 ff.), examines 'sea', 'shield', and 'helmet', and Page, *HHI* 266 ff., 'sea', 'wine', 'shield', 'spear', 'sword', 'bow and arrows', and various ethnics.

[2] This is recognized at *ET* 25, cf. 131, but is brushed aside from the first of the *HSCP* articles.

[3] This point was put by Chantraine, *R. de Ph.* iii (1929) 299, the acutest as well as the most sympathetic of *ET*'s reviewers.

[4] *HSCP* xli (1930) 77–80: N.B. it is only in these few pages that Parry felt it appropriate to use the analogical argument.

other circumstances do you need to defend yourself with such precaution against the possibility of breakdown? I need hardly add that this is in perfect accord with all that the early epic itself says about ἀοιδή, the art of poetry. It is corroborated by the presence of certain special features in the epics, agglomerations, haplologies, and aural echoes,[1] which are best explicable in terms of an *oral* improvising technique.

Parry saw that his concept of the formula-type might provide a bridge between the principal elements of improvised verse recognized at that date, i.e. the formulae and the stylized patterns of phrase, sentence, and stanza composition. This is nothing less than a theory of improvisation. The criteria on which a formula-type is set up include those of common meaning and related syntax, and it therefore follows that a formula-type is nothing but an incomplete statement of a pattern on which sentences are constructed. The statement Parry usually completes in his discussion of each formula-type. Thus it is pointed out (*ET* 64–7) that the noun-epithet formulae for gods and heroes in the nominative case between the 4th foot caesura and the verse-end are preceded by:

(a) the verbs προσέφη or μετέφη with a predicate filling the first half of the verse;

(b) the connective ἀτάρ;

(c) a preposition and connective, e.g. μετὰ δέ, παρὰ δέ;

(d) iambic or anapaestic verbs, e.g. βάλε̄, ἕλε̄, ἀπέβη;

If at this point we are willing to grant, as Parry demands, that the whole Homeric diction, predicates as well as subjects, is formulaic, it is easy to see that the addition of a number of regular sentence-patterns to the poet's equipment means that creative activity can be almost completely eliminated. Improvisation was

---

[1] Agglomeration: C. J. Ruijgh, *L'Élément achéen dans la langue épique*, Assen 1957, 21, 57; haplologies: Hainsworth, *CR* xiv (1964) 127–9, with retort from M. L. West, *CR* xv (1965) 139–42; aural echoes: *ET* 90 ff. and *HSCP* xli (1930) 140 ff. L. Ph. Rank, *Etymologiseering en verwante verschijnselen bij Homerus*, Assen 1951, 28 ff., has some interesting notes on assonance. If allowed, these corroborations may counter Hoekstra's observation, *MFP* 17, that Homer may still be literate, since a literate poet may adopt, though he cannot create, a formulaic diction. The presence of inconsistences (neatly dealt with by Kirk, *SoH* 212 ff.) are most readily accounted for by oral composition without directly suggesting it. Glosses, cf. Parry, 'The Homeric Gloss', *TAPA* lix (1928) 233–47, prove in themselves only that the diction is traditional.

seen as the arrangement of data, and it was not considered per-
missible to improvise the parts any more than one is allowed to
carve one's own pieces in building a jigsaw puzzle.[1] In Parry's
own words: 'In composing he (i.e. the oral poet) will do no
more than put together for his needs phrases which he has often
heard or used himself, and which, grouping themselves in accor-
dance with a fixed pattern of thought, come naturally to make
the sentence and the verse.'[2]

With a carefully chosen example this equipment can seem deva-
statingly adequate. Consider the sentence pattern 'X—προσέφη
—Y', a favourite for this purpose, where X represents a prono-
minal object with connecting particle and a nominative participle
and Y represents a noun–epithet formula as subject extending
from the fourth foot caesura to the verse-end, e.g.

$$\left.\begin{array}{l} τὸν\ δ'\ ἀπαμειβόμενος \\ τὸν\ δ'\ ἄρ'\ ὑπόδρα\ ἰδὼν \\ τὸν\ δὲ\ μέγ'\ ὀχθήσας \end{array}\right\} προσέφη \left\{\begin{array}{l} νεφεληγερέτα\ Ζεύς \\ κορυθαίολος\ "Εκτωρ \\ ξανθὸς\ Μενέλαος \end{array}\right.$$

In the *Iliad* and *Odyssey* there are twenty-two values for X (including one or two strictly analogous phrases) and twenty-one
for Y used in this structure alone, so that in principle these formulae alone and this sentence-pattern provide the material for
462 verses. Add to this that there are many anapaestic or spondaic
verbs which might replace προσέφη in the structure and many
more values for X and Y, and it is easy to persuade oneself that
one is well on the way to composing the 15,000 verses of a major
epic. In fact, what we should have are several hundred introductions to speeches, most of which we should not require, and some
analogous verses.

It is easy to speak of sentence-patterns in the plural, but the
fact is that since *ET* little work has been done on this twin
foundation of the oral style in Homer. We have no idea how many
sentence-patterns are present,[3] whether they too are econo-

---

[1] To adapt Van Gennep's metaphor, *La Question d'Homère*, Paris 1909, 52, 'Les
poésies des guslars sont une juxtaposition des clichés. . . . Un bon guslar est celui
qui joue de ces clichés comme nous avec des cartes, qui les ordonne diversement
suivant le parti qu'il veut tirer.'

[2] *HSCP* xli (1930) 77, cf. *HSCP* xliii (1932) 7.

[3] At *HSCP* xli (1930) 126 it is stated that the sentence-patterns are 'very many'.
This may be so, but it is dangerous ground. For if the patterns are not limited in
number the structure of the diction will be no different from that of other hexameter poetry, and so of no aid towards improvisation.

mically reduced to the necessary minimum, whether they respond as sensitively to the metre as does the diction, or indeed whether they extensively apply to other parts of the diction than personal names in the nominative. In fact since *HSCP* xli the sentence-pattern has until very recently quietly sunk out of sight. No recent writer concedes it a separate heading: all hasten from formula to theme, and from theme to the whole poem.[1] Parry himself began this neglect, for as soon as the Homeric text was compared with the model of improvisation a more glaring discrepancy forced itself on the attention. The content was *not* all formulaic, as formulaic had been defined, i.e. as a verbal repetition. This was felt to be serious, more serious than it really is, for two reasons. It was believed *a priori* that the formula was a *necessary* condition for successful improvisation[2] and Parry had begun to slip more and more into a quantitative sort of argument, claiming that Homer is oral poetry because it is more formulaic and more schematized than later poems.[3] So some attempt must be made to count the unique expressions as formulae with a show of reason. If the expression falls into a normal formula-type one argues from the regular pattern to the regular content.[4] But this will not take care of many phrases, chiefly because formula-types of the sort found among personal names are not demonstrable in quantity elsewhere. Many new 'formulae' will be uncovered, however, if we tacitly change the sense of 'formula' from a repetition of words to a repetition of structure, so that a formula becomes any expression constructed according to a regular phrase pattern. For Parry this meant counting as a formula any expression that shared a common term with a regular formula:

[1] 'Theme' means a regularly used group of ideas, cf. Lord, 'Composition by theme in Homer and Southslavic Epos', *TAPA* lxxxii (1951) 71–80. For its function see Lord, *SoT* 68 ff. A theme does not require verbal repetition, though this may occur giving the so-called 'typical scenes' exhaustively studied for Homer by W. Arend, *Die typischen Scenen bei Homer*, Problemata 7, Berlin 1933. A poem, in so far as it is a repeated poem, is a regularly used group of themes, *SoT* 99 ff.

[2] This seems to have been the view of the comparativists known to Parry, who also was unduly impressed by Meillet's dictum, 'L'épopée homérique est toute faite de formules que se transmettaient les poètes', *Les origines indo-européennes des mètres grecs*, Paris 1923, 61, cf. *ET* 10 and the quotation from Parry's field-notes given at *SoT* 11–12.

[3] e.g. at *HSCP* xli (1930) 74, 87, 132.

[4] *HSCP* xli (1930) 122, 'It is the nature of an expression that makes of it a formula'. Contrast the deliberate caution at *ET* 55 where Parry was not under pressure to prove so much.

thus ἄλγε' ἔθηκε, κῦδος ἔθηκε, τεύχε' ἔθηκε, and εὖνιν ἔθηκε are all grouped together.[1] I have examined this procedure elsewhere, for I do not entirely concur with it.[2] Yet it does provide an element of control in that it insists on the common term, and such control is imperative in a sound method of study. However, in a more speculative mood Parry professed to find a similarity between τεῦχε κύνεσσιν (A 4) and δῶκεν ἑταίρῳ (P 698), in that both combine an aorist verb with an indirect object to give the rhythm – ∪ ∪ – ⌣.[3] Nevertheless he shrank from attributing formulaic status to τεῦχε κύνεσσιν on these grounds. Inevitably, later scholars have been less reticent.[4] Yet even with these auxiliary aids it is far from clear that *all* Homer is made up of regular formulae deployed in a regular way. In the published analyses about one-tenth of the *lines* are without any demonstrably formulaic element. No refinements of method have yet been devised comprehensive enough to catch every phrase.

A parallel erosion has meanwhile eaten away the strictness of the old formula-type. The common syntax is no longer insisted on when we are asked to group together γιγνώσκω σε, θεά E 815 and μῆνιν ἄειδε, θεά A 1.[5] Certainly these are the same length and (ignoring word length and order) similarly constructed, but they require quite different complements. Different syntax is required also when noun–epithet formulae are in a different grammatical case. For comparison no more is now required than that the expressions be of the same over-all shape and embody some terms of the same grammatical class. But what reason have we for assuming that the poet would, or could, associate such expressions? By using these lax criteria we can mark very many more phrases as formulae in our charts: in fact we can mark far too many. It is impossible to conceive of a line most of which we

---

[1] *HSCP* xli (1930) 128. Under the term 'formula-system' this procedure is now general among American Parryists.

[2] 'Structure and Content in Epic Formulae: the Question of the Unique Expression', *CQ* xiv (1964) 155–64. See also W. W. Minton, 'The Fallacy of the Structural Formula', *TAPA* xcvi (1965) 241–53.   [3] *HSCP* xli (1930) 133.

[4] Especially bold is J. A. Notopoulos in his series of papers on non-Homeric early epic: 'Homer, Hesiod, and the Achaean Heritage of Oral Poetry', *Hesperia* xxix (1960) 177–97; 'The Homeric Hymns as Oral Poetry', *AJP* lxxxiii (1962) 337–68; and 'Studies in Early Greek Oral Poetry', *HSCP* lxviii (1964) 1–77.

[5] J. A. Russo, 'A Closer Look at Homeric Formulas', *TAPA* xciv (1963) 235–47, would separate these, but on the grounds that μῆνιν ἄειδε fails to conform to localization tendencies. (One would expect it at the verse-end.) Otherwise Russo's position is the same as that of Lord and Notopoulos.

should not have to count formulaic, no matter what its origin was known to be. In this way the term formula becomes vacuous and so useless for the construction of an illuminating picture of the poet's art.

Parry himself seems to have believed that even his looser criteria usually detected real formulae, that is, pre-existent phrases that chanced to appear but once. This belief, along with the rest of 'hard Parryism'[1] has not stood up well against the results of comparative studies, and A. B. Lord has satisfactorily demonstrated its implausibility. The unique but formula-like phrase is a creation of the individual bard, yet not a complete novelty. A quotation will explain the matter: 'A study of sung texts indicates considerable formula deviation. We know now that creation and re-creation occur on the formula level much more actively than Parry thought. Each singer has a group of formulae which forms the basis of his style. These change but seldom; on them he patterns others.'[2] For the derivative phrases Lord uses the term 'formulaic expression'.[3] The mode of derivation, as explained in *Singer of Tales*, turns out to be the substitution of variables within a common frame, as before.[4] Creation and re-creation are South Slavic contributions to the theory of improvisation, but it is clear that they are applicable to parts of the Homeric diction. The whole usage of the generic epithet can be viewed in this light with advantage. A minor gain is that the qualms caused by occasional breaches of economy are soothed. For the poet might, by a venial human error, exercise his creative skill where there was no call for it. The principal gain, it is supposed, is that an ingenious suppleness replaces the repellent rigidity of Parry's first model. It is this generative technique that Lord and others have in mind when they speak of the flexibility of the formulaic technique or the internal flexibility of the formula. However, we must be careful that this improvement does not explain too much. The Homeric generic epithet system is a special kind of phrase pattern which shows its intimate connexion

---

[1] The phrase is that of T. C. Rosenmeyer: see his paper 'The Formula in Early Greek Poetry', *Arion* iv (1965) 295–311, for a useful critique of the methodologies pursued by Parry and his successors.

[2] *TAPA* lxxxiv (1953) 127.

[3] *SoT* 4. The term does not seem to me very happy, as being virtually tautologous with 'formula'. Notopoulos's term is 'formula by analogy'.

[4] See notes to the chart, *SoT* 291–3.

with metre in other ways than merely possessing a shape that coincides with a natural portion of the hexameter. On the other hand, to group together σκῆπτρον, τεύχε', and αἰγίδ' with ἔχων as an interrelated set of phrases does not seem to be so useful or illuminating. Patterning of this sort is a necessary part of *le langage*, or at least of hexameter language, and does not in itself prove anything about Homer.[1] It could be made to prove something if it were shown that the patterning has restrictions beyond those that are naturally imposed by the hexameter: if we could say, as we can say of the decorative epithets, that Homer uses these and those many times but *never any others*. This negative side of the original Parry and Witte arguments has never been investigated.[2]

As it is, we are offered a poetical diction which differs from *prosa oratio* only in having special rules, mostly metrical, over and above those of normal speech. There is indeed no reason why the additional rules should not be mastered by singers in the same way as the additional rules of rhetoric are mastered by orators. It is possible that some singers, in some traditions, operate in this fashion.[3] In that event we should likely have trouble in separating the products of oral and literary composition, unless the difficulty of the verse put special constraints upon the improviser, leading him to give an excessive preference to certain patterns.[4] Happily the Homerist is spared this embarrassment. There is no real basis at this point for analogical reasoning from modern traditions to the Homeric. In Homer it must be obvious that besides whatever phrase-patterns we admit the core of regular formulae is very large, so large that it cannot be eliminated as one of the most potent instruments of the poetical technique.

The construction or recollection of the appropriate phrase by no means ends the improviser's toil. The phrase must then enter the sentence. To ease the task the regular sentence-pattern, not always and indeed not necessarily distinguished from the phrase-pattern, has been described. There can be no doubt that this is

---

[1] This is excellently put by Pope, *Acta Classica* vi (1964) 16–17.

[2] Parry himself was aware of the need for this, *HSCP* xli (1930) 89. Russo, 'The Structural Formula in Homeric Verse', *Yale Classical Studies* xx (1966) 219–40, observes (p. 226) that 'extent and economy would be extremely difficult to measure', and then concentrates on a purely quantitative argument.

[3] This is Lord's view of the South Slavic tradition, *SoT* 35–6.

[4] Pointed out by G. E. Dimock, *Arion* ii (1963) 47–9.

a portion of the Homeric art where the explanations will not be simple. Without dwelling on the innate complexity of the material, the question must be met of the relation between the regularities in sense and the rhythmical regularities described by the colometry of the hexameter. If one accepts the Fränkel–Porter thesis of a verse falling into four cola,[1] it is possible to postpone the question at the formula level, because the relation between colon and formula is so obscure that as an element in composition it may well be irrelevant. Some cola, e.g. $- \cup$ before the 'A' caesura and $\cup -$ before the 'C' caesura, are too short to hold any formulae, and some formulae are too long to fall into any single colon. This does not mean that Fränkel's view of the colon as a sense-unit is flatly contradicted by formulae which are also sense-units, but it must be qualified.[2] Porter's opinion that the colon is a rhythmical unit having a normative effect on the shape and length of sense-units within the verse is persuasive, but requires only that certain formula-types are favoured in certain positions without being inadmissible elsewhere. This, as it will appear, is precisely what happens. However, whatever form and nature of colometry we accept, if it has effect on sense division at all, this must appear somewhere in the sentence. Is then the relation between sense-structure and verse-structure regularized and exploited? On the one hand a limited number of sentence-patterns in Homer are used with impressive frequency and must be accepted as part of the poet's technical equipment.[3] Yet I am doubtful if we can progress much further than these simple quantitative observations. On the other hand the Homeric verse is more variable, that is, has more patterns of word arrangement, than the literary hexameter of later times.[4] There is also a striking

---

[1] H. Fränkel, 'Der kallimachische und der homerische Hexameter', *NGG* (Phil.-hist. Kl.) 1926, 197–229, and *Wege und Formen frühgriechischen Denkens*[2], Munich 1960, 100–56; modified in detail by H. N. Porter, 'The Early Greek Hexameter', *Yale Classical Studies* xii (1951) 3–63; and further modified, to the point of refutation, by Kirk, 'The Structure of the Homeric Hexameter', *Yale Classical Studies* xx (1966) 76–104.

[2] I cannot believe Fränkel's suggestion (*Wege u. Formen*, 107 n. 4) that colometry is such that φάρμακον ἐσθλὸν ὅ τοι δώσω, κ 292, and ἄνδρα γέροντα δύῃ ἀρημένον σ 53 have a sense boundary between noun and adjective.

[3] Several of the patterns listed by Russo, *Yale Classical Studies* xx (1966) 236–40, are partial statements of sentence-patterns rather than phrase-patterns.

[4] Increasing rigidity in the localization of words—E. G. O'Neill, Jr., *Yale Classical Studies* viii (1942) 117 with Table XXX: in the placing of caesuras—Porter, *Yale Classical Studies* xii (1951) 19 and 34.

contrast between the care lavished on the inner metrics of the formulae and the indulgence extended to metrical faults at their junctures with other words or formulae.[1] Thus it seems that the ordering of their phrases, once these had been created or brought to mind, was not in practice the most exacting task confronting the poets of the Greek epic.

I have therefore turned again to the core of indisputable formulae in the Homeric tradition from which attention has been diverted in the search for means to improve the quantitative arguments for the oral character of early Greek epic. It is more than twenty years since Severyns's neat survey of the Homeric technique[2] mentioned such points as the mutability in length of basic formulae, their mobility within the verse, and their expansion. Yet we do not know how much of this sort of flexibility is present, nor how it arises, nor how to integrate it into our theory of Homeric improvisation. The current practice is to make no integration at all, but to label the adapted phrase anti-traditional or anomalous.

A modern analogy can furnish a suggestion. Of several modern traditions it has been said: 'Though this poetry abounds in formulae it is hardly ever entirely formulaic'.[3] In such cases the use of the formula cannot be to supply the fragmented pieces of the whole poem but can only be an auxiliary aid. It holds up the pace of the narrative so that the poet is able from time to time to think slightly ahead or to rest momentarily while familiar words are enunciated. Since the value of such formulae is entirely their familiarity, there is no absolute need for them to be fixed in shape and place if they are to perform their function. The Homeric technique is far more schematized than most of its modern counterparts, but this is a matter of degree. The dactylic hexameter is by any standards no easy metre, and in comparison with some modern lines almost intractable. The greater range and

---

[1] Strikingly in the frequent failure to ensure the quantity of word-final syllables, cf. *Les Formules*, 6 ff., and most recently A. G. Tsopanakis, 'Problems in the Homeric Hexameter', Ἀριστοτέλειον Πανεπιστήμιον Θεσσαλονίκης, 'Επιστημονικὴ 'Επετηρὶς Φιλοσοφικῆς Σχολῆς ix (1966) 337–74.

[2] A. Severyns, *Homère II: le poète et son œuvre*, Bruxelles 1946, 49–61, cf. J. Labarbe, *L'Homère de Platon*, Liège 1949, 16–19.

[3] Bowra, *HP* 230, of the Russian, Jugoslav, Kirghiz, Kalmuck, and Yakut traditions. For Bowra a formula is a 'set of words which is used, with little or no change, whenever the situation with which it deals occurs', *HP* 222.

organization of the Homeric formulae are the response to the greater difficulty of improvising in hexameters, and the freedom and flexibility which they still display far from being anomalies, are perhaps a glimpse of a more basic technique about which it would be useful for Homerists to know more.

II

PERSONAL NAME FORMULAE:
SOME IRREGULARITIES

THE neatly fitting system of formula-types and sentence-patterns was established in a favourable quarter, the personal name formulae. Its extension to other parts of the diction depends on the recognition by analogy of fragments of formula-types whose extension and economy cannot be proved by counting the examples in the text. This is a sound enough methodology provided that the base of the analogy is accurately described, that the correct correlations are made, and that there are no recalcitrant features in the new material. Of the two fundamental properties of formula-types the principle of economy in my view is rightly discerned in all parts of the Homeric diction. Among the common nouns, for example, are met the same very frequent formulae to which the poet never seems to consider any alternative, e.g. δολιχόσκιον ἔγχος 25×, πατρίδα γαῖαν 78×, or φίλον ἦτορ 40×. Where metrical equivalents do occur it is often the case that one is an occasional use which has the air of a mere aberration, e.g. νηυσὶ θοῇσι 10×, but νηυσὶν ἐΐσῃς 1× only, cf. πόδας ὠκὺς Ἀχιλλεύς 31×, but μεγάθυμος Ἀχιλλεύς 1×. This point is generally admitted. However, it is not so clear to me that all parts of the Homeric diction are equally organized into formula-types with fixed position and used only in certain regular sentence-patterns. Much of the material seems to be recalcitrant to this treatment, in ways that I shall deal with fully. The base of the analogy, moreover, merits testing. Are the personal name formulae used themselves only in regular sentence-patterns? Or is it that the idea of a formula fixed in shape and position arises from the dazzling effect of the longer formulae and a preoccupation with those in the nominative case? The easiest point to test is that of fixed position. The concordances seem to bear out the Parry–Lord hypotheses: the personal name formulae in the nominative case are indeed fixed, with only inconsequential exceptions. But fixed by what?

As far as I can see there are two positive factors that might keep a formula in one place, (1) metrics, and (2) habitual use within a limited number of sentence-patterns. To these we must add (3) placing habits for particular formulae which are more obscurely conditioned but equally effective. It is a tricky matter to disentangle these factors, but I do not despair. The presence of sentence-patterns is most obvious in the second half of the verse, but certain special usages of formulae in this area merit attention.

The longer a formula is, the more striking it is to the investigating scholar—and the less easy it is for the poet to vary its position in the verse. Thus the notable and numerous formulae that fill the whole second half of the verse between the feminine caesura and the verse-end are only liable to displacement if they embody certain accidents of word-division and metrical quantity ($\cup - \cup$ | $\cup - \cup\cup - \cup$—a very unusual division—or $\cup - \cup\cup - \cup$ | $\cup - -$ assuming a feminine caesura in the new position, and $\cup -$ | $\cup\cup - \cup\cup - \cup$ or $\cup - \cup\cup -$ | $\cup\cup - -$ with a masculine caesura), for in their medial placing the formulae would have to give a caesura, either strong or weak, in the 3rd foot and at the same time avoid giving a weak caesura in the 4th. Of the seventy-six expressions—personal names—of this length in the nominative case and beginning with a consonant thirty-six fulfil the requirements.[1] But because the medial position is possible does not mean that it is desirable. It is likely to be both cramping and inelegant: cramping, because little space is left at the beginning of the verse; inelegant, because so many expressions in medial use would give a spondaic rhythm before an observed bucolic diaeresis, a heavy measure much out of favour. It is not odd therefore that none of the expressions of this class are found medially. However, I do not press the point, for it is evident that the expressions of this class behave very much as the theory demands that they should. They are interchangeable units used in a particular sentence-frame, viz. a whole-line sentence the first half of which is constituted by the predicate. Very significant is the rarity of these formulae in any other sort of sentence-frame, for example, with the verb in the preceding or following line. Thus the formula-type

---

[1] All totals in this chapter are my own count and include expressions with special, generic, patronymic, and determinative epithets and epithet phrases, as well as periphrastic expressions for persons: the character of the phrase is not relevant for its placing in the verse.

and the sentence-pattern are realities, but by stating them at this level of generality, as is usually done, we obscure a characteristic of their use. The predicates are of very unequal popularity. The majority of occurrences are in the lines that introduce *oratio recta* or resume narrative after it, the types

τὸν δ' αὖτε προσέειπε ⎫
ὣς φάτο· γήθησεν δὲ ⎭ πολύτλας δῖος 'Οδυσσεύς.

This sort of line is not as good an illustration of Homeric technique as it is sometimes taken to be. Granted the epic prejudice in favour of whole-line introductions and transitions some such pattern of use would be bound to emerge. Having emerged and being used with great frequency in connexion with *oratio recta* its analogical power would be great. We might then be inclined to regard such a line as

ἀλλὰ σφέας κόσμησε Ποδάρκης ὄζος Ἄρηος   B 704

as immediately derivative from the introductory lines. The more a certain type of formula is restricted to a given context, the smaller is the poet's need for any sort of flexibility as he builds up in effect a series of whole-line formulae, e.g.

τὸν δ' ἠμείβετ' ἔπειτα Γερήνιος ἱππότα Νέστωρ
τὸν (τὴν) δ' αὖτε προσέειπε περίφρων Πηνελόπεια
ὣς ἔφατ', οὐδ' ἀπίθησε θεὰ λευκώλενος Ἥρη—etc.

Thus all three of our factors combine to fix this class of formulae in their verse-end position. It is idle to apportion responsibility more precisely, but lest the effect of the sentence-pattern should be exaggerated the behaviour of two closely related classes may be taken into consideration.

The type of the same dimensions as the preceding but beginning with a vowel has twenty-three members, of which nine could be used in a medial position. No advantage is taken of the possibility. However, the restricting factors, in so far as the shortness of the list permits them to appear, cannot be the same as those that restricted the first class. Since the types with initial vowels and consonants are usually taken as alternants whose use is determined by the final sound of the preceding formula, this needs some explanation. We have seen, however, that the consonantal type is prevailingly used in the introductory lines, in which the first-half formula always terminates in an open short vowel. An alternant with initial vowel is thus quite unnecessary, and expressions which are proved to be alternants are not used in that sentence-pattern.[1] A few formulae that have no consonantal alternant enter in defiance of metre or by leave of the *v*-movable: Ὀϊλῆος ταχὺς Αἴας, Ἀλέξανδρος θεοειδής, and Ὀδυσσῆος φίλος υἱός. Otherwise the use is unpatterned, except for a few instances of co-ordination by καί with other personal names.

The slightly longer type normally found between the strong caesura of the 3rd foot and the verse-end has only twenty-seven members counting together those with consonantal and vocalic initial sounds. Thirteen could be used medially. One,[2] υἱὸς Φρονίοιο Νοήμων δ 630, 648, is only medial, two others are found medially, υἱὸς Πετεῶο Μενεσθεύς N 690, and υἱὸς Δολίοιο Μελανθεύς χ 159, which are also found finally. There is no discernible reason why this type should be easier to move than its two congeners,[3] a warning that the low frequencies at this point are statistically insufficient to eliminate the random and fortuitous. At the verse-end the use of these formulae is mostly unpatterned, the principal exception being that those with the vocalic initial can enter the introductory and transitional line pattern through the elision of the first-half formulae, τοῖσι δὲ βοῦν ἱέρευσ' ἱερὸν μένος Ἀλκινόοιο ν 24, cf. B 402.

Where unpatterned uses prevail the inherent awkwardness of the metrics must be the factor that keeps these bulky formulae in their verse-end position in the majority of cases.

Special preferences in the use of certain formulae are sharply visible in the case of those name-formulae that normally lie between the 4th foot caesura and the verse-end. These also are regularly used in the construction of a certain type of introductory line which, having the predicate a foot longer than the preceding pattern, has the verb (προσέφη or μετέφη) expanded by a participle, e.g. the familiar τὸν δ' ἀπαμειβόμενος προσέφη . . . To this pattern some of the formulae are strikingly confined: πόδας ὠκὺς Ἀχιλλεύς (27 instances against 4 elsewhere), κρατερὸς

---

[1] An exception is τὸν δ' ὡς οὖν ἐνόησεν ἀρηΐφιλος Μενέλαος Γ 21, cf. A 580. The different usage of the consonantal and vocalic types bears out Hoekstra's contention, *MFP* 71 ff., that *v*-movable is a relatively late intruder into epic diction, otherwise we should expect a more decisive breakdown in the regularity.

[2] υἱὸς Τελάμωνος ἀγανοῦ P 284 has, in effect, *ἀγανόο. ἀγανοῦ like μεγαθύμου is not placed finally.

[3] ἦρχ' at N 690 is clearly no easier than ἦρχε(ν): but there is a pattern of use for υἱός-formulae without an epithet in the first half of the verse: τὸν δ' υἱὸς Καπανῆος Δ 403, cf. E 319; τὸν δ' υἱὸς Οἰνῆος I 543; τόν ῥ' υἱὸς Τελαμῶνος N 177, cf. P 293.

Διομήδης (10:2), νεφεληγερέτα Ζεύς (22:8), and πολύμητις
Ὀδυσσεύς (72:9).[1] When a formula is thus associated regularly
with another word, it is reasonable to speak of a *complex formula*,
here *verb*+(*name*+*epithet*). When it is part of such a complex
formula the place of the simple formula is naturally determined
by the factors that govern the placing of the whole, and since
a longer formula is normally less movable than a shorter one the
formation of complex formulae tends to restrict mobility. Not all
formulae of this type coalesce so decisively with προσ- or μετέφη;
cf. κρείων Ἀγαμέμνων (10 instances against 16 elsewhere), γλαυκῶπις Ἀθήνη (7:19), κορυθαίολος Ἕκτωρ (10:15), and ξανθὸς
Μενέλαος (5:12).[1] Besides the introductory line the usage is
generally patterned, the preceding word being either a connective or a verb.[2] The patterns and the complex formulae exert
a firm grip: out of 55 usable expressions only three are found
medially: πολύβουλος Ἀθήνη Ε 260, Ὀδυσεὺς πολύμητις Γ 268 etc.,
and κρατερὸς Διομήδης Ε 151, also finally *passim*. Being shorter
this type is more versatile metrically than the longer groups, and
only 13 expressions are absolutely immovable from the verse-end.
The type with initial vowel is rare (6 expressions) compared with
the consonantal classes (19 with single consonant, 43 with double).
In practice these differences have little effect on usage.[3]

The third important group in the second half of the verse,
that used between the diaeresis and verse-end, is smaller than
the preceding. The usage is tightly patterned.[4] Of the thirty ex-

---

[1] Further examples in Parry's table, *ET* 64.

[2] *ET* 65–6, with examples.

[3] There is no objection to the surallongement of the preceding syllable, which
will be the *arsis* of the fourth foot. As for lengthening a *brevis*, the two initial consonants overlap with other artifices, chiefly the ν-movable and the particles: so
βάλε γλαυκῶπις Ἀθήνη but πέφνεν πόδας ὠκὺς Ἀχιλλεύς; τὸν δὲ κρείων Ἀγαμέμνων
but τὸν δ' αὖ κορυθαίολος Ἕκτωρ. Pairs with single *versus* double consonant are rare.
Parry, *ET* 64, noted only three (four, if we add πολύβουλος Ἀθήνη). But there is
very little clear functioning of these as metrical alternants: κλυτότοξος Ἀπόλλων
ρ 494 and μεγάθυμος Ἀχιλλεύς (with lengthening μ-) Ψ 168 are used without metrical
necessity: πολύβουλος Ἀθήνη may be *ad hoc*, arising from the disturbed formulaic
character of Ε 260, but cf. π 282 for the epithet.

[4] See *ET* 48–63, where seven sentence-patterns are given, defined in terms of
the preceding words (verbs in -ετο, -ατο, verb+connective, etc.). Of twenty instances of φαίδιμος Ἕκτωρ only three fall outside these patterns. Yet the schematization of this diction can too easily be exaggerated or its nature misapprehended.
What sentence-structures has the poet omitted? If he eschews none that he might
reasonably employ, then we have no right to say that the structures discovered are
not part of verse-language generally but a sign of an oral poetical language.

pressions that might in principle occur medially five are so found, all in 2nd–3rd feet: one is very likely a nonce phrase, *Ἶρος Ἄϊρος σ 73 : three are of the υἱός+genitive type, Πηλέος υἱός Φ 139, Τυδέος υἱός E 376, Λ 338 and finally *passim*, and Νέστορος υἱός γ 448, δ 186 and finally *passim* in *Iliad*: lastly the half-personified natural phenomenon δῖα Χάρυβδις μ 104 and finally μ 235. All these have the final syllable short, a metrical advantage shared by only seven other expressions in this class. If we dare to assume that this proportion is not fortuitous—and it will be borne out by results elsewhere—three points emerge much more sharply than in the two preceding types. First, the usage is very sensitive to the rhythm of the line. It is not enough that an expression may occupy a given place, it must occupy that place according to certain standards of elegance if the possibility is freely to become a reality. The formulae with long final would give a ponderous rhythm both in 1st–2nd feet and especially in 3rd–4th feet. Second, for the first time a quotable proportion of medial occurrences is built up. In the type under discussion the freely movable sub-class gives seven medial occurrences against twenty-five final. Third, medial placing is used with expressions that would never be chosen as typical of their group. The typical expression, typical for us, that is, is a name–epithet formula for a principal hero, δῖος Ἀχιλλεύς or φαίδιμος Ἕκτωρ, the dazzling class that quantitatively is quite a small proportion of the total Homeric diction.

In addition to the three positive factors noted, metrics, patterning, and complex formulae, there is a negative factor also that makes for fixity in position. This is the poet's need, and is related to the degree of patterning a group of formulae shows. Supposing, *per impossibile*, that there were no sentence-patterns in the poet's usage, it would be reasonable to expect that a given type of formula would be randomly distributed throughout all sorts of sentence. A given type would be just as common in, for example, narrative sentences as in the introductions to speeches. That is to say, the poet's need for a formula of a given shape would arise without any correlation with the type of sentence he was composing. As sentence-patterns develop, however, each pattern favours one formula-type and *excludes the others*. The poet has no need of them since he can express his thought just as well and far more easily by using the favoured type of expression. The more efficient the patterning is, the less need there will be in a given area for formulae of various shapes used in various positions. It is only where sentence structure is unorganized that subject and predicate are likely to find themselves in competition for the same part of the verse and so one or other must be shifted, or that otherwise unsuitable formulae come to mind.

Clearly it would be most useful to have a substantial class of unorganized and freely movable expressions whose behaviour we could inspect, but the personal names do not provide material in convenient quantity. The nominative is frequent but well-patterned. The oblique cases bring about a sharp reduction in the extent of the formula-types, e.g. the $- \cup \cup - \smile$ type has only 16 members in the vocative case, 17 in the accusative, none in the genitive, and 5 in the dative. Nor does inflexion improve metrical versatility. On the contrary it may reduce it, for the dative case will quite regularly produce a long final syllable with consequent difficulties in medial positions. It would therefore be rash to speak of proofs, but at least one can see in which direction the available evidence points. I set out the distribution of the freely mobile class in the accusative case, listing formulae used twice or more, for the $- \cup \cup - \cup$ shape.

Position by feet of verse

	1st–2nd	2nd–3rd	4th–5th	5th–6th
ὀξὺν Ἄρηα	0	1	0	6
θοῦρον Ἄρηα	0	2	0	7
Ἕκτορα δῖον	2	4	2	19
Ἠῶ δῖαν	0	1	2	9
Νέστορα δῖον	0	0	0	3
Τυδέος υἱόν	0	4	1	3
Νέστορος υἱόν	1	1	0	3

There are seven more expressions, all occurring finally, which are unique in this shape and case: οὖλον Ἄρηα, Δῖον ἀγανόν, οὖλον Ὄνειρον, νήδυμον Ὕπνον, Φυλέος υἱόν, Μέμνονα δῖον, Μέντορα δῖον. Including these unique expressions in the count the proportion of medial to final occurrences is 21 to 57, or approximately 27 to 73 per cent. In these circumstances at least, to say that formulae are *confined* to a given position badly overstates the poet's preference.

The $- \cup \cup - \underline{\smile}$ shape provides the clearest picture because it has the highest innate versatility, but the same pattern of use, in a more fragmentary form, can be seen in the longer $\cup \cup - \cup \cup - \underline{\smile}$ group. The nominative case gives three expressions used medially; the oblique cases provide ten: Ἀγαμέμνονα δῖον, Δία τερπικέραυνον, Ἕχετον βασιλῆα, Ζῆνα Κρονίωνα, Θρασυμήδεα δῖον, κήρυκα Μέδοντα, Ὀδυσῆα ἄνακτα, Πριάμοιο ἄνακτος, Προῖτον βασιλῆα, and Σαρπήδονα δῖον, all having the final syllable short and totalling thirteen occurrences.[1] The $\cup - \cup \cup - \cup \cup - \underline{\smile}$ type, however, has no medial occurrences in the oblique cases.

Up to this point I have sought to keep within the terms of Parry's own definitions, and within those limits it is not possible to go further. The movement of formulae or their placing in positions of second preference is the sole manifestation of flexibility that his formulations permit. Anything more drastic is ruled out on the ground that it must imply thought and not habit on the part of the poet.[2] I hope to show presently that this is an arbitrary and crippling exclusion. Meanwhile, if the use of formulae is viewed with a more liberal eye, various sorts of adaptation will be discovered in some abundance in the three major formula-types I have been discussing, especially in the longer classes. It would be wrong to dismiss these treatments as aberrations without significance. They are evidence for the workings of the poet's mind.

It is too readily assumed within the terms of Parry's theory that because a formula is supposed to be called to mind when it is required so it comes to mind *only* when required. This is psychologically improbable. In ordinary circumstances all speakers are aware that thoughts crowd into the mind in a most disorderly fashion. A poet's linguistic habits ought not to be more regular, and I assume that from time to time formulae force themselves upon his attention which he can only deploy in the verse by bending them out of their normal shape, by trimming them down to a shorter length, or by intruding other words between them.[3] Another device, too regular to be itemized, is the boosting of the

---

[1] Omitting, since their status is unclarified, the elided Πηλῆα ἄναχθ' I 480, and βροτολοιγον Ἄρη' (v.l. Ἄρην) E 909, and the correpted χρυσόθρονον Ἠῶ (or elided *'Ηό') τ 319.　　　　　　　　　　　　　　　　　　[2] See HSCP xli (1930) 84.

[3] In all classes epithets may be added or deleted with some freedom. For modifications that preserve the word-association note the following:

(i) The $(\cup) \cup - \cup \cup - \cup \cup - \underline{\smile}$ class: shortening (εὐρυ)κρείων Ἀγαμέμνων, (περι)-

length of a formula by piling on additional epithets: e.g. Καπανήϊος υἱός > Καπανῆος ἀγακλειτοῦ φίλος υἱός, and the not infrequent
'whole line formulae' πότνι᾽ Ἀθηναίη ἐρυσίπτολι δῖα θεάων, Αἶαν
διογενὲς Τελαμώνιε κοίρανε λαῶν, Ἀτρεΐδη κύδιστε ἄναξ ἀνδρῶν
Ἀγαμέμνων, etc.

My purpose here has been to make out a prima facie case for
impeaching the uncritical analogical extension of the technique
of use of nominative personal names to the whole diction of the
epics. The base of the analogy, it is clear, is by no means
solid unless a special context is in question also. The flaw in the
analogical argument is that the special context drops out of view
and no factor corresponding to it is sought in the new field. Were
such a factor sought, then it would be seen at once that the
analogy breaks down. If to preserve the analogical argument we
delete the special context (the nominative case and the associated
sentence-patterns) then we find that the personal names in all
contexts generally are moved, modified, inverted, and split: not
to the extent that such versatility should be considered typical,
but enough to make it implausible to set the unconforming
examples down to the poet's human fallibility in handling an
almost mechanical technique. But if the poet's technique is not
mechanical (placing fixed formulae in fixed sentence-structures)

κλυτὸς Ἀμφιγυήεις, Πηληϊάδεω Ἀχιλῆος—Πηλεΐδεω Ἀχ., (βοὴν) ἀγαθὸς Διομήδης,
(εὐρυ)κρείων Ἐνοσίχθων, (βοὴν) ἀγαθὸν Μενέλαον, Ὀδυσσῆος θείοιο—θείοιο Ὀδυσῆος;
slight lengthening ἑκηβόλου Ἀπόλλωνος—ἑκατηβόλου Ἀπ.; making a dactylic ending
Ὀδυσσῆα πτολίπορθον—Ὀδ. πτολιπόρθιον; inversion Ἀγαμέμνονος Ἀτρεΐδαο—
Ἀτρεΐδεω Ἀγ., δαΐφρονος Ἀλκινόοιο—Ἀλκ. δαΐφρονος, ἀρηΐφιλος (-ον) Μενέλαος (-ον)
—Μεν. ἀρήϊος (-ον), διοτρεφὲς ὦ Μενέλαε—(ὦ) Μεν. διοτρεφές, μεγαθύμου Τηλε-
μάχοιο—Τηλεμάχου μεγαθύμου; for straddling the caesura βίη Ἡρακληείη—β.
Ἡρακλῆος; separation Ἀπόλλωνι . . . κλυτοτόξῳ, Ἡφαίστοιο . . . πολύφρονος,
Ἶρις . . . ποδήνεμος cf. π. ὠκέα Ἶρις, Νέστωρ . . . Γερήνιος cf. Γ. ἱππότα Νέστωρ,
Ὀδυσῆος . . . θείοιο, γέρων . . . Πηλεύς cf. γ. ἱππηλάτα Πηλεύς, Σθενέλοιο . . .
Περσηϊάδαο cf. Σθενέλου Π., Σθένελον . . . Καπανήϊον υἱόν.

(ii) The ◡◡ – ◡◡ – ◡ class: shortening Ζῆνα Κρονίωνα—Δία Κρ., (πόδας)
ὠκέα Ἶρις cf. the two Achilles formulae (πόδας) ὠκὺς Ἀχιλλεύς; inversion Βρισηΐδα
κούρην—κούρῃ Βρισηΐδι and κούρην Βρισῆος, Διὸς αἰγιόχοιο—αἰγ. Διός, ἐριούνιος
Ἑρμῆς—Ἑρμείας ἐριούνιος, Θέτις ἀργυρόπεζα—ἀργ. Θέτις, πολύμητις Ὀδυσσεύς—
Ὀδυσεὺς πολύμητις; separation Τελαμώνιος . . . Αἴας, Ἀγαμέμνονι . . . δίῳ, πολύβουλος . . . Ἀθήνη, ἑκάεργος . . . Φοῖβος Ἀπόλλων, βροτολοίγῳ . . . Ἀρηΐ, Δία (-ὶ) . . .
τερπικέραυνον (-ῳ), and Ζεὺς . . . τερπικέραυνος, Διός . . . αἰγιόχοιο, κορυθαίολος . . .
Ἕκτωρ, χρυσόθρονος . . . Ἥρη, χρυσόθρονος . . . Ἠώς, πολύμητις . . . Ὀδυσσεύς,
Πεισίστρατος . . . ἥρως.

(iii) The – ◡◡ – ◡ class: lengthening Παλλὰς (-άδ᾽) Ἀθήνη (-ην)—Π. Ἀθηναίη
(-ην); inversion Φοῖβος Ἀπόλλων—Ἀπ. Φοῖβος, δῑ᾽ Ἀφροδίτη—Ἀφρ. δῖα, δῖος
Ὀδυσσεύς—Ὀδ. δῖος.

what is it? We noticed above that some formulae were *moved*, others *modified*, yet others *separated*. These are the unexamined techniques, the extent of which it is obviously necessary to explore before a more complete description of Homeric formulaic usages can be drawn up.

III

WHAT IS A FORMULA?

THE personal-name formulae on the whole show a highly
evolved usage. Being undeniable, this has come to be regarded as the basis of the formulaic technique. Yet there
should have been misgivings. I prefer to consider that the narrow
limitations of position and context are the form towards which
the handling of a formulaic diction tends, the consequence but
not the starting point of the technique. To develop this suggestion
we clearly need different material to work on from Parry's and
to look at it, if possible, in a new way. The first pitfall is a ter-
minological difficulty which, though a tedious beginning, has
nevertheless to be resolved, because the whole study of flexibility
among formulae depends on what is included under, and excluded by, this term.

1. Criticisms of Parry's concept of the formula

The nature of Parry's work demanded of him an exact formulation: 'Dans la diction des poèmes aédiques la formule peut
être définie comme une expression qui est régulièrement employée, dans les mêmes conditions métriques, pour exprimer
une certaine idée essentielle' (ET 16).[1] This is repeated without
change (except for translation) in HSCP xli (1930) 80, and seems
to have obtained general acceptance along with the rest of Parry's
work.[2] Yet it was intended to identify expressions which, subject
to certain tests, could be proved to be traditional. It is not without

---

[1] As Hoekstra points out (MFP 12 n. 6) the French term 'expression' may apply
to single words as well as phrases: a useful ambivalence to the student of sentence-
patterns, since, for instance, ὀβριμοπάτρη may be aligned with Παλλὰς Ἀθήνη as
ὄβριμος Ἄρης is with χάλκεος Ἀ. But I see no sign that Parry was aware of the point,
or at least that he exploited it.

[2] The influence on Labarbe, L'Homère de Platon, 17, is obvious. ('Une locution
figée, qui couvre exactement une portion de l'hexamètre et que l'usage appelle,
au lieu d'une locution originale, chaque fois qu'il s'agit de rendre l'idée précise
dont elle est le support, orné ou non.') Lord is still repeating it at SoT 30.
Severyns gives no definition.

objection that a formulation which was not concerned with the techniques of composition has been applied to one of the basic elements of the improvising style. All my complaints spring from this root.

Parry mentioned meaning in his definition only to raise the point that his formulae incorporated words (i.e. ornamental epithets) superfluous in the context of use. This point was vital in *ET*, for its strict application sorts out the material there required for establishing the extension and economy of the formula-types. But from the first paper in *HSCP* the net has always been cast more widely so as to include expressions in which all constituent words were functional. There is no avoiding this extension once the use of the formula in composition replaces its antiquity as the focus of interest. For the study of shifted and modified expressions it is of no consequence whether an epithet is ornamental or not, provided it is regular. In any case the line between the two categories is much harder to draw among common-noun formulae than among personal names.[1] There is no difficulty in finding formulae in which almost all the content is borne by the epithet and scarcely any by the noun, e.g. φίλον ἄνδρα, κακὰ ἔργα, or in which the noun is only weakly functional, e.g. νηλέες ἦτορ, ταλασίφρονα θυμόν. Again, epithets may be weakly functional and at the same time obviously useful metrically, e.g. ἀπερείσι᾽ ἄποινα, χρυσάμπυχας ἵππους, μήδεα πυκνά. Accordingly I have not sought to exclude any adjectives of quality, demonstratives, numerals,[2] πᾶς, or ἄλλος from participation in noun–epithet formulae. It must be conceded, however, that a regular association is harder to establish for a functional epithet and indeed can never be finally proved. For an ornamental epithet there is nothing but the noun to suggest the adjective, for a functional one there is always in the nature of the case the context.

Must a formula be fixed in shape and position? Fixed position, conveyed by the phrase 'dans les mêmes conditions métriques', is an implicit assumption in *ET*. It does no harm to the argument there because the material, with very few exceptions, happens to

---

[1] L. Bergson, *L'Épithète ornementale dans Eschyle, Sophocle et Euripide*, Lund 1956, 9 ff. has some useful criticisms of our concept of ornament. See also p. 76 n. 1 below.

[2] The numerals severely strain our now traditional categories: they cannot be purely ornamental, yet are very often habitual, cf. G. Germain, *Homère et la mystique des nombres*, Paris 1954, 5 ff.

be fixed, for the most part by the shape and length of the formulae under discussion. But when formulae and sentence-patterns are made the basis for a theory of improvisation the assumption is more perilous, for it concentrates our attention on a limited part of the diction and biases the argument in such a way that certain conclusions are bound to be drawn. To escape the hazard of any such circularity the fixity of the formula ought not to be made a defining feature, that is, part of the meaning of the term. It might still, of course, turn out to be a property of the formula. In the practical study of Homeric diction qualifications soon began to creep in. At one point Parry himself allowed that some formulae were not tied completely to one position.[1] From any flexibility in shape, however, he shied away. A formula may decline or conjugate, 'but any less simple alteration in the word-group supposes thought of some length on the part of the poet'.[2] I object that one does not know *a priori* what requires thought and what does not. How can we assert that a change from ἕταρον φίλον to ἑτάρῳ φίλῳ needs hardly any thought at all while the change to ἑτάροιο φίλοιο needs considerable thought?

2. *A revised definition*

It is obvious that the formula in Homer is a special feature and needs special definition.[3] In any field the essence of a formula is repetition. In literature, as opposed to the sciences, the repetition is normally of the matter and not of its arrangement. This is a convenient practice, for it permits the application of the term 'formula' to be confined to the poet's diction with the least departure from normal usage, and leaves the terms 'pattern' and 'theme' free to be used for repetitions respectively in the arrangement of the words and the subject-matter of the poems. The genus of the formula is thus a 'repeated word-group'.[4]

[1] *HSCP* xli (1930) 129, apropos of α 1, 'Μοι ἔννεπε Μοῦσα is one of the rare cases of a formula of any length which is found in more than one place in the verse'.

[2] *HSCP* xli (1930) 84.

[3] In the extra-Homeric field one may refer to O. Jespersen, *Philosophy of Grammar*, London 1924, 18–24. Is it necessary to add that the Homeric formula is not the same thing as a cliché, either in the sense that it is an ossified expression or that it is a defect of style?

[4] If the formula is a word-group we cannot use the term to designate the repetition of a single word at the same point in the verse, as is done, for example, by Kirk, *SoH* 67, and Notopoulos, *AJP* lxxxiii (1962) 355 ff., and *HSCP* lxviii (1964) 28 ff. We need a term for this regularity.

By the differentiae other kinds of repetition at this level, the accidental and the deliberate, are marked off. This may be done from a consideration either of the way in which the formula is used or of the way in which it is held together. Parry's differentiae are of the former type.[1] Unfortunately such differentiae are likely to be too narrow, to be too subjective and psychological, and may be circular. In fact the only datum the scholar has is the text of the poems. There the occurrences of word-groups can be counted, and it is obvious that some groups are very frequent. Even if the text were in an unknown language, it would be natural to call such groups formulae. In doing so we should not be committing ourselves to any evaluation of the author's mental processes, but stating only that the use of one word created a strong presumption that the other would follow. This degree of mutual expectancy I choose as the best differentia of the formulaic word-group.[2] By this terminology we say nothing about the function, shape, manner of use, or position of the formula, nor about the order, proximity, or syntactical relations[3] of the words in it. No flexibility is legislated into limbo before the investigation begins.

3. *When are word-groups the same?*

'Word' is a very fluid term, scarcely worthy to be a technical expression. To define it further I postulate that for present purposes the following accidents permit words and word-groups to be counted the same:

(*a*) Changes in metrics, e.g. $\mu\acute{\epsilon}\lambda\ddot{\iota}\ \chi\lambda\omega\rho\acute{o}\nu$, including synizesis and lengthening *metri gratia*, e.g. $\chi\rho\epsilon\iota\acute{\omega}$—$\chi\rho\epsilon\acute{\omega}$, $^{"}O\lambda\nu\mu\pi\sigma\varsigma$—$O\ddot{\nu}\lambda\nu\mu\pi\sigma\varsigma$.

(*b*) Elision and correption.

(*c*) Inflexion, including the usual cases of suppletion, e.g. $\delta\acute{\epsilon}\sigma\varsigma$ $\alpha\acute{\iota}\rho\epsilon\hat{\iota}/\epsilon\hat{\iota}\lambda\epsilon$.

---

[1] And deliberately developed in that direction in order to cover expressions of questionable status. 'We could not observe certain phrases found only once in different places, and thus prove their regular usage, but we saw that they belong to particular artifices of versification which have a fixed place in the diction. We have thus brought into the category of formulas not only the repeated expressions, but those which are of the same type as others' (*HSCP* xli [1930] 132–3).

[2] This was the older opinion, if it was thought useful to express it, e.g. van Gennep, *La Question d'Homère*, 13–14, before its phrase-pattern became the essence of a formula.

[3] A syntactical relation, e.g. noun+adjective, is normal (but flexible, see below pp. 38 f.): sometimes it is absent, e.g. $\alpha\dot{\nu}\tau\grave{\alpha}\rho\ \dot{\epsilon}\gamma\acute{\omega}$ and variants 122 ×, $\theta\nu\mu\grave{o}\varsigma\ \dot{\epsilon}\nu\grave{\iota}\ \sigma\tau\acute{\eta}$-$\theta\epsilon\sigma\sigma\iota$ 61 × ($\dot{\epsilon}\nu\grave{\iota}\ \sigma\tau$. is adverbial), etc.

(d) Fluctuations in adjectival inflexion (or gender in nouns), e.g. ἠέρα πολλήν/πουλύν.

(e) Shifts in meaning (i.e. within the same semantic field—actual homophones must be separated), e.g. μάρμαρον (adj. Π 735) ὀκριόεντα—μαρμάρῳ (noun M 380) ὀκριόεντι. These are accidents that may overtake a word in the Greek poetical language generally, but there are others which are characteristically Homeric. The *Kunstsprache* arms the poet with many alternative forms. They are invoked where (a), (b), and (d) above are not available. Hence the following Homeric accidents will not separate words and phrases:[1]

(f) Alternative inflexions, e.g. -οιο/-ου, etc., including the observance or neglect of contraction or diectasis.

(g) Alternative forms of suffix. The problem here is one of demarcation. If the metrical alternants μαχείομενος—μαχεούμενος are admitted, then suffixes giving just the same effect though in fact at different stages of their phonological evolution, e.g. κήδειος—κήδεος, may not be excluded, since the poet cannot be supposed to have distinguished the two types. Again such a pair as οἰνοχοεύω—οἰνοχοέω give the same result, but the means, the exploitation of similar but formally distinct suffixes, is different. However, in a study devoted in part to the modification of formulae it would be misleading to exclude this last category. To the poet they are clearly another sort of metrical alternant.

(h) Presence or absence of prefixes, including the augment. Performing the same duty at the head of the word are prefixes which, when semantically insignificant, are optional, e.g. the prepositional compounds of many verbs and the intensifying prefixes (whose force is often much weakened) of adjectives: κλυτός—περικλυτός and ἀγακλυτός. Compounded epithets also may have very little additional force, e.g. (νεό)πριστος, (ποδ)ωκύς.

(i) Alternative forms of the stem. These arise through the analogical extension of a certain grade throughout a paradigm, e.g. μητέρος for μητρός from the accusative μητέρα; from the dialect mixture, e.g. ἤμβροτε and ἅμαρτε; from the continued coexistence of older and newer formations, e.g. νῆες and νέες, and from metrical lengthenings, e.g. ἀπειρέσιος and ἀπερείσιος.

---

[1] Most of these points have been widely discussed, most recently by L. R. Palmer, *Companion to Homer* (edd. Wace and Stubbings) 106 ff., and Chantraine, *Gram. Hom.* 94 ff., but usually in terms of the single word only.

Outside the same paradigm, however, it cannot be assumed that there was any perception of the underlying unity in different grades or modifications of the same root.

It is clear that same word and synonym are not in practice sharply distinguished, but merge through a series of modifications. Consequently, wherever the line is drawn, there is bound to be something of the arbitrary. Thus I have not ventured to equate words with differences in both suffix and prefix together.

The modifications listed will be regarded as making variants of the same word, so that the word-groups in which they appear will not be separated, but will constitute modifications of the same formula. Besides these there are modifications which the word-group itself may undergo, independently of any modification of its members, without upsetting the bond of mutual expectancy by which it is cemented. Four categories may be set up:

(a) Rearrangement of the word-order, e.g. χεῖρας ἀάπτους and ἀάπτους χεῖρας.

(b) Separation of the constituent words, e.g. βροτὸς ἀνήρ but βροτὸς ⟨οὔτασεν⟩ ἀνήρ. Separation may also take place even across the verse-end, e.g. χάλκεον ἔγχος and ἔγχος | χάλκεον.

(c) Insertion, omission, or change of particles or prepositions. The syntactical links of formulae are normally indicated by the inflexions, but these may be supplemented by the prepositions. Because the prepositions perform this syntactical function, their addition to a formula does not turn it into a different formula. Likewise the introduction of connectives does not change a word-group. If the connective is prefixed, it is scarcely noticed, but it is of no more consequence if the connective is infixed, e.g. ἄναξ ⟨δ'⟩ ἀνδρῶν Ἀγαμέμνων. Some formulae are especially common in a prepositional or connective construction, but such developments are accidental, like the frequent use in certain case-forms of other formulae.

(d) Special cases of inflexion. Several formulae have in them a personal adjective or pronoun, the person of which (whether first, second, or third) must vary according to circumstances. This is a special case of declension or conjugation, and expressions which incorporate such words are counted as variants of the same formula.[1] Exceptionally inflexion may affect only part

[1] This is Parry's view also, HSCP xli (1930) 84; but the personal adjectives and

of a formula, so that the internal syntax is changed without the association of the words being impaired, e.g. δῖα θεάων and δῖα θεά, ἕρκος Ἀχαιῶν and ἕρκος Ἀχαιοῖσιν. These too will not be separated.

There is nothing of course to prevent two, or even all four of these modifications being applied to the same formula at once.

Finally, there is one other accident that may overtake a formula, an accident which need not modify its original constituents, namely its expansion by the addition to it of further terms, e.g. ὄβριμος Ἄρης is used five times by itself and once preceded by βριήπυος. Influenced in his thought by the system of formula-types, Parry separated these into two formulae, because they are of different over-all lengths.[1] But this is to ignore the obvious relation between the two, and in the present study such phrases will not be separated: the formula is the smallest recurrent word-group, but is a unit capable of extension.

The above criteria of identity, therefore, have been deliberately framed to admit all possible material relevant to the study of the formula's flexibility. In marginal cases it is not impossible that their scope will allow unworthy expressions to be elevated to formulaic status. But no matter how skilfully a definition is drawn such marginal cases are bound to arise, for flexibility in the formulae is but one technique out of several for meeting the problems of improvised composition, and merges into other techniques, particularly the use of synonymous words and formulae.

4. What is a repetition?

The high antiquity of some formulae and so the traditional association of the words may be inferred from lexical, archaeological, or linguistic criteria,[2] but such criteria are available for

---

pronouns are not perfectly interchangeable (e.g. (ϝ)ός will lengthen even a naturally short open final syllable, σός will not, and the first person has no monosyllable). Thus just as in normal declension the shape of the formula may have to be transformed in order to preserve the word-association.

[1] *ET* 50–51, Tableau I.

[2] Many, indeed most, items are controversial, and the literature correspondingly voluminous, see *Lustrum* i (1956) 18 ff., v (1960) 651; T. B. L. Webster, 'Early and late in Homeric diction', *Eranos* xiv (1956) 34–48; Kirk, 'Objective dating criteria in Homer', *Mus. Helv.* xvii (1960) 189–205. By lexical items are meant the glosses, cf. Parry, 'The Homeric Gloss: a study in word sense', *TAPA* lix (1928) 233–47,

but a small proportion of the sum of Homeric formulae. For the rest the sole valid criterion is that of repetition in the same or in a modified form, and from this the element of chance is inseparable. There are in Homer three specific reasons for this, the effects of inadequate representation, conventions of narration, and certain phrase-patterns.

(a) Inadequate representation

Despite their generous bulk (27,800 verses) the two Homeric epics cannot be more than a sample of the production of Greek heroic verse in its heyday.[1] This matters little where an incident is regular, e.g. the formulae of the fighting scenes, but some themes and so much phraseology are quite rare. Hence among the wholly unique expressions are doubtless some formulae,[2] but these are scarcely to be picked out by any criteria of technique, for any resemblance they may have to other formulae may be grounds for questioning the traditional association of the words. The great variation in the popularity of themes also makes it impossible to fix a quota of repetitions which a phrase must fulfil to be counted a formula.[3] Outside the special area of the personal names expressions that occur but two or three times are a numerous class. Often, if the epithet, say, of a noun–epithet formula is of a typically Homeric sense and formation, and if the occurrences are widely spaced so that one is not the immediate inspiration of the other, then it is hard to deny a formulaic status: e.g. σπόγγοισι πολυτρήτοισι α 111, χ 439 = 453, the last pair being an order and its execution.

and the so-called Arcado-Cypriot words, now supplemented by Mycenaean, cf. J. Chadwick, 'Mycenaean elements in the Homeric dialect', *Minoica: Festschr. f. J. Sundwall*, Berlin 1958, 116–22, with G. P. Shipp's evaluation, *Essays in Mycenaean and Homeric Greek*, Melbourne 1961, 1–14 (both papers now reprinted in *Language and Background of Homer*, 119 ff. and 126 ff.). The whole field is compendiously surveyed by Page, *HHI* 218 ff.

[1] Parry insists on this matter strongly. The essential point is whether or not the two epics are a representative sample of Greek heroic verse. There seems no reason to doubt that they are.

[2] Some unique expressions even contain glosses, e.g. αἵμονα θήρης E 49, which increases the probability of their antiquity.

[3] Pope, *Acta Classica* vi (1963) 14–15, operates with the idea of a quota of three occurrences and concludes that the poet of the similes had very little prefabricated terminology available to him. But the topics of the similes are prime examples of relatively rare themes. 184 different similes in the *Iliad* give 665 lines, a total insufficient to prove much about technique.

(b) Conventions of narration

Some repetitions are deceptive, the true repetition being in the structure and above the level of diction.[1] First, in the epic direct speech is the rule.[2] When a message or command is reported to another character, it is repeated verbatim or with only slight condensations. Similarly, when the execution of a command or the fulfilment of a prophecy is reported, the original words of the command or prophecy are used with only the necessary changes of person and tense. The convention is prevalent in most oral traditions,[3] but though it amply proves the capacity of the poet to retain extensive passages in the mind over a short period, it proves nothing about the mutual expectancy of words which chance to occur. Second, an archaic device extensively used in Homer to organize and coordinate the narrative is ring-composition, by which a given passage is framed by identical or similar expressions and so is clearly marked off from its context.[4] Similes are very commonly embedded into the narrative by this device, which, being purely structural, can tell nothing of the internal relations of the words that happen to be so repeated.

(c) Phrase patterns

Mutual expectancy admits of infinite gradations. Words, at first fortuitously combined, by re-creation slowly become regularly associated.[5] Conversely, a firm association, by desuetude, unintelligibility, or competition from other formulae, becomes slack and sporadic. Created and re-created expressions may follow a familiar phrase-pattern, with the result that any rare expression

---

[1] The refrain is of this type, the repetition of the phrases being due to the chance of their inclusion in the refrain-structure. Parry's idea that 'regular repetition' could be equated with 'habitual' and then 'useful repetition' (*HSCP* xli [1930] 80–82) was not happy: the utility of the formula is what we are trying to elucidate. Refrain-like effects are Homeric, e.g. ἔνθεν δὲ προτέρω πλέομεν ἀκαχήμενοι ἦτορ ι 62 = 105 = 565 = κ 77 = 133. Are we to say that, (e.g.) ἀκαχήμενος (-οι) ἦτορ is a very frequent formula with nine occurrences altogether, or that it is a moderately frequent formula with four occurrences in the body of the text plus an occurrence in a refrain?

[2] The only considerable piece of *oratio obliqua* is ψ 310–43.

[3] Bowra, *HP* 254–64.

[4] Ring-composition has been the especial study of W. A. A. van Otterlo. For its use in Homer see his *De Ringcompositie als Opbouwprincipe in de Epische Gedichten van Homerus*, Amsterdam 1948, and B. A. van Groningen, *La Composition littéraire grecque*, Amsterdam 1958, 51 ff.

[5] On this see Lord, *SoT* 43–45.

must lie under suspicion if it is constructed on such a schema, especially if the occurrences are in close proximity. Phrases incorporating a generic epithet, i.e. an epithet used indifferently with a whole class of nouns, are a prime example of this ambiguous status. Such phrases are constructed on a pattern in which one element, the generic epithet, is a constant, and the other, any noun of a certain shape, is a variable. Thus κρατερός is used with seven proper names to make useful phrases after the 4th-foot caesura. Now κρατερὸς Διομήδης 18× may be formulaic on grounds of much repetition, but what of κρατερὸς Μεγαπένθης and κρατερὸς Πολύφημος, both twice only?

The deceptive results of the conventions of narration can be detected and corrected, but there are no general rules by which the effects of haphazard re-creation and inadequate representation can be eliminated. These are opposite dangers, Scylla and Charybdis. Setting up a quota of occurrences would exclude chance repetitions, if it were set high enough, but as was pointed out, this would exclude much material that was not only formulaic but also interesting from the point of view of flexibility. It is the rarer phrases that are particularly liable to modification. Moreover the quota might have to be set unexpectedly high. Even quite frequent formulae are sometimes found to be lacking in enough cohesion to prevent their disruption. Thus θεοὶ Οὐρανίωνες 6× ought to represent a firm association. But the pattern, pyrrhic word before diaeresis and pentasyllable in the 5th and 6th feet, is a very marked one, and a favourite with the poet. Re-creation would thus be easy. For lack of cohesion compare the following lines:

ὤχθησαν δ' ἀνὰ δῶμα Διὸς θεοὶ Οὐρανίωνες   Α 570,
ὤχθησαν δ' ἀνὰ δῶμα Διὸς θεοί· ἡ δὲ γέλασσε   Ο 101.

Which pitfall is likely to prove the least uncomfortable? It seems to me that too much concern about re-created expressions is going to exclude far too much material without any obvious gain. In the first instance therefore I place together both developing and developed formulae and count as a formula any expression occurring at least twice in the Homeric text.[1]

---

[1] 'Homeric text' means *Iliad* and *Odyssey* in the editions of Munro–Allen and Allen of the Oxford Classical Texts series. I exclude the Hymns (and, of course,

Since there are few verses in Homer which on this definition do not contain at least one formula it is obviously necessary to extract from this material some classes of expressions representative of the poet's natural practice and comparable with each other in the factors controlling their use.

It is this matter of comparability that poses the severest problems. The personal names are a true class, governing the same predicates as each other and utilizing the same generic epithets: but common nouns, for example, are not such a class. Helmets, horses, ships, and mountains appear in quite different contexts, share no epithets, and give rise to no analogies between each other. Consequently many common-noun formulae have been studied according to meaning, with useful results in every field but that of the technique of composition. We have marked time at this point because helmets, horses, etc., give rise to very small groups of formulae constituted in the same way as the very large group of heroes. We thus discover again the economy of the diction, the special fixed and (sometimes) generic epithets, complex formulae, and (occasionally) sentence-patterns: but the evidence is usually very fragmentary and needs the analogy of the personal names to elucidate it. To advance a little we must bring together all the common-noun formulae (or all the verbal formulae, or whatever our chosen class is). How do we sort them out? The technical problem of the poet is that of fitting expressions into a certain rhythmical shape. His immediate datum is a word or expression of a certain shape. Shape therefore must be the first classifying factor to introduce comparability. However, a list of expressions compiled solely on the basis of shape, besides being impossibly long, would not consist of comparable expressions. Suppose the poet gets into some technical difficulty and cannot use a formula in the way he normally does. He may (i) abandon the formula, (ii) move it, (iii) modify it, or (iv) keep it and move or modify some other element. Ideally the members of the list should be comparable in the ease with which they and their associated words may be subjected to these alternative treatments: an

the Hesiodic corpus) as representing different and in some respects more developed schools, but I see no point, in the first instance, in separating the two epics and still less in separating parts of them (e.g. the Odyssean 'Continuation'). As M. I. Finley reminds us (*World of Odysseus*, London 1956, 32–33), 'the style and language of the poems . . . are essentially indistinguishable apart from certain interesting preferences in vocabulary', whatever other differences there may be, cf. *ET* 238–9.

impossible demand, since formulae vary in cohesion and their elements may have many, few, or no alternant forms or synonyms. These are points also on which information can never be known to be complete. The best that can be done is to use a grammatical criterion (nouns are more likely to be comparable with nouns than with verbs), which at the same time cuts down numbers to a manageable but still significant quantity. From these considerations it is easy to see that the noun–epithet formulae consisting of a noun (common, abstract, or collective) with an attributive epithet, a numerous and usually unambiguous class, provide the most convenient material. On these I concentrate, but the field can with advantage be narrowed further. What shape or shapes can be most usefully analysed? Among personal names this question was answered by the prominence of at most five shapes. Yet even in that field, though the point is not stressed by the exponents of the formula-type theory of composition, expressions are found of almost every possible shape and length. The same is true of common-noun expressions except that the spread is more even and shorter formulae are possible, because disyllabic and trisyllabic common nouns are more numerous than personal names of such dimensions and there is less use of compounded epithets with common nouns. One has no difficulty in compiling substantial lists of formulae of at least the following shapes (⌣⌣ is normally equivalent to –) :

1. – ⌣ ⌣ – αἰνὸν ἄχος
2. – ⌣ ⌣ – ⌣̱ ἔγχεα μακρά
3. – ⌣ ⌣ – ⌣ ⌣ αἷμα κελαινεφές
4. – ⌣ ⌣ – ⌣ ⌣ – αἰετὸς ὑψιπέτης
5. – ⌣ ⌣ – ⌣ ⌣ – ⌣̱ θηλυτέρῃσι γυναικί
6. ⌣ – ⌣ ⌣ κακὸν μόρον
7. ⌣ – ⌣ ⌣ – ἁλὸς πολιῆς
8. ⌣ – ⌣ ⌣ – ⌣ ἀεικέα ἔργα
9. ⌣ – ⌣ ⌣ – ⌣ ⌣ ἀρήια τεύχεα
10. ⌣ – ⌣ ⌣ – ⌣ ⌣ – ⌣̱ διϊπετέος ποταμοῖο
11. ⌣ ⌣ – ⌣̱ φίλον ἦτορ
12. ⌣ ⌣ – ⌣ ⌣ δόρυ μείλινον
13. ⌣ ⌣ – ⌣ ⌣ – ξίφεϊ μεγάλῳ
14. ⌣ ⌣ – ⌣ ⌣ – ⌣̱ δολιχόσκιον ἔγχος
15. ⌣ ⌣ – ⌣ ⌣ – ⌣ ⌣ λιμένος πολυβένθεος
16. ⌣ ⌣ – ⌣ ⌣ – ⌣ ⌣ – ⌣̱ ὑπερώϊα σιγαλόεντα.

I should hesitate to assert that any metrically possible shape is wholly neglected.

It would be an unnecessarily repetitive proof of Homeric technique to work out the usage of each shape in detail, and I select only the classes $- \cup \cup - \underline{\cup}$ and $\cup \cup - \underline{\cup}$, as used in the two epics, for close inspection here. Several reasons determine this choice. Both classes are large, they exemplify very well the various devices of flexibility, and the shorter of the two has been unjustly neglected. But my principal motive springs from the part played by the mobility of formulae in this study, for it would be illogical to scrutinize material for freedom in placing if there are grave difficulties besetting its use in more than one position. With a short final syllable the shapes chosen can be used in as many as four positions (1st–2nd, 2nd–3rd, 4th–5th, and 5th–6th feet),[1] and in two or three with perfect facility. Ease of use, it may be said, is more important in this connexion than possibility, for although some shapes with favourable word-division, e.g. $\cup \cup - \cup \cup$ and $- \cup \cup -$, may also theoretically be placed in at least four different positions, at the margins of the verse and near the caesura they create difficulties in the choice of words to be juxtaposed which in practice seem to limit their flexibility severely. Thus $\cup \cup - \cup \cup$ effectively belongs to 3rd–4th and 4th–5th feet only. The same factors largely confine the other shapes also to a pair of positions. The two chosen classes also mark two different relations to the inner metrics of the hexameter. The $\cup \cup - \cup$ shape coincides with only one of the more weakly defined natural portions of the hexameter (in 2nd–3rd feet), whereas shape $- \cup \cup - \underline{\cup}$ at the verse-end is one of the most obvious subsections into which the verse breaks. Since the natural portions of the verse have at various times been supposed to influence the development of formulae, it is useful to inspect the behaviour both of a class that must have been affected by the verse-structure, if any was, and of one that may have escaped.

---

[1] This notation means that the expression in question begins at a point in the first foot and ends at a point in the second, etc. Other notations are used for special purposes, but none seems so clear and convenient for my present needs as that adopted.

IV

MOBILE FORMULAE

THE question posed is: how much freedom should we expect the poet to enjoy in positioning formulae? My method is first of all to eject from the material all remaining expressions that are confined to one position by metrical but not compositional factors. This preliminary operation has not been entirely circumvented by selecting the $- \cup \cup - \underset{\smile}{}$ and $\cup \cup - \underset{\smile}{}$ classes. The members of these sets, especially the first, frequently are declined into grammatical cases that give a long final syllable χεῖρα βαρεῖαν > χειρὶ βαρείῃ, θεὸς αὐτός > θεοὶ αὐτοί. This at once deprives them of the greater part of their potential mobility. In any count of occurrences such 'long' case-forms and all other expressions having a long final syllable must be segregated. The point is obvious, but because the quantity of the final syllable is of no consequence at the verse-end, it has been ignored in specifications of formula-types that extend to that point. Yet the use in medial positions is critically affected by this quantity, for a formula with a long final is longer in effect, since medially it takes up more space, than one with a short final. The quantity to be attributed to a final syllable in listing formulae (or at least my two classes of formulae) is its natural quantity. There is no need in practice to entertain the possibilities either of correption or of positional lengthening *in thesi*. Both are exceptional.[1]

When we speak of the poet's freedom in placing formulae we allude to those artifices of composition which tend to fix formulae in one position. We are asking how far he is free from these constraints. But even if these artifices were non-existent the poet would not, owing to constraints of a different order, be free to place his formulae wherever he wished. Next therefore we must discover, or plausibly conjecture, what the scatter of expressions would be within the verse but for the interference of compositional pressures. Even without committing oneself to any particular

[1] See below pp. 58 f.

colometric theories, it would be uncritical to assume that the distribution would be equal throughout all theoretically possible positions. The average word length in the Homeric vocabulary and the average phrase length in the diction conspire with the metrical breaks (which need not all be colometric in nature) to load the dice in favour of certain positions. It is thus easy to guess that if the poet takes the line of least resistance more $- \cup \cup - \cup$ expressions will fall in the 5th–6th feet than elsewhere, with 2nd–3rd feet as a second favourite position, and that the 2nd–3rd feet will be the first position for the $\cup \cup - \cup$ class, since the commonest cuts in the hexameter leave cola of the required shape in those positions. But such deductive reasoning cannot tell even approximately what proportions may be expected to fall in which positions. It is better to approach from the opposite direction and to examine at a favourable point the poet's response to metrical pressures. My method is to sort the expressions of a given shape into three classes: (1) regular formulae, (2) derivative or doubtful formulae that occur only once in the shape in question but whose words are elsewhere associated in another shape, and (3) unique expressions. It is likely that a good proportion of the expressions falling into the last two categories are *ad hoc* creations. This is clear from their large numbers in every class. All cannot be under-represented formulae. *Ad hoc* creations, however, are likely to be less affected by compositional devices (though they must be to some extent) than regular formulae, since they lack predetermined associations with other words and phrases. The distribution of these unique phrases thus gives an easily ascertained approximation to the natural distribution of formulae, as far as this is governed by metrical considerations. This method is applicable to formulae of any shape or length, but our choice of two relatively short shapes allows a further check: a comparison with the distribution of single words of the same length. If the scatter of the unique phrases is then compared with that of formulaic expressions (not occurrences of formulae) the effect of sentence-patterns will be exposed by the increase at certain points. For the principle of the extension of formula-types means that more formulae are used in a given position than would otherwise be the case. If we then compare the scatter of the occurrences of the formulae we obtain not only a confirmation of the grip of the sentence-patterns but also an indication of the presence of complex groupings or special preferences from the increase at a given point. Inspection will then reveal the formulae that depart most violently from the norm so as to elucidate particular cases.

1. *The* – ∪ ∪ – ≍ *class*

The shape – ∪ ∪ – ≍ is one of the shortest to fill a sharply marked natural portion of the hexameter, that between the diaeresis and the verse-end. There is a great concentration of words and phrases of all sorts at this point which exactly fill the space available, and many seem to have been deliberately made with this portion of the verse in mind. Some peculiarities in language and diction, such as the anomalous accusative singular εὐρέα πόντον, were early noted by J. E. Ellendt and Düntzer, but it is to Witte that we owe the fullest exposition of the effect of metre at this point of the verse on the use of -αο, -οιο, -άων, -εσσι, the voices of the verb, and the formation of compounds. The work of these scholars showed that it was important to the poet to fill the space after the diaeresis even at the cost of archaism, dialect, and anomalous declension, conjugation, and word-formation. Not surprisingly the formulae of this shape are the most numerous class of common-noun formulae in Homer.[1]

There are almost 300 regular formulae and over 230 unique expressions of the two categories. All the grammatical cases are well represented, and many formulae occur in more than one case-form. The accusatives are most numerous, followed closely by the nominatives. The genitive is relatively infrequent,[2] and the vocative, as may be expected in a group that for the most part denotes material objects, is rare.

A long final syllable in this group, as in others, is unlikely to lead to a flexible use. In his paper on the localization of word-

---

[1] Reversing the proportions of the personal-name formulae the common-noun expressions decrease in number with increasing length. It is strange that Parry should have based his belief that the formulaic technique began between diaeresis and verse-end on the poet's equipment for personal names. While it is true that the principal characters have a formula for this space, the extension of the type (*c.* 50 expressions) is more limited than that of the longer formulae following the third- or fourth-foot caesuras.

[2] There are no personal name formulae of this shape in the genitive. I put down the rarity to conservatism, since the contracted -ου would give many convenient phrases. As usual the handling of personal names is under better control than other parts of the diction, where an occasional ἡδέος οἴνου aut sim. makes its appearance.

types in the hexameter O'Neill[1] found that in Homer none of the words in his sample scanned $- \cup \cup - -$ occurred anywhere but finally. Theoretically an expression, i.e. a phrase of two words, should be more versatile, since it can be made to straddle the caesura if its first word is of one or two syllables only. No great advantage, however, is taken of this possibility. The reason for this is that such a placing would result in the slow and ponderous rhythm which the poet avoids. It has been calculated that only some 2·3 per cent. of Homeric lines have a word scanned $\cup \cup - -$ or $\cup - -$ by nature in the 3rd–4th feet,[2] and only 11·7 per cent. of words so scanned are ever found there.[3]

The few medial examples are given in Table I. Since their numbers are so small, only seven expressions, it is almost otiose to spend any ingenuity on reducing them further, but the Homerist is bound to observe that the three genitives in -ου and the dative in -οι are contracted formations and that the placing reflects habits appropriate to the disyllabic stage in the evolution of these terminations. The usage of ἀγανός reflects this very sharply and is doubtless itself traditional; the placing of the others we may prefer to regard as derivative, following the pattern of more ossified phrases. Other explanations of the medial position are discernible: thus ἵνα μή μιν λιμὸς ἀτερπὴς γούναθ' ἵκοιτο T 354 is an expanded version of the normally constructed half-line ἵνα μή μιν λιμὸς ἵκηται T 348; in τούτου ἀέθλου πειρή-σεσθε (-σθον) 3× and μακρὸν ἐέλδωρ ἐκτετέλεσται ψ 54 long words claim a prior right to the verse end. It is worth noticing also that some of these expressions are for practical purposes rather longer than the simple noun–epithet group: τόδε μακρὸν ἐέλδωρ, τοῦ παιδὸς ἀγανοῦ, παρὰ τάφρον ὀρυκτήν. This additional length considerably simplifies the structure of the first half-verse by providing a caesura after the arsis of the second foot which is not easily

<hr/>

[1] E. G. O'Neill, Jr., 'The Localisation of Metrical Word-types in the Greek Hexameter: Homer, Hesiod, and the Alexandrians', *Yale Classical Studies* viii (1942) 105–78.

[2] H. N. Porter, 'The Early Greek Hexameter', *Yale Class. Stud.* xii (1951) 3–63. The figure is taken from Table XIX, p. 61. Porter's calculations are based on 1,000 lines each from *Iliad* and *Odyssey*, beginning with Book V in each case.

[3] O'Neill, op. cit. The figure is taken from Tables X and XVI, pp. 142 and 145. Since O'Neill counts *syllaba anceps* in the sixth foot as long, it has been necessary to correct his figures from his Table XXIX where he distinguishes the natural quantities. O'Neill's material comes from A 1–B 453 and α 1–γ 170, i.e. 1,000 lines from each epic with the omission of repeated verses.

obtained with the simple shape. This break occurs in more than 60 per cent. of Homeric lines. Here for once the longer formula is more versatile than the shorter.

In sharp contrast with these very limited uses expressions scanned – ∪ ∪ – – in 5th–6th feet number 166 (Table II). Fifty of the ninety-seven regular formulae have word-divisions that would permit a medial placing, but it is scarcely worth while making the calculation, because no formulae are mobile, that is to say, are found medially as well as finally, except by leave of certain accidents and artifices (see Table VII at end).

This group of formulae therefore presents a picture of great rigidity, but it is not a rigidity that the poet can be said to have chosen. It is imposed on him by the inherent intractability of his material.

Of very different potential are the expressions with the final syllable short by nature. Four positions are available. The scatter together with that of the control group of words of this shape is given below:

Feet	1st–2nd	2nd–3rd	4th–5th	5th–6th
Words	8·4	25·4	17·8	53·4 (%)
Unique phrases	8·0	24·6	14·8	52·6 (%)
Regular Formulae	7·5	26·9	15·6	50·0 (%)
Occurrences of formulae	3·3	15·3	12·6	68·8 (%)

The parallelism between the distribution of single words and that of the uniquely occurring phrases is close. The fall in the 4th–5th feet is accounted for by the special difficulties created for the phrases by the ban on the weak fourth-foot caesura. The type with trochaic first word cannot be placed here at all. The deficiency appears to be made up by an increase in the 1st–2nd feet. It is not clear why this should be so, and in view of the very small numbers involved the increase may be most safely taken as fortuitous.

How much of a grip, generally, do sentence-patterns have on the use of the formulae? Evidently, since the number of formulaic expressions shows no decisive increase at any point, not very much. But before we explore further we must ask a question or two about the patterns supposed to govern expressions of this shape. For the personal names in the nominative case Parry defined six patterns:[1]

(i) with a verb filling the whole space between caesura and diaeresis, e.g. προσεφώνεε, ἐκέκλετο, μεταύδα;
(ii) with a verb, appositional pronoun, and connective, e.g. ὁ δ' ἐπεύξατο;
(iii) with a verb and object, e.g. τά οἱ πόρε, δόλον ἤγαγε;
(iv) with a verb, connective, and preposition in tmesi, e.g. ἀνὰ δ' ἴστατο;
(v) with a verb and connective, e.g. νόησε δέ;
(vi) coordinated with a second noun, e.g. Τρῶες καὶ φαίδιμος Ἕκτωρ.

Some of these sentence-patterns are reproduced by the common noun, and there are others. I single out four for mention:

(i) with a verb of which the formula is more often the object than the subject extending from caesura to diaeresis, e.g.

$$\left.\begin{array}{l}\text{ἀνείλετο}\\\text{ἠλεύατο}\\\text{ὑπέρπτατο}\end{array}\right\}\text{χάλκεον ἔγχος,}\qquad\left.\begin{array}{l}\text{ἀναφαίνεται}\\\text{πεφήσεται}\\\text{κιχάνεται}\\\text{τετεύξεται}\end{array}\right\}\text{αἰπὺς ὄλεθρος;}$$

(ii) with a pyrrhic verb, often with a connective, e.g. δόσαν ἀγλαὰ δῶρα, φέρε δ' ὄβριμον ἔγχος;
(iii) co-ordinated with a second noun, e.g. ὄϊς καὶ πίονας αἶγας;
(iv) with a preposition, e.g. ἐς πίονα δῆμον, ἐπὶ νῆα μέλαιναν.

It has not been sufficiently noted that the number of sentence-patterns assigned to the personal-name formulae increases as the formulae become shorter. The longest class has only two patterns allotted to it—a predicate to complete the verse and the resumptive line after direct speech;[2] the ∪ ∪ – ∪ ∪ – ⌣ class is given four;[3] the shortest class six. Thus the more space is left in the verse the greater is the syntactical versatility. Something of this progression might be expected on the grounds that the long formulae are unduly restricting. But I remain suspicious. If the sentence-pattern is to be given a meaningful role in a theory of

---

[1] ET 48–63. Parry's Type vii (ET 62), a corrected verb followed by a formula with initial vowel (βιάζεται ὠκὺς Ἀχιλλεύς) is a sub-type of (i).
[2] ET 67–69.
[3] ET 63–67, or rather three, if προσέφη is grouped with other ∪ ∪ – or ∪ – verbs.

improvisation it must occupy at the level of sentence-structure
a place corresponding to that of the formula at the level of diction.
The use of formulae is a limitation of choice of expression:
sentence-patterns should show a comparable selection and concentration on a limited range of syntagmata. Let us then ask
concerning the shortest formulae: what usages has the poet
eschewed? Ingenuity will discover possibilities,[1] but it is clear
that the poet's self-denial is not exercised in this direction. Hence
to say that the usage is patterned is not meaningful, because
there is no practical possibility of its being other than it is. Accordingly the scatter of formulae parallels that of unique phrases
and words of the same length.

On the other hand there is a rise in the proportion of occurrences of formulae at the verse-end which is much too high to
be fortuitous. The complex formulae responsible are easily sifted
out, e.g. φίλην ἐς πατρίδα γαῖαν 28×, καὶ σὴν (ἐὴν) ἐς πατρίδα
γαῖαν 9×, βόες (-ας) καὶ ἴφια μῆλα 10×, Μενοιτίου ἄλκιμος (-ον)
υἱός (-όν) 12×, and many more.

The scatter of occurrences might seem at this stage to be
sufficiently explained, but the consolidated totals are not to be
passed without inspection. Despite the slight fall of formulaic
occurrences in the 4th–5th feet there are two very frequent complex formulae that bring two of the – ∪ ∪ – ∪ expressions into
that position: πατρίδα γαῖαν with parts of ἱκέσθαι 15×, and τοὶ (οἵ)
οὐρανὸν εὐρὺν ἔχουσι 18 ×. Consequently the real popularity of the
4th–5th feet position is less than that indicated. The placing has
its problems. The weak caesura must be avoided, and a monosyllabic or pyrrhic word has to be found to precede the formula.
This does not favour those with initial consonant, the majority
group.[2] On the other hand elided δ' makes a neat combination
with an initial vowel: νῦν δ'/τὰ δ' ἀθρόα πάντα, ἐπὶ δ'/ὁ δ' ἄλφιτα
λευκά, περὶ δ' ἤματα μακρά, περὶ δ'/κατὰ δ' ἠέρα πουλύν.

A diminution of the real total in the 4th–5th feet means a corresponding increase at the verse-end and perhaps in the 2nd–3rd
feet, the position of second popularity. But the distribution in

---

[1] e.g. verb in first half of verse with object between caesura and diaeresis, cf.
ἔρριψε καλαύροπα βουκόλος ἀνήρ Ψ 845; or appositional phrase terminating with
ἀγανοῦ or μεγάθυμον at the diaeresis, Π 571, P 284, Φ 579. How many examples
must we have before we set up a pattern?

[2] Fifty of the 73 expressions found in the 4th–5th feet begin with a vowel. At the
verse-end the proportions are reversed.

the 2nd–3rd feet is remarkably even, and the only complex formula of any consequence is εἵλετο δ᾽ ἄλκιμον ἔγχος 8×.

There is nothing in the distribution and usage of these expressions, apart from the operation of some complex formulae, that would suggest they are naturally confined to any one position. In fact a very large number are found in two or more places in the verse. Table VII lists 92, or about 47 per cent. of the total of regular formulae of this shape, which is about the proportion which a random distribution would give. This is not quite the full number of mobile formulae, for the varying length of case-forms in declined formulae complicates the scholar's categories. Thus ἔγχεϊ μακρῷ 7× and νηλέϊ θυμῷ 3× must fall at the verse-end, but the nominative ἔγχεα μακρά 1× falls in the 4th–5th feet and the accusative νηλέα θυμόν 1× in the 1st–2nd feet: rather oddly it is the genitive τούτου ἀέθλου that is medial and the accusative τοῦτον ἄεθλον 1× that is final.[1]

From this outline of an important class of expressions I advance the following provisional conclusions: (i) expressions are found wherever the configuration of the verse allows in proportion to the ease or difficulty of the position; (ii) the scatter of the formulae is predictable from the scatter of single words and unique expressions of the same shape; (iii) the number of mobile formulae is not correlated with any factors of technique; and (iv) developed complex formulae cause a build-up of occurrences of formulae at the most favoured position.

2. The ∪ ∪ – ⌣ class

The brief expressions of this shape have received little attention from scholars, and were only by the narrowest margin counted as formulae at all by Parry, who made virtually no use of them,[2] perhaps because they include hardly any proper-name formulae (only Διὶ πατρί, Κρονίδης Ζεύς, φίλε Φοῖβε, and ταχὺς Αἴας).[3] Nevertheless the ordinary noun–epithet formulae of this shape constitute a very numerous class, showing all the features of construction that appear in more impressive classes, such as the

---

[1] I count the mobile formula ἀνδρόμεα κρέα, final with synizesis at ι 347 but initial with elision at ι 297, as belonging to the – ∪ ∪ – ∪ ∪ class.

[2] Parry's wish was to cut out fortuitous repetitions liable to arise among brief collocations of particles and connectives, cf. HSCP xli (1930) 84 n. 2. Severyns omits these short formulae altogether.

[3] Only in the complex formula ᾽Οϊλῆος ταχὺς Αἴας 7×.

generic and special epithets, consonantal and vocalic alternants, and the absence of superfluous equivalents.

If the final syllable is long, the only portion of the hexameter marked out by the normal divisions that seems fitted to receive an expression of this shape is that between caesura and diaeresis. But for reasons already indicated the use of $\cup\cup--$ in that position is regarded with marked aversion. The little group of medial expressions is given in Table VIII, to which must be added the medial occurrences of the four mobile formulae of Table X.[1] All the rest are final. The usage is thus very similar to that of the $-\cup\cup--$ expressions, and for the same reasons.

Again the short final syllable makes all the difference. The available positions are comparable to those of the $-\cup\cup-\cup$ class, but the normal divisions of the verse leave a space $\cup\cup-\cup$ only in the 2nd–3rd feet, and this is in fact the preferred placing rather than the verse-end. An analysis of the scatter of these expressions follows:

Feet	1st–2nd	2nd–3rd	4th–5th	5th–6th
Words[2]	2·0	40·0	24·2	33·1 (%)
Unique phrases	3·9	52·6	19·8	23·7 (%)
Regular formulae	2·8	40·0	29·8	27·4 (%)
Occurrences of formulae	1·2	41·3	26·0	31·5 (%)

The proportions are not so neatly parallel as those of the $-\cup\cup-\cup$ class, and in particular the discrepancy between the single words and the unique phrases demands inquiry. It is due, I consider, to the very popularity and versatility of the formulae which form a very large proportion of the material in this group and leave too small a number of unique phrases for the clearest possible picture: two or three more phrases in the last two positions would be enough to bring words and phrases into parallel. The scatter of single words therefore is likely to give the truest impression of the natural distribution.[3] In any case

---

[1] The causes of displacement are sometimes evident: οὐδέ κεν ἀμβαίη βροτὸς ἀνὴρ οὐδ᾽ ἐπιβαίη μ 77, a common pattern of co-ordination; ἱερὴ ἲς Τηλεμάχοιο β 409 etc. 7× after ἱερὸν μένος Ἀλκινόοιο / Ἀντινόοιο; three have a long word or formula finally, πόσιος οὗ κουριδίοιο ψ 150, ἕλικας βοῦς βουκολέεσκες Φ 448, and πυρὶ κηλέῳ νῆας ἐΐσας Θ 217. [2] 0·7% of the single words fall in the 3rd–4th feet.

[3] A check on the distribution of single words shaped $\cup\cup-\cup$ in Ω gives 2 : 32 : 18 : 26 in the four positions. This is strictly comparable with O'Neill's result.

the increased number of regular formulae in the 4th–5th feet, inverting as it does the preferences in position in the second half of the verse, is the striking feature. We may safely attribute this to a sentence-pattern, the construction of the formula, usually as subject or object, with a verb scanned ∪ – ∪; forty-one out of fifty-two formulae are so used.

The occurrences of the formulae are boosted at the verse-end so as to restore a distribution very like that of the single words. But the contrast is with the third line of the table and suggests the development of complex formulae at the verse-end: e.g. ὑψερεφὲς μέγα δῶμα 5×, ὅπως ἔσται τάδε ἔργα 7×, κατεκλάσθη φίλον ἦτορ 7×, ἐρυσσάμενος ξίφος ὀξύ 4×, ἐρύσσομεν (-αμεν) εἰς ἅλα δῖαν 5×, λύτο γούνατα καὶ φίλον ἦτορ 9×, κρέατ' ἄσπετα καὶ μέθυ ἡδύ 6×, and Ὀδυσσῆος φίλος υἱός 9×. These outweigh the effect of some notable complex formulae that locate the ∪ ∪ – ∪ element in the 4th–5th feet: e.g. κακὰ πολλὰ+μογήσας or parts of πάσχω 8×, φρεσὶ σῇσι μελόντων 5×, μέγα κῦδος Ἀχαιῶν 9×.

The favoured position in the 2nd–3rd feet is less dominant in this class than the verse-end position in the – ∪ ∪ – ∪ class. The proportion of formulae that are not confined to any one place is correspondingly larger: Table XV lists sixty formulae, many found in three different positions, some even in all four possible places. That is almost 64 per cent. of the regular formulae. In addition to the contents of Table XV we notice the declined formula ταχέ' ἵππω 5th–6th feet but ταχὺν ἵππον 2nd–3rd feet; χθόνα δῖαν 4th–5th feet has its nominative χθὼν δῖα (a rare shape) in 2nd–3rd feet:[1] βροτὸς ἀνήρ 3rd–4th feet falls in the 4th–5th feet in the oblique cases and nominative plural: κύνες ἀργοί 4th–5th but κύνας ἀργούς at the verse-end: and πύρα πολλά in 2nd–3rd feet but πυρὶ πολλῷ at the verse-end.

The pattern of use of the two shapes is thus closely similar, with the shorter formulae somewhat freer than the longer. This link between flexibility and length has already been noted in the case of the personal names. But the shorter formulae show one deviation. It was natural to assume that complex formulae would form themselves most readily about phrases used in the most popular position. With the ∪ ∪ – ∪ class this is not so. However,

---

[1] Expressions naturally shaped – – ∪ are usually – – – by position, and so not the metrical equivalents of ∪ ∪ – ∪. The most striking exception is κρῖ λευκόν 4× before caesura, 1× in 4th–5th feet, and 1× at the verse-end.

in the nature of the case a complex formula is a group of some length and also, since otherwise it would not become established, a group that the poet can use easily. Consequently complex formulae are a feature of the second half of the verse, most filling the whole half-verse. In the $- \cup \cup - \cup$ class the pull of the favoured position and the convenience of the complex formulae reinforce each other, in the $\cup \cup - \cup$ class they are in conflict.

The formulae of the two shapes considered present the brightest picture of free mobility, but this is only in proportion to the opportunities afforded. Other shapes, though more restricted, are equally as free as the verse permits them to be. My count of five common shapes is as follows:

Shape	Movable	Moved	Proportion
$(\cup) \cup - \cup \cup - \cup \cup - \underset{\smile}{\cup}$	25	2	8·0 (%)
$\cup \cup - \cup \cup - \cup$	132	30	22·7 (%)
$\cup \cup - \cup \cup$	90	18	20·0 (%)
$- \cup \cup - \cup \cup -$	74	22	30·0 (%)
$- \cup \cup - \cup \cup - \cup$	66	10	15·1 (%)

Thanks to the attention lavished on structural patterns in recent studies the purely metrical factor has been unduly neglected, but it is fundamentally important for the distribution of formulae. Some shapes are simply more convenient at one point in the verse than anywhere else and at other points may be very inconvenient indeed should they obliterate a natural boundary within the verse or lead to a sluggish and ponderous rhythm. Therefore the observed scatter of readily moved formulae is the natural result of random placing. What needs explanation is the heavy concentration of occurrences of some formulae in certain positions.

A theory of improvisation based on the rigorous confinement of formulae to a fixed place and their use in equally rigorous sentence-patterns cannot, outside certain limited areas, be a complete account of the versifier's craft. We can even point to instances where the fixed position and the fixed pattern are in collision, e.g. the sentence-frame ʽῥέπε+αἴσιμον ἦμαρ+genitive of the doomed party' gives ῥέπε δ' αἴσιμον ἦμαρ Ἀχαιῶν at Θ 72 but ῥέπε δ' Ἕκτορος αἴσιμον ἦμαρ at Χ 212. A fuller picture of versification cannot be drawn until the practices of modification, expansion, and separation have yielded their contribution. But there is one feature of formulae inherent in their nature that the mere fact of mobility brings out, their coherence. When a word-group has been cemented into a formula, the group has a certain autonomous existence. It does not come into mind only if a certain space is available. If the context suggests, say, the noun, then the epithet suggests itself also. That is the equivalent in psychological terms of the observable mutual expectancy of the terms of a formula.

V

MODIFICATION

THE study of the mobility of the formula necessarily operates with classes of formulae of the same length. We have noted, however, that there is no reason to suppose that length and shape are magically preserved constants. The next question must therefore be: to what extent are formulae flexible in shape as well as in use? It is convenient to use the same material, the formulae shaped $- \cup \cup - \underline{\cup}$ and $\cup \cup - \underline{\cup}$, but although the degree of coherence between the members of a formula was not of much consequence for their positioning in the verse, it is clearly a factor when formulae are adjusted in shape in any way. Unfortunately coherence is not a predictable quality and can only be inferred from the formulae's use. Hence it is not possible to separate our material into say, formulae of low coherence and formulae of high coherence, in a way roughly comparable to our separation of formulae into those easily moved and those moved with difficulty. Willy-nilly, for studying modification all must be placed on the same level.

Paradoxically the material that showed the flexibility possible in the use of formulae seems at first sight to emphasize the firm stability of the formula itself. Noted in passing was the virtual invariability of the natural quantity in a final syllable.[1] The exceptions to this rule may be conveniently dealt with here, because the rule is sufficiently absolute for departures from it to rank as modifications of some consequence. The examples of correption and lengthening are listed in the Tables. In the $- \cup \cup - \underline{\cup}$ class there are ten correptions and two lengthenings, in the $\cup \cup - \underline{\cup}$ class five correptions and no lengthenings. Although three of the longer formulae ($\dot{\alpha}\nu\delta\rho\grave{\iota}$ $\dot{\epsilon}\kappa\dot{\alpha}\sigma\tau\omega$, $\pi\dot{\alpha}\nu\tau\epsilon\varsigma$ $\dot{\alpha}\rho\iota\sigma\tau\omega\iota$, and $\pi\rho\dot{\omega}\phi\rho\omega\nu\iota$

---

[1] This applies to formulae of all dimensions normally extending to the verse-end. Positional lengthening *in arsi* is, of course, common enough, e.g. in the normal placings of the $- \cup \cup -$ and $- \cup \cup - \cup \cup -$ classes. Correption is never anything like so common among medial formulae ending with . . . $\cup \cup$, e.g. 12 out of *c.* 250 expressions shaped $\cup \cup - \cup \cup$.

θυμῷ) and one of the shorter (κύνες ἀργοί) are moved into their medial positions by correption, it is obvious that the poet has little liking for the great possibilities of this artifice and even less liking for enhancing the convenience of short final syllables by metrical lengthening (ἐννέα νῆας and νηυσι θοῇσιν). The reluctance to lengthen is obviously part of the prosodical habits defined by Wernicke's Law and its extensions.[1] But those who counted spondees in the fourth and, more rarely, in the second feet of the verse and noted the rarity of positional lengthening of final syllables drew no distinction between words in isolation and words in formulae. But it seems the distinction must be drawn. A compositional factor, the stability of some sorts of formulaic group, operates on the formulae as well as the prosodical preference.

Two more constants complete the picture of the stable formula. First, elision is used on medially placed formulae without obvious inhibition, but only in positions where the formula could stand in its complete form. Thus αἴσχεα πόλλ' may stand in the 1st–2nd or 4th–5th feet (it does), but not in the 3rd–4th feet where the complete formula would give a weak caesura.[2] Here it would seem is another opportunity forgone. Second, in formulae where the equivalence of two short syllables to one long is freely admitted the fall of ictus is fixed. Thus there is no interchange between the spondaic forms of the verse-end type ⏑⏑ – ⏑⏑ – – and

---

[1] Discussion in O'Neill, op. cit. (see p. 49 n. 1) 168 ff. The metrical rules state the avoidance of long word-final syllables in the 2nd and 4th feet, the prosodical rules the rarity of positional lengthening in those positions. Thus the vulgate reading ' Ὀδυσσῆα πτολιπόρθιον is preferable at ι 530 to ' Ὀδ. πτολίπορθον (Manuscript families f g k and Bentley), in spite of following ϝ-.

[2] There is an expression καλὰ λέπαδν' in 3rd–4th feet at T 393, but nothing like it in the ⏑⏑ – ⏑ class. At E 909 therefore Herodian's βροτόλοιγον Ἄρην in 2nd–4th feet would seem to be better than β. Ἄρη' (Family g, Venetus A) if that, not Ἄρη, is in fact the tradition. Nor need we assume that antevocalic ἄλλοισι θεοῖς A 597, μακάρεσσι θεοῖς E 819, Z 141, πάντεσσι θεοῖς μ 337, κτεάτεσσιν ἑοῖς a 218, ξεστοῖσι λίθοις Σ 504, and ἀθανάτοισι θεοῖς E 130, etc., in the same position are concealed elisions (-οισ'). The only class in which elision is exploited to any degree at all is ⏑⏑ – ⏑⏑. The secondary position for this shape is in the 4th–5th feet. There elision is possible in the normal way (nine expressions), producing coincidence in shape with the ⏑⏑ – ⏑ class. Since the latter shape is normally placed in the 2nd–3rd feet we find that four of the elided expressions follow it there, χαλέπ' ἄλγε', φίλα γούνατ', τάδε εἵματ', κακὰ φάρμακ' (the last three formulae are always elided). κάκ' ἐλέγκε' is the only elided formula of this class that does not also occur with elision in the 4th–5th feet. Evidently these elided formulae are ambiguously classified in the poet's mind. I have discussed this matter further in BICS xiv (1967) 17–21.

the initial type $-\smile\smile-\smile\smile-$. θνητῶν ἀνθρώπων ($-\underline{}-\underline{}-$) cannot be used initially, nor ἄλλων ἀνθρώπων ($\underline{}-\underline{}-\underline{}$) finally.[1]

Since drastic modifications of formulae occur often enough it is hard to say why slight modifications like the above do not. If it has to do with the conditions of improvisation we can only guess. It is possible, for example, that in the production of familiar material the slight adjustments are just those that it is most difficult to make, because the enunciation is automatic and needs positive effort to change it.

The more considerable modifications examined here mean (i) the use of alternative case-forms and suffixes, non-significant changes of number and gender, and alternative metrics;[2] (ii) rearrangements of word-order; and (iii) a combination of (i) and (ii). I do not consider the important technique whereby flexibility is obtained by using synonymous words: for a different word means a different formula. Nor are the uses of movable -ν in dative plurals and elision examined;[3] they are too ubiquitous to be put in the same class as the major adaptations here considered. Some of the more consequential adjustments were examined by Witte,[4] who correctly diagnosed the powerful influence of metre as their cause. The 'influence of metre' in Homeric diction can usually be restated in terms of the technique of composition, and perhaps ought always to be stated in such terms. If it seemed that this could not be done for such alternants as ἠέρα πολλήν (final) and ἠέρα πουλύν (medial) that was because mobility was not recognized as part of the technique of the formula. The modification of ἠέρα πολλήν and of many other formulae is an artifice for making a fixed expression movable. Naturally there are other uses: a short formula may be expanded, a long one contracted; adaptation to adjacent words secured; the position of word-divisions changed, and so on.

---

[1] Of longer shapes among the noun–epithet formulae only ἄλλοι πάντες is variable, $\underline{}-\underline{}\smile$ 3× but $-\underline{}-\underline{}$ 2×, for which the existence of ἄλλοι μὲν πάντες 9× is undoubtedly relevant. πάντων τ' ἀνθρώπων Ξ 233 at the verse-end against π. ἀνθρώπων 2× initially reflects the problems presented by phrase and sentence connexion.

[2] For details see above pp. 36 ff. None of our formulae are affected by changes in internal syntax. The particles (γε, δή, ῥα, περ, etc.) play no part in the modification of noun–epithet formulae.   [3] On ν-movable see Hoekstra, MFP 71 ff.

[4] Glotta iii (1912) 106 ff., following Düntzer and Ellendt. The modifications considered by Parry in Les Formules et la métrique, 10 ff., are all internal (type μερόπων ἀνθρώπων > μέροπες ἄνθρωποι) and do not affect the over-all shape of the formula.

But the evidence must precede its evaluation. To present it in a reasonably orderly fashion I must make a few provisional assumptions.

The simplest account of modification as a compositional artifice is to assume that the poet desires to use a certain formulaic word association. He naturally thinks of this in its most familiar form, and this form we may call the primary shape of the formula. If then the primary shape is impossible since the positions in which it might be used are already occupied, the poet adjusts its shape to make it fit the space that is available. This secondary expression is thus transient, a response to an emergency in composition and in no way part of the regular stock of formulae. Needless to say, this oversimplifies and must be later qualified, but has certain advantages for exposition. With this account or something like it in the background we must distinguish between modifications which the poet chooses to make in order to ease the use of a formula and modifications which are forced upon him by the use of a formula in an unusual case-form. The former are a matter of technique and illustrate the handling of material that the poet already possesses, the latter are evidence of the persistence of formulaic associations. An example will elucidate the distinction. Let the context have suggested the sense 'citadel' in the dative case. The regular formula is πόλει ἄκρῃ, and falls at the verse-end. If this position is difficult, being pre-empted for some other expression that the poet wishes to use, then the formula can be modified by the use of the superlative degree of the epithet, πόλει ἀκροτάτῃ and shifted to a position before the caesura. That is voluntary modification of existing material. However, the context at another time might suggest the genitive singular for which the poet has no regular formula at hand to use or to modify. He must therefore create one, and declines into the genitive the existing πόλει ἄκρῃ, but in so doing is obliged to modify it since πόλιος (or πόληος) ἄκρης is unmetrical. Hence ἀκροτάτης πόλιος, with inversion of the word-order. This chapter, and the two succeeding chapters, are concerned only with the handling of existing formulae, that is to say, with the voluntary adjustments. The primary and derivative expressions quoted are therefore either both in the same grammatical case or else the case of the derivative expression is possible in the primary position.

1. *Modifications to the* – ∪ ∪ – ⌣ *class*

(i) > ⏖ – ∪

Since the – ∪ ∪ – ∪ formulae are found in the same pairs of feet as those of the ∪ ∪ – ∪ shape one might expect some interchange between the two. It is not easy for the poet to contrive it, for his alternative forms are mostly alternative ends to words, not alternative beginnings. The few examples exploit chance opportunities: φίλτατοι ἄνδρες—φίλοι ἄνδρες; ἄντιτα—τιτὰ ἔργα; πῆμα μέγιστον—μέγα πῆμα; and σοῖσι πόδεσσι—ποσὶν οἷσι. Giving a similarly shaped result are ἀνέρι τῷδε—τῷδ' ἀνδρί, also in acc. Γ 166 etc. 6×; παιδὸς ἑοῖο—οὗ παιδός Ζ 466 etc. 8×; and πατρὸς ἑοῖο—οὗ πατρός A 404, η 3.

Elsewhere the modification of these formulae is a response to the exigencies imposed by the first half of the verse and by the caesura. The position in the 1st–2nd feet is the least popular for the unmodified formula, since the space that is left before the caesura is inconveniently cramped. Nor is a mid-verse location very convenient for this important class of formulae. They cannot lie immediately after the caesura, and the rhythm of the fourth foot gives rise to the well-known difficulties. Modification is used with some freedom to surmount these troubles.

(ii) > – ∪ ∪ – in 1st–2nd or 2nd–3rd feet[1]

ἧς ἀλόχοιο—ἧς (σῆς) ἀλόχου ν 336, etc. 3×; παιδὸς ἐμοῖο (ἑοῖο)— π. ἐμοῦ (ἑοῦ) A 496, etc. 3×; πατρὸς ἐμοῖο (ἑοῖο)—π. ἐμοῦ (ἑοῦ) γ 83, etc. 5×; and ἀμβροσίη νύξ—ν. ἀβρότη Ξ 78. Some of the short genitives may be regarded as elisions (-οι'), but seven instances, including all three of ἀλόχου, are ante-consonantal.[2] Moreover the position in the 1st–2nd feet is a very usual one for *words* scanned – ∪ ∪ – in the genitive singular.[3] It is odd that none of the short datives are used similarly, for the poet uses them with some freedom in other classes of formula.[4]

---

[1] The artifice is unknown to the personal name formulae (it is probably impossible), but is common in other types, e.g. δῖα θεάων—δ. θεά, δεύτερον αὖτις—δ. αὖ, ἀλλὰ καὶ ἔμπης—ἀλλ' ἔμπης, αὐτὰρ ἔγωγε—αὐτὰρ ἐγώ(ν), ἀχνύμενος κῆρ—κ. ἀχέων, κεῖτο τανυσθείς—κ. ταθείς, χεῖρας ὀρεγνύς—χεῖρ' ὀρέγων.

[2] M 403, γ 83, ζ 256 and 299, ν 336, ψ 165 and 346.

[3] Cf. Witte, *Glotta* v (1914) 13 ff., showing that the proliferation of the -ου genitive is assisted by the metrical usefulness of the shape.

[4] Chiefly in medial placings of the ∪ ∪ – ∪ ∪ – ∪ class shortened by a syllable, see p. 59, n. 2 and add the anteconsonantal μεγάροισιν ἐμοῖς τ 490.

(iii) $> - \underline{\cup\cup} - \underline{\cup\cup} - (\cup)$ in 1st–3rd feet

Elongation by sufficient syllables gives a total solution to the problems of the first half-verse, but noun–epithet formulae are not usually sufficiently elastic.[1] ἄνδρας ἀρίστους—ἄ. ἀριστῆας, also in gen. sing. O 489 etc. 5×; πᾶσι δόλοισι—παντοίοισι δόλοισι γ 119, 122, and with a preposition ἐν πάντεσσι δ. ν 292; and ὠκέας ἵππους—ἵ. ὠκύποδας E 732.

(iv) $> - - - \cup$ in 1st–2nd feet

The artifice is an inversion of the word-order together with the elision of the second word: ἠέρα πολλήν—π. ἠέρ᾽[2] η 140; κτήματα πολλά—π. κτήματ᾽ γ 312; πότνια νύμφη—ν. πότνι᾽ α 14; and χρήματα πολλά—π. χρήματ᾽ ξ 385. πολλὴν ἠέρα η 15 occurs also without the elision. This neat device seems confined to noun-epithet expressions. Here I enter the isolated ἄλλοι ἄπαντες— ἄλλοι πάντες (– – – ∪) T 190 etc. 3×, but put into the 2nd–3rd or 4th–5th feet, cf. (vii).

For medial placing a modified formula of only moderate length quite easily makes the caesura its starting point or (more rarely) its finishing point. Actually to make the formula straddle the caesura is to place it in the very two feet of the verse where the metrical requirements are most stringent. However, the *Kunstsprache* exists for coping with metrical problems and the creation or preservation of forms scanning $(\cup) \cup - \cup \cup$ for use between the caesura and diaeresis is one of its specialities,[3] so that the adaptation of a formula is more readily achieved than may be thought.

(v) $> - \cup \cup - \cup \cup$ in 3rd–4th feet[4]

αἷμα κελαινόν—αἷμα κελαινεφές[5] Δ 140 etc. 4×; ἔργον ἀεικές —ἔργα ἀεικέα Ω 733; εἴκοσι φῶτες—φῶτας ἐείκοσι Π 810. The

---

[1] The shorter shape – ∪ ∪ – ∪ ∪ – is easier to obtain. The artifice is known in only one personal name Παλλὰς Ἀθήνη—Π. Ἀθηναίη, and in acc. similarly, but is not unusual in a wide variety of formulae, e.g. Ἴλιον αἰπύ—Ἴλιος (-ον) αἰπεινή (-ήν), τείχεος ἐκτός—τ. ἔκτοσθεν, ἀσκελὲς αἰεί—ἀσκελέως αἰεί, τίπτε δέ σε χρεώ— τ. δέ σε χρειώ, ἀντίον ἐλθεῖν—ἀ. ἐλθέμεναι.

[2] Not an equivalent of ἠέρα πουλύν whose initial vowel is necessary (περὶ δ᾽, κατὰ δ᾽ E 776, Θ 50).

[3] See Meister, *Hom. Kunstsprache*, 13–23, for details.

[4] The alternation of active and middle voices makes this a common trick in the verbal formulae, e.g. γούναθ᾽ ἱκάνω—γ. ἱκάνομαι, ἔντε᾽ ἔδυνε—ἔ. ἐδύσετο, θυμὸν ἔτερπε—θ. τέρπετο, χαλκὸς ἔλαμπε—χ. ἐλάμπετο. Other examples: ἔλπετο θυμός— θ. ἐέλπετο, ἔργα τέτυκται—ἔ. τετεύχατο (also with πάντα instead of ἔργα), θῆκεν ἄεθλα —θ. ἀέθλιον, χεῖρας ἀνασχεῖν—χ. ἀνασχέμεν.

[5] Whatever the merits of Leumann's derivation of this word (*Homerische Wörter*,

same modifications reappear with inverted word-order, cf. (vii) below.

(vi) > – – ∪ ∪ in 3rd–4th feet[1]

With one exception the pattern is the simple inversion of conveniently shaped words: ἄλγεα πολλά—πόλλ' ἄλγεα ζ 184; ἄλφιτα λευκά—λεύκ' ἄλφιτα[2] Σ 560; ὀστέα λευκά—λεύκ' ὀστέα[3] α 161, ω 76; and υἱὸς ἑοῖο—οὗ υἱέος Ω 122.

(vii) > ∪ – ∪ ∪ – ∪ or ∪ ∪ – ∪ ∪ – in 1st–3rd or 3rd–5th feet[4]

Inversion of the word-order is the simplest means of securing the new shape: hence μελαίνη κηρί ρ 500; ἐρεβεννὴ νύξ E 659 etc. 3×; ὀρυκτὴ τάφρος Π 369 (the primary form is accusative); ἀάπτους χεῖρας A 567; and βαρείη χειρί Λ 235 = P 48; all after the caesura. ἑκάστῳ φωτί β 384 = θ 10 and ἕκαστον φῶτ' ι 431 lie before the caesura. With the exception of the very last example all these have a final long syllable in the primary form and consequently do not require a positional lengthening *in thesi* in the modified form. This shows a nice sensitivity to rhythm, especially in the case of βαρείη χειρί, which occurs also in the genitive singular and nominative and accusative plural cases in that word-order, but not in the accusative singular, where χεῖρα βαρεῖαν 2× is normal.[5] The only positional lengthening in the 3rd–4th feet, where it is particularly objectionable, is in a weak formula with the demonstrative, ἄεθλον τοῦτον τ 576 cf. τοῦτον ἄεθλον. Other-

---

202 ff.), from the synchronic point of view, which is my point of view here, κελαινεφής is an alternant of κελαινός.

[1] This artifice of modification is confined to noun–epithet formulae.

[2] The full phrase is λεύκ' ἄλφιτα πολλὰ πάλυνον Σ 560, a variant of the complex formula ἄλφιτα λευκὰ πάλυνε (-ον, -ειν) 4×. It is hard to see why πολλά should have displaced λευκά. H. Amann, *Glotta* xii (1923) 110–11, detects an emphatic word-order become ossified.

[3] Also (once with elision) in the 4th–5th feet, thus functioning as a regular member of the ∪∪ – ∪ ∪ class. At λ 221 the modified formula is drawn into a formulaic complex: λίπε δ' ὀστέα θυμός M 386 etc. 3×, λίπε δ' ὀστέα θυμὸς ἀγήνωρ μ 414, λίπη λεύκ' ὀστέα θυμός λ 221.

[4] Cf. the three personal name formulae noted at ch. ii, p. 30 n. 3 (iii). At ET 102 Parry explains the displacement of 'Οδυσσεὺς δῖος β 27 as the consequence of a conflation of ἐξ οὗ 'Οδυσσεύς τ 596, ψ 18 with the normal δῖος 'Οδυσσεύς. The inversion is not frequent in other sorts of formula, but note κῦμα θαλάσσης—θ. κῦμα(τ'), νῆας (-σὶν) Ἀχαιῶν—Ἀχ. νῆας (-σίν), χεῖρ' ἐπὶ καρπῷ—ἐπὶ καρπῷ χεῖρα (-ας).

[5] Observe the striking absence of inversion of the very frequent accusative κῆρα μέλαιναν 17×. F. Sommer, *Glotta* i (1909) 198 ff., stressed the rarity of positional lengthening here even within the word-group.

wise where the primary formula terminates in a naturally short syllable the use of by-forms is considered necessary, usually with inversion also:[1] αἷμα κελαινόν—κελαινεφὲς αἷ. Π 667 etc. 3×; ἔργον ἀεικές—ἀεικέα ἔ. π 107, υ 317;[2] οὗ ἑτάροιο—ἑοῦ ἑ. Ω 416; καλὰ πρόσωπα—προσώπατα κ. σ 192; εἴκοσι φῶτες—ἐείκοσι φῶτας[3] δ 530, 778; and μῆτιν ἀμείνω—ἀμείνονα μ. Ε 107. Before the caesura are ἄλλοι ἅπαντες—ἅ. πάντες ξ 478, ρ 411 (‒ ⏑ ‒ ⏑); and Τρώϊοι ἵπποι—ἵ. Τρῳαί Π 393.

(viii) > ⏑ ⏑ ‒ ⏑ ⏑ ‒ ⏟ in 4th–6th feet[4]

ἄλλοι ἅπαντες—σύμπαντες οἱ ἄλλοι Χ 380; ἔργον ἀεικές—ἀεκήλια ἔ.[5] Σ 77; ἱερὰ καλά—ἱερήϊα κ. ρ 600; εἴκοσι φῶτες—ξυνεείκοσι φωτῶν ξ 98; plus five dative plurals taking advantage of the Aeolic -εσσι (-έεσσι): πᾶσι βροτοῖσι—πάντεσσι β. ν 397; πᾶσι θεοῖσι—πάντεσσι θ. Τ 100; νηυσὶ θοῇσι—νήεσσι θ. Μ 112, Ν 320; σοῖσι τέκεσσι—τεκέεσσιν ἑοῖσι Μ 222; and χερσὶ φίλῃσι—χείρεσσι φ. Ρ 620.

(ix) Various

Changing a long final syllable to a short: ἠέρα πολλήν—ἠ. πουλύν Ε 776, Θ 50; κίονα μακρήν—κ. μακρόν θ 66 etc. 3×; and ὄσσε φαεινώ—ὄ. φαεινά Ν 435. For straddling the caesura (cf. (v) above): πάντας ἀρίστους—π. ἀριστῆας Κ 117; ἡμέτερον δῶ—ἡμ. δόμον Σ 406; and πᾶσι θεοῖσι—πάντεσσι θεοῖς μ 337.

[1] Since the effect of modification in this group is to contrive an additional short syllable at the head of the formula, the verbal formulae are at an advantage, because a prepositional compound can be introduced or augmented, e.g. ἵκετο πένθος—καθίκετο π., ὤλεσε λαόν—ἀπώλεσε λ., (ἐκ-)φύγε κῆρα—ὑπέκφυγε κ., ἀντίος ἦλθε—ἐναντίος (-η) ἦλθε.

[2] Also (+καὶ) at the verse-end at δ 694, a placing which, augmented by connective or preposition, enjoys a mild popularity in the Odyssey.

[3] This and the first two formulae listed appeared also in section (v). For the reasons stated at the beginning of this chapter these are listed as modifications of the shape ‒ ⏑ ⏑ ‒ ⏑, but the class of formulae shaped ⏑ ‒ ⏑ ⏑ | ‒ ⏑ has many autonomous formulae and its conversion to ‒ ⏑ | ⏑ ‒ ⏑ ⏑ by reversing the word-order is an established artifice. Besides the three formulae noted the following are inverted: ἀνάλκιδος ἀνδρός, νεώτερον ἄνδρα, ἀνέψιον ἐσθλόν, ἀγακλυτὰ δώμαθ', ὀλέθριον ἦμαρ, ἀπηνέα θυμόν, ἀθέσφατον ὄμβρον, νοήματα πάντα, ἀρήϊα τεύχε', παλίντονα τόξα, ἀρίστερον ὦμον.

[4] An easy extension for verbal formulae by compounding, e.g. (ἐπι-)ἥνδανε βουλή. Witte, Glotta iv (1913), 11 ff., related this artifice to the desire for a dactylic 4th foot, but the extension is not always ⏑ ⏑, cf. (ἐξ-)ἦρχε γόοιο.

[5] A doubtful instance, see Lexicon des frühgriechischen Epos, s.v. ἀεκήλιος, but the techniques of modification support Bechtel's connexion with ἀεικέλιος, Lexilogus 13. For the suffixation see Risch, Wortbildung 113.

Prolonging the formula by a syllable: ἄλκιμον ἄνδρα—ἄλκιμοι ἀνέρες Φ 586 (4th–5th feet); and ἄρσενος οἰός—ἄρσενες ὄϊες (or ὄϊες) ι 425 (1st–2nd feet).

The consonantal or vocalic character of the initial sound of a formula has an important bearing on its use anywhere except at the beginning of the verse. Yet in the class of noun–epithet formulae just considered no attempt is made to convert the one into the other by modification. However, the will may not be absent. For the noun–epithet formulae it is the means that is lacking, unless it is possible to invert the formula and elide the last syllable of the new second term. The treatment ἠέρα πολλήν—π. ἠέρ' exactly illustrates the conditions, but that modification was made for a different reason and the expression is placed at the head of the verse. Nor would this device be of any help at the point where presumably it would be most useful, at the verse-end. Verbal formulae are definitely more versatile in this respect.[1]

2. *Modifications to the* ∪ ∪ – ⌣ *class*

For interchange with the – ∪ ∪ – ⌣ class see 1 (i) above.

The formulae of this class are found almost exclusively at the verse-end if the final syllable is long and principally in the 2nd–3rd feet if the final syllable is short by nature. The two most obvious needs are therefore for a shape that can begin the verse and for one that can follow the caesura. Lengthened shapes would also be useful in the first half of the verse.

(i) > – ∪ ∪ –

Provided the formula begins with a single consonant and terminates in a short open syllable, or begins with a vowel and ends in a short closed syllable, the poet has only to invert the word-order to obtain the new shape. The artifice is well exploited, principally to fill the 1st–2nd foot position, but also the 2nd–3rd and the 3rd–4th feet across the caesura.

In 1st–2nd feet: by simple inversion αἷμα μέλαν Λ 813, Π 529; ἀνδρὶ φίλῳ Ξ 504; ἄστυ μέγα I 136 = 278; αἰνὸν ἄχος Π 55;

---

[1] The optional character of the Homeric augment and the alternation of -σ- and -σσ- in some sigmatic aorists combine to give some neat modifications, e.g. ἤλασε χαλκόν—χ. ἔλασσε, ὤλεσε θυμόν—θ. ὄλεσσε, ὤπασε λαόν—λ. ὄπασσε. ὤπασα πομπόν—π. ὄπασσε.

ὀξὺ βέλος Λ 392, 845; ἔγχος ἐμόν Π 618 (dat. sing. Ξ 483, Χ 271);
πολλὰ κακά Σ 455; κῦμα μέγα μ 60; υἱὸν ἐμόν Α 510 (and υἱεῖ ἐμῷ
Σ 144): with a change of case or some further modification δύο γ'
ἄνδρε—ἄ. δύω Ψ 659 etc. 6×; νέον (-ου) ἄνδρα (-ός)—ἀ. νέῳ π
210; and ἐὸν οἶκον—οἶ. ἐμόν α 251, π 128.

In 2nd–3rd feet: all by simple inversion, ἄστυ μέγα Χ 251;
αἰνὸν ἄχος Δ 169 etc. 9×; ὠκὺ βέλος φ 138 = 165; and υἱὸν ἑόν
Μ 292 (and υἷες ἐμοί γ 325).

In 3rd–4th feet: by simple inversion αἷμα μέλαν Ν 655 = Φ
119; ἄστυ μέγα Β 332 etc. 7×; υἱὸν ἐμόν Ο 67; τέκνα φίλα γ 418;
and with a slight modification δύο δοῦρε—δ. δύω Λ 43 etc. 3×.

Where the final syllable is long inversion is possible only in
the rare event of the second word of the formula being a monosyllable: we have σὴν (ἣν, ἧς) ἀρετήν (-ῆς) Θ 535 etc. 3×; πᾶν
πεδίον Π 79 etc. 4×, (both distributed into 1st–2nd, 2nd–3rd,
and 3rd–4th feet); πῦρ ὀλοόν Ν 629 in 1st–2nd feet.[1]

Many of the ∪ ∪ – ∪ formulae have a pyrrhic first word with
an open final syllable. After inversion positional lengthening
according to the normal Homeric practice may take care of the
final open short vowel, e.g. ἄστυ μέγα Πριάμοιο Β 332 etc.). But
the short vowel may be elided and the ensuing dactyl used in
1st, 3rd, or (in a single complex formula) 5th feet. There is no
other modification.

In 1st foot: ἄστυ τόδ' Ζ 329; κῦμα μέγ' ε 416; λαῖτμα μέγ' η 35;
πάντα τάδ' Ο 159; and τέκνα φίλ' δ 78.

In 3rd foot: ἔργα κάκ' ρ 226, σ 362; ἔργα τάδ' Α 573; πολλὰ
κάκ' Ω 518 etc. 4×; πῆμα τόδ' Ω 547.

In 5th foot: only in (οἰῶν) μέγα πῶυ—πῶυ μέγ' (οἰῶν) Λ 696
etc. 3×.

Altogether twenty-five formulae are inverted in these ways.

(ii) > ∪ – ∪∪ –

Normally for 1st–3rd feet, so ὃν ἑταῖρον—ἑ. ἑόν Λ 602; μέλῐ
χλωρόν—μέλῐ χλ. Λ 631 with the usual positional lengthening;[2]
δύο νύκτας—δύω ν. ε 388, ι 74; πατέρι ᾧ—ἑὸν πατέρα χ 355 (and
ἐμὸν π. Ε 639) and ἑὸν πατέρ' Ω 511, ω 236 in 3rd–4th feet, also
ὃν (σὸν) πατέρ' α 195 etc. 4×; ποσὶν οἷσι—πόδεσσιν ἑοῖς ξ 23.

─────────

[1] Cf. the divine name Κρονίδης Ζεύς—Ζ. Κρονίδης Λ 289, Π 845. Though noun-
verb formulae shaped ∪∪–∪ (verb –∪) are common enough, this inversion is not
exploited.
[2] Cf. the similar alternation of πολὺ μεῖζον and κατὰ μοῖραν.

(iii) > ∪ ∪ – ‿ – in 1st–3rd feet

All the examples have a preposition in the first half of the verse, and may be already prepositional in their primary position: (ἐν) πόλει ἄκρῃ—ἐν π. ἀκροτάτῃ X 172; πόλις (-ιν) ὑμή (-ήν)—ἐν πόλει ὑμετέρῃ E 686; and (ἐν) πυρὶ κηλέῳ—σὺν π. κηλείῳ O 744.

(iv) > ‿ – ∪ ∪ or ∪ – ∪ ∪ mostly in 3rd–4th feet[1]

Simple inversion will in many cases give the shape needed, so ἄλλον θεόν ε 104 = 138; αὐτὴν ὁδόν θ 107 etc. 3×; τέκνον φίλε ο 125, also τ. φίλον ψ 26, and φίλον τέκος Γ 162 etc. 15×; υἱὸς (-ὸν) φίλος (-ον) K 50 etc. 5×; φᾶρος μέγα ε 230 = κ 543; and σῇσι (ἧσι) φρεσί K 237 etc. 5×. εὐρὺ σπέος ε 77 etc. 3× falls in the 2nd–3rd feet.

The rest make use of various alternative forms: βροτὸν (-ῷ) ἄνδρα (-ί)—β. ἀνέρος Σ 85; similarly δύο γ' ἄνδρε—δύ' ἀνέρε (-ας) M 421 etc. 4×; and φίλου (-οι) ἀνδρός (-ες)—φ. ἀνέρος (-ες) Δ 41, δ 169; ἕλικας βοῦς—ἕ. βόας λ 289; πυκινὸν δῶ—π. δόμον K 267 etc. 5×; τόδε δῶμα—τάδε δώματα ρ 264 etc. 4× (twice, with δώμαθ', in 4th–5th feet); ὀπὶ καλῇ—ὄπα κάλλιμον μ 192; πτέρα πυκνά—πυκινὰ πτέρα[2] ε 53; μέλαν ὕδωρ—ὕδωρ μέλαν B 825; χρόα καλόν—χ. κάλλιμον λ 529. μέγα τεῖχος—μ. τειχίον π 165, 343 falls in the 4th–6th feet.

(v) > ∪ – ∪ ∪ – ∪ in 3rd–5th feet

A useful post-caesural shape: θοὸν ἅρμα—βοηθόον ἅ.[3] P 481; κλυτὰ δῶρα—περικλυτὰ δ. I 121, Σ 449; τιτὰ ἔργα—παλίντιτα ἔ. α 379=β 144; ποσὶν οἶσι—πόδεσσί γε οἶσι[4] P 27.

---

[1] This adjustment is popular with verbal formulae, e.g. πάθεν ἄλγος (-εα)—πάθεν (πάθ') ἄλγεα, σχεδὸν ἦλθε (-ον)—σχ. ἤλυθε (-ον), φρένας εἷλε—φ. εἵλετο and ἕλε φρένας, δέος (nom.) εἷλε—δ. (acc.) εἵλετο, δέος ἴσχει—δ. ἰσχάνει, κτύπος ὦρτο—κτ. ὤρνυτο. The modified shape is desirable owing to the number of sentence-patterns that locate a verbal phrase in the 3rd–4th feet.

[2] πυκινά because πυκνός is not used with the first syllable *in thesi*. Szemerényi, *Syncope in Greek and Indo-European*, Naples 1964, 82 ff., takes the words as related by syncope, that is, πυκινά is an older form than πυκνά, in which case it may be noted that the diction has had time to sort the two forms according to their maximum metrical utility, in contrast with the imperfect exploitation in formulae of recent linguistic developments such as the quantitative metathesis (cf. Hoekstra, *MFP* 36).

[3] There is an ancient variant βοῇ θοόν (as also at N 477), which would make θ. ἅρμα an expanded formula in its secondary position, extended by a rather infrequent technique.

[4] But the γε has point, as always in Homer.

(vi) Various

Changing the character of an initial or final sound: τάδε ἔργα[1]—
τόδε ἔργον I 527 etc. 6×; πόλις ἥδε—πτόλις ἥδε X 118; τόδε τόξον
—τάδε τόξα E 215, φ 349; φίλον υἱόν—φ. υἷα δ 765, ν 259. Making
a dactyl ἑὸν ἄνδρα—ἄνδρ᾽ ἐμόν T 295. Giving – – ◡ πατέρι ᾧ—ᾧ
πατρί Θ 406, ν 265. Giving – ◡ ◡ – ◡ ◡ κρέας ὀπτόν—ὀπτάλεα
κρέα[2] Δ 345.

It is not easy to summarize the evidence for modification of
formulae in a way that is at once lucid and free from built-in
prejudice. Our troubles are basically two, doubts about the direction in which the modification is made, and doubts about the
derivative status of some of the expressions provisionally counted
as adaptations of primary formulae. The evidence has been presented in a consistent way, as if the formulae of the two classes
examined were basic formulae or part of the poet's permanent
stock. There is, of course, no reason *a priori* why these shapes or
any others should be so favoured, but the assumption is very
often demonstrably true when formulae are attested several times
in one of the two selected shapes and only once in the modified
shape, e.g. πάντες (-ας) ἄριστοι (-ους) 16× > π. ἀριστῆας 1×, or
μέλαν ὕδωρ 6× > ὕδωρ μέλαν 1×. But the same evidence shows that
the direction of modification is occasionally quite the opposite,
e.g. ἄλλοι πάντες 5× > ἄλλοι ἅπαντες 1×, or αἰνὸν ἄχος 10× > ἄ.
αἰνόν 1× : or it may be quite indecisive, e.g. μέλι χλωρόν 1×—μέλι
χλωρόν 1×. Nor may we be inclined to be assertive about the character of a formula that appears twice only in one form and once in
another; too much depends upon chance. But these are problems
which bedevil our judgement of particular formulae. As a class
each of the two considered classes consists of primary formulae
and was chosen for that reason. The really doubtful cases are
those expressions that embody a regular association of words
once only in the shapes examined. These are inherently trouble-
some, since nothing can be *proved* about them. Might not both occurrences, for example, of ὀλοὸν πῦρ—πῦρ ὀλοόν be *ad hoc* creations?
Of course, if they are both *ad hoc* creations this implies that there

---

[1] Not so obviously a plural in form only, as δώματα *v.* δῶμα, but it is hard to see
any difference in sense between the plural and singular forms: the former are
mostly final (12× out of 16×), the latter medial (5× out of 6×).

[2] In the 2nd–3rd feet. The placing arises through contamination with the
verbal formula κρέα ἔδμεναι.

is no bond of word-association present: and if this is so what are we to say, for example, of λάσιον κῆρ and all the other word-groups whose association is only twice attested, albeit in the same shape? The evidence for word-association is really the same in both cases. With a sigh for the loss of the epic literature that would give all formulae their proper representation we must say that ὀλοὸν πῦρ—πῦρ ὀλοόν conceals a formula which, being modified, must have a real existence, like a proved regular formula, in whatever its primary form happens to be.[1] In most of these doubtful cases the direction of the modification is probably the same as that of the majority of clear cases.

Even when the direction of modification is not disputable some of the 'modified' forms listed occur more than once. There are times when this need not be disturbing: φίλος υἱός occurs sixty-five times in three grammatical cases, the inverted modification occurs five times; μέγα κῦμα seventeen times, inverted twice. Obviously if a formula is frequently needed the hazards that induce modification arise with corresponding frequency. In such cases I should be inclined to regard the modifications as genuinely such, because one form is so manifestly dominant. Yet whatever its source the effect of repetition can never be wholly denied: it is consolidating the word-association in a particular shape, and quite likely consolidating wider associations with other words. Thus ἠέρα πουλύν occurs in two almost identical lines E 776 and Θ 50. When this is the situation, whatever may be the historical development, the poet's equipment really contains two related but autonomous expressions.

Finally, granting the poet such a pair of expressions, which are we to choose as the source if a third form, apparently a genuine modification, is attested? Such a set is ἔργον ἀεικές 6×, ἀεικέα ἔργα 3×, and ἔργα ἀεικέα 1×. ἔργον ἀεικές is the dominant member of the whole group, but ἔργα ἀεικέα is closer to ἀεικέα ἔργα both in plural number and in type of modification. It would be reasonable enough to argue that despite its importance ἔργον ἀεικές does not enter into the flexibility of this word-association.

In the face of such complexity it seems best to summarize the

---

[1] It remains possible that a case like ὀλοὸν πῦρ—πῦρ ὀλοόν represents a word-association that has not crystallized into any dominant shape, cf. also πυρός τ' ὀλοοῖο μ 68. It may be so, yet we must recognise that the majority of the 'possible and derivative' expressions are clearly derivative. The amorphous word-association cannot be more than a minute element in Homeric technique.

extent of modification among Homeric formulae in terms of a maximum and a minimum. For the maximum possible extent we assume that the direction of adjustment is from the shape we are studying to some other shape and that the relationship *is* one of modification: for the minimum extent we load the dice against us, counting repeated 'modifications' as autonomous or primary expressions. We obtain the following result:

Shape	Total formulae	Modifications Maximum	Minimum	Proportion (%) Maximum	Minimum
$-\cup\cup-\underline{\cup}$	319	47	30	15	9
$\cup\cup-\underline{\cup}$	140	56	26	40	19

We naturally wish to know which of the two estimates is closer to the truth. This depends on our choice of material. By choosing two shapes which are basic in the poet's technique we have a strong base for analogical reasoning: the doubtful cases are not really doubtful, and many repeated modifications will be re-creations remade as many times as they are needed. Here therefore the maximum exaggerates less than the minimum understates: for other shapes less favoured by the basic stock of formulae the position might be very different.

The calculation assumes, of course, that all formulae are modifiable, and modifiable with equal facility. Obviously this cannot in fact be the case. For most formulae that are not modified there is no certainty whether appropriate by-forms existed or might be created. Nor can words of a formula always be inverted.[1] Thus the potential extent of modification, unlike potential mobility, is imponderable. We can only say that the poet's willingness to modify those formulae that he has the means to modify is greater than our detective methods can discover.

What exigencies of composition induce modifications? Many that result in the movement of the expression appear to arise in the same way as the simple movement of formulae, from competition for the same placing in the verse which results in the squeezing out of the more flexible expression. This situation arises when the system of sentence-patterns is insufficiently developed to pre-

---

[1] Assuming no internal elisions or correptions, the combinations of word-division and initial and final sounds exemplified by the following expressions are irreversible: αἷμα κελαινόν, ἄνδρα γέροντα, ταῦτα ἕκαστα, αἴθοπι χαλκῷ, ἄλκιμον ἔγχος, ἵα πάτρη, ὁδὸς ἥδε.

vent it: e.g. ἔρρεεν αἷμα κελαινεφὲς ἐξ ὠτειλῆς Δ 140, where ἐξ ὠτειλῆς is seven times final. Though four times (Δ 140, 149, E 870, Λ 266) it is a matter of blood coming from the wound the poet does not have αἷμα κελαινόν in the line. But this explanation will often be too simple, for it overlooks what there may be besides context to suggest the displacing word. The context properly suggests an idea not a word, and since the diction is very copiously supplied with synonyms the idea does not always have to be expressed by any particular word. However, it sometimes happens that a given word insists, as it were, on appearing because it is closely associated with one of the terms of the formula. The picture is then that of a word realizing two of its associations, the shape or order of one being necessarily disturbed: e.g. among the formulae built around the word νύξ are νὺξ ἐρεβεννή and νὺξ ἐκάλυψε, both naturally placed at the verse-end. There are synonyms for all three words, but the association between the three is strong. But if all three are to be used one of the usual formulae must be modified, hence ἐρεβεννὴ νὺξ ἐκάλυψε E 659 etc.

But such competition for a given space is by no means always in evidence, e.g. οὓς ἀέκοντας ὀρυκτὴ τάφρος ἔρυκε Π 369. Why not ἐρύκανε (cf. κ 429) τάφρος ὀρυκτή? Of if the poet can bring himself to put πιθήσας after the caesura at X 107, why must he say βαρείῃ χειρὶ πιθήσας at Λ 235 = P 48, with no improvement in rhythm as a result of the modification? Much the same can be said of many expressions brought into the first half of the verse: they could have been kept at the verse-end if only the poet had been willing to pad out the verse. One can only say that the modified expression falls where it does because it just happens to be convenient to use there. This will not be surprising to those who are willing to believe that Homer is a master of language and an artist in the deployment of a formulaic diction.

The existence of modification of formulae as a technique in Homer has a consequence for the theory of a formulaic diction. For it implies a gap in the system of formulae for a given idea. But such a gap is precisely that which according to the original model of Parry did not, or ought not, to exist. For it was the function of the memory technique of verse-making to provide a formula for all the poet's needs. That was overstated because it was not appreciated how large a system would have to be—

a dozen expressions or more—to supply a formula for every need that might be reasonably anticipated. What a formula-system usually does is to provide an expression for the principal needs only. Most systems of common-noun formulae with epithets have obvious gaps, some of which are doubtless real gaps and not just the consequences of under-representation. Thus the sword has no shape ∪ – ∪ – ∪, the bow no ∪ ∪ – ∪ ∪ – ∪ or ∪ – ∪ ∪. A complete set of pre-existent formulae is certainly not attested.[1] However, if gaps are present in all systems it follows that the means must exist for filling or circumventing them as required. The formula by analogy or substitution-system has now replaced the memorized formula in the most modern statements of improvising methods,[2] and might be thought to perform this service. But in a controllable form it is hard to apply to the Homeric noun–epithet phraseology and cannot be a complete account. A gap is not in practice as dangerous as it appears if the formula-system is considered in isolation, for a certain number of gaps can be tolerated if the missing parts of different systems are complementary. In a diction as extensive and complex as that of Homer this cannot be relied on altogether. Some techniques for the rapid production of phraseology are a necessity. In the case of personal names it is likely that the comprehensive substitution-systems provided by the generic epithets take care of most contingencies: among common nouns generic epithets are rarer, but there are synonyms in some abundance and there is modification. The principle of economy in the epic diction thus reappears at a new point: thanks to these artifices the mass of remembered formulae need not be larger than the principal requirements demand.

[1] The sword system supplies regular formulae for six shapes (ignoring intermittent provision of vocalic and consonantal intitials) in the nominative and accusative singular and unique expressions for more: the wine system in the accusative singular has regular formulae for five shapes and unique expressions for four others. Various grammatical cases of 'ship(s)', 'horses', 'spear', and 'sea' are also very well provided for, cf. ET 135 ff., Page, HHI 267 ff., a useful source for checking the scope of the most common systems.

[2] Lord, SoT 35 ff.

VI

THE EXPANSION OF FORMULAE

THE ability to expand or contract the content put into a theme is a recognized part of oral technique,[1] but it has not been widely noticed that in Homer at least the technique of 'ornamentations' extends down to the level of the formula.[2] Ornament, from the point of view of meaning, is superfluous, and its use is a technical device whereby a formula is made, not by modification but by the addition of further words, to occupy more space than did its primary form. Though similar in structure, i.e. (A+B)+C, an expanded formula is thus different in origin from a complex formula into which a new *significant* term has been introduced.

Expansion may be simple, where no source other than the sense of the context is apparent for the ornamentation, or (and more usually) may result from the conflation of two different formulae that share the same term. In a conflation it is often clear that one member is much more important than the other, so that the technique does not differ much from simple expansion. But knowing the source of the supplement we can understand it better.

1. *Expansion by means of epithets*

Among noun–epithet formulae the most obvious, and the commonest, variety of ornamentation is another epithet, for which the evidence is presented in this section. For the purposes of ordering the material certain assumptions have been made. I have supposed that a simple formula, i.e. a noun with one epithet,

---

[1] The term ποικιλία is well known to the B and T scholia without, of course, any implication that this might be a technical rather than an artistic matter. The connexion with oral composition was first made by Parry, *Class. Phil.* xxi (1936) 359; cf. Lord, 'Composition by theme in Homer and South Slavic Epos', *TAPA* lxxxii (1951) 71–80, *Serbo-Croatian Heroic Songs* (Cambridge, Mass. 1954) 239–41, and *SoT* 88, for detailed explanation.

[2] J. La Roche, *Wiener Stud.* xix (1897) 175–80, collected instances of nouns qualified by more than one epithet, but characteristically drew no conclusions.

is primary, and that the extended formula with two or more epithets is secondary, and in fact an expansion. But it must be admitted that this history is not necessary, and that some primary formulae may have two epithets or otherwise present an expanded appearance, and be subject to apocope or contraction by the omission of one epithet or its equivalent.

The examples listed are expansions of formulae of the two shapes $- \cup \cup - \underline{\cup}$ and $\cup \cup - \underline{\cup}$. The provisional assumption is that these are the shapes of the primary formulae, an assumption which we shall re-examine. Only juxtaposed epithets (with a few exceptions of interest) are admitted: ornamentation by means of τε and καί, which is not frequent, is omitted as being rather part of the construction of sentences than formulae, and where epithets are separated by infixed connectives or other words the motivation for the use of the additional epithet may be complicated.

Like changed position and modification, expansion is an adjustment that may be imposed on the poet by the declension of a formula (e.g. ὑψόροφον θάλαμον but θαλάμοιο ⟨θυωδέος⟩ ὑψορόφοιο), but this is indicative of the stability of the formula not of its flexibility. Such expressions are not noted here.

The clearest instances of expansion are seen in phrases constructed with two or more non-functional epithets. These cannot be complex formulae in the sense just defined. But what is a non-functional epithet? One may distinguish four main types of epithet:

(a) special (i.e. confined to one noun): ποντοπόρος νηῦς;
(b) generic: βέλος ὀξύ, ξίφος ὀξύ, ὀξεῖαι ὀδύναι;
(c) determinative (i.e. (a) or (b) used of a sub-class within the broadest denotation of the noun): ἰφθίμους ψυχάς;
(d) functional (i.e. not predictable from metre and context): εἴκοσι φῶτας.

There is much overlapping, and the vitality of function may vary from example to example.[1] The difficulty is type (c), which

---

[1] This is strangely denied by Parry: 'l'épithète employée dans une certaine expression nom-épithète ne peut pas avoir tantôt le sens ornemental, tantôt le sens particularisé, *mais doit toujours avoir soit l'un soit l'autre*', ET 196 (Parry's italics). But this cannot be the case when there is fluctuation between attributive use, which may be ornamental, and predicative use, which must be functional: examples in Bergson, *L'Épithète ornemental*, 35-37.

pace Parry (*ET* 204) it is hard for the student of common-noun formulae to take as meaningful,[1] so prominent is their ornamental character. They are here grouped with (*a*) and (*b*). Adjectives of material and colour are mostly determinative: numerals are taken as meaningful throughout.

When a functional epithet is part of the 'expanded' phrase its analysis is more complicated. The most favourable case is when there is no question of conflation and the kernel phrase is securely and independently attested. One may then venture to separate the complex expression (in which a functional epithet has been attached to a noun–epithet formula with an ornamental epithet) and the truly expanded expression (in which an ornamental epithet has been used to supplement a noun–epithet formula whose epithet, though regular, is necessary and significant for the sense). The former do not concern us here. Statistical criteria can be applied to conflations but with much less safety. In the nature of the case both components are pre-existent. But it is only too often the case that the functional phrase is rare, the decorative phrase well established. We are then confronted by the impossible question whether context (which suggests the priority of the functional phrase) is to be preferred to epic custom (which would insist on the cohesion of the ornamental word-group). Were the question important it could only be settled example by example by scrutiny of the context, for most formulae are members of wider and looser word-associations. Here conflations are noted only as phrases *involved* in expansion without implication of the direction of the process. Word-groups displaying two or

---

[1] Cf. Bergson's criticisms, op. cit. 21 ff. Parry's discussion of the functional epithet, *ET* 192 ff., is throughout extreme and polemical, inspired probably by a wish to reinforce the case for economy in formula systems. By 'meaningful' I intend that something is added to the content of the expression. Confusion has arisen through the equation of such ideas as meaningful and appropriate, or conventional and meaningless, which are in fact different levels of evaluation. There is no reason why conventional epithets should not be either meaningful or decorative, or indeed both simultaneously. The decorative epithet is not intended to inform, but neither is it intended to confuse: therefore it must be appropriate generally (οὐ τὸ τότε ὄν τι ἀλλὰ τὸ καθόλου, as the scholiasts say). I cannot agree therefore with Whallon, *Yale Classical Studies* xvii (1961) 134 ff., that a carefully appropriate use of certain epithets implies that they are meaningful in the sense required. A word is never mere noise (as if the poet were to sing *tra la la*) but has certain compatibilities with other words and incompatibilities built into it. Respect for the compatibilities, like respect for grammar, allows inattention: incompatibility, like anacoluthon, causes puzzlement, and in good epic style must be avoided.

more functional epithets cannot be expansions, except in the very rare event of both epithets being synonymous when one can be looked upon as an ornament of the other. Otherwise the functional phrases do no more than illustrate the use of a formula in a given contextual situation.

(i) > (◡) ◡ – ◡◡ – ◡◡ – ◡ in 3rd–6th feet

If no epithets are functional the technique is easily understood: it is a matter of simple addition. This sort of expansion, though unremarked,[1] is quite common among personal names where frequent need has often consolidated the expansion into a new formula, e.g. βριήπυος ὄβριμος Ἄρης 1 × on the one hand but πολύτλας δῖος Ὀδυσσεύς 42 ×. Of c. 100 expressions for personal names between caesura and verse-end twenty-three are expansions.[2]

Simple expansion:[3] ⟨ἰονθάδος⟩ ἀγρίου αἰγός ξ 50; ⟨γερούσιον⟩ αἴθοπα οἶνον Δ 259, ν 8.

Conflation: (καὶ) ⟨εἰλίποδας⟩ ἕλικας βοῦς Ι 466 etc. 5 ×, (and 1 × in 2nd–4th feet), cf. εἰλίποδας β.; ἕλικας βόας ⟨εὐρυμετώπους⟩ λ 289, cf. ἕλικας βοῦς and καλαὶ β. εὐρυμέτωποι 1 ×; (καὶ or καθ') ⟨ὑψερεφὲς⟩ μέγα δῶμα Ε 213 etc. 5 ×, cf. ὑψ. δῶ; ⟨ἐρυσάρματες⟩[4] ὠκέες ἵπποι Π 370, cf. ἐρ. ἵππους 1 ×; ⟨μεγακήτεϊ⟩ νηὶ μελαίνῃ Θ 222 = Λ 5, cf. μ. νηί 1 ×; (καὶ) ⟨αἴθοπα⟩ οἶνον ἐρυθρόν μ 19; ⟨μελιηδέα⟩ οἶνον ἐρυθρόν ι 208, cf. μ. οἶνον 6 ×.

[1] Pope, *Acta Classica* vi (1963) 11, seems to be the only scholar who has seriously objected that the commonly quoted formula-systems offer 'what are in effect the same goods under a different label or in a different size'.

[2] Ten with γέρων, three with θεά, two with μέγας, eight (all – ◡ ◡ – ◡) with miscellaneous epithets, all added at the head of the formula. Parry asserts 'le style héroïque ne permet pas d'intercaler dans le même vers le nom d'un personnage entre deux *adjectifs* épithétiques', ET 72 (Parry's italics). This restriction by no means applies to common nouns and is probably accidental, for personal names are very usually final. The insistence that adjectives are different in this respect, I suppose, from appositional nouns (cf. θεὰ Θέτις ἀργυρόπεζα and γέρων Πρίαμος θεοειδής) seems arbitrary. In any case the restriction is not absolute, cf. χρυσήνιος Ἄρτεμις ἀγνή ε 123.

[3] Here and subsequently I quote components only if the term is of a shape not listed in the Tables or if it has undergone some modification.

[4] This word has caused undue mystification. Parry, ET 140 n. 1, wants it to make 'une distinction entre les chevaux de char et les chevaux de trait'. But the Homeric draught animal is the mule. For Delebècque, *Le Cheval dans l'Iliade*, Paris 1951, 153, the epithet marks a contrast with 'chevaux destinés non à l'attelage mais à la selle'. But the Homeric saddle is as rare as the carthorse. In the contexts, O 354 and Π 370, it is a decorative epithet, ruinous as this may be to the economy of the formula-series for 'horses'.

A number of noun–epithet formulae are used so regularly in construction with prepositions and coalesce so firmly that their expansion takes place outside the preposition, which is not displaced from its position. All are conflations. Most are used with several prepositions, all occurrences of which I have added into the totals: ⟨φίλης⟩ ἀπὸ πατρίδος αἴης B 162 etc. 4×, cf. φίλην ἐς πατρίδ᾽ 8× in acc. sing. only; ⟨φίλην⟩ ἐς πατρίδα γαῖαν B 140 etc. 7× ; ⟨θοὴν⟩ ἐπὶ νῆα μέλαιναν β 430 etc. 7×, cf. θοὴν ἐπὶ νῆα 3× ; ⟨κοίλην⟩ ἐπὶ νῆα μέλαιναν δ 731 etc. 4×, cf. κοίλην ἐπὶ νῆα 4× ; both ship-formulae are treated in exactly the same way in the genitive singular (with νηὸς ἐΐσης); ⟨θοὴν⟩ διὰ νύκτα μέλαιναν K 394 etc. 4×, διὰ νύκτα θοήν 1×.

Of word-groups incorporating a functional epithet as well as a decorative term the following are, or may be, expansions.

Simple expansion: ⟨μεγαθύμου⟩ σοῖο φονῆος Σ 335, presumably an expansion, but no simple component is attested.

Conflation: ⟨ἐπιχθόνιος⟩ βροτὸς ἄλλος Ω 505, cf. β. ἐπιχθόνιος 1× ; (ἠδ᾽ or καὶ) ⟨ἀθάνατοι⟩ θεοὶ ἄλλοι Γ 298 etc. 9×, cf. ἀθάνατοι θ. 1× ; ἐμὸν ⟨δολιχόσκιον⟩ ἔγχος, erratically placed in the 2nd–5th feet, Z 126, cf. δολιχ. ἔγχος 24× ; ἑοῦ ἑτάροιο ⟨φίλοιο⟩ Ω 416, cf. οὗ ἑτ., ἑτ. φίλοιο 3× ; πόσιος οὗ ⟨κουριδίοιο⟩ ψ 150, cf. κουρίδιον ... πόσιν 1× ; ἐείκοσι φῶτας ⟨ἀρίστους⟩ δ 530, 778, cf. εἴκοσι φ.

I include here two expanded phrases that intrude beyond the caesura into the first half of the verse: ⟨ἀμφιβρότην πολυδαίδαλον⟩ ἀσπίδα θοῦριν Λ 32, cf. ἀσπίδος ἀμφιβρότης 3× ; πάντας ⟨ἐϋκνήμιδας⟩ ἑταίρους κ 203, cf. ἐϋκν. ἑταῖροι (-ους) 4×.

(ii) Expansions in mid verse

The neatest artifice is to add an epithet scanned ∪ – ∪ ∪ after a formula placed in the 2nd–3rd feet so as to continue it to the diaeresis.

Expanded: ἄττα γεραιὲ ⟨παλαιγενές⟩ P 561;[1] and involving functional epithets πολὺν ὄμβρον ⟨ἀθέσφατον⟩ K 6, cf. ἀθέσφατον ὄ. 1× ; δέρμα βόειον ⟨εὐχροές⟩ ξ 24; ζυγὸν οἷον ⟨εὔξοον⟩ N 706. No simple components are attested for the last two expressions.

Conflated: οὗ παιδὸς ⟨ἀμύμονος⟩ Ω 85, cf. π. ἑοῖο and π. ἀμύμονες 2× ; σάκος εὐρὺ ⟨παναίολον⟩ N 552, cf. σ. αἰόλον 2× ; τόδε τόξον ⟨εὔξοον⟩ τ 586, φ 92, cf. τ. εὔξοον 7×.

---

[1] P 561, v.l. διοτρεφές, which is read at I 607 in a similar verse and is there to be construed with the name Φοῖνιξ, not with ἄττα.

It is easy for the poet to improve on this artifice by continuing the expression as far as the verse-end. In so doing he merges the technique of expansion with a habit of phrase-construction. Paired epithets in the second half of the verse are very usual, e.g. ἀμύμονος ἱπποδάμοιο, δαΐφρονα ποικιλομήτην, χαλκήρεος ἱπποδασείης, etc.[1] Hence ⟨ἄλκιμα⟩ δοῦρε δύω ⟨κεκορυθμένα χαλκῷ⟩ Λ 43, χ 125, cf. δύο δοῦρε and δοῦρε δύω κ. χ. I ×; τὰ μῆλα ⟨ταναύποδα⟩ πίονα ⟨δημῷ⟩ ι 464, cf. πίονα μ.; φάσγανα καλὰ ⟨μελάνδετα κωπήεντα⟩ Ο 713, without any simple component attested.

The remainder are a mixed class: two expressions are brought up to the diaeresis by adding epithets in front of the noun: ἄλλοι ⟨μάκαρες⟩ θεοί ε 7 etc. 4×, a conflation, cf. θεοὶ ἄλλοι and μάκαρες θ. 7×; and ⟨ἀργύφεον⟩ φᾶρος μέγα ε 230 = κ 543, cf. μέγα φ. Four expressions acquire the shape (∪) ∪ – ∪ ∪ – ∪, useful in the 3rd–5th feet and found also before the caesura: ⟨λεύκ'⟩ ἄλφιτα πολλά Σ 560, but cf. ἄ. λευκά; ⟨πυκινὸν⟩ δόλον ἄλλον Ζ 187; and two conflations: τάδε δώματα ⟨κάλ'⟩ ρ 264, cf. τόδε δῶμα; τεὸν (ἑὸν) ⟨φίλον⟩ υἱόν Ε 314 etc. 4×, cf. ἑὸν υἱόν; the shorter σὸς (ὃν) φίλος (-ον) υἱός (-όν) occurs 8×. In 2nd–5th feet is οἷς ἑτάροισι ⟨φιλοπτολέμοισι⟩ Ψ 5; and in the 2nd–4th feet ῥάκος ἄλλο ⟨κακόν⟩ ν 434, ξ 342, which has no simple components attested.

(iii) In the first half of the verse

Expansions in the first half of the verse are quite unusual. The reason is by no means obvious, since the shorter formulae are already prominent in the 2nd–3rd feet and an expression to fill the whole half-verse has a manifest utility—many simple formulae fill this space. Four examples only: ὀξὺ βέλος ⟨περιπευκές⟩ Λ 844, cf. β. ὀξύ; ⟨πορφύρεον⟩ μέγα φᾶρος Θ 221, θ 84; ⟨ἄκρον⟩ ὑπὸ λόφον αὐτόν Ν 615, without attested simple components; and a conflation πατρὸς ἑοῖο ⟨φίλοιο⟩ ξ 177, cf. π. φίλου 3×.

In all, twenty-four expressions of the – ∪ ∪ – ◡ class, and eighteen of the ∪ ∪ – ◡ class, are involved in expansion by epithets.

2. *Expansion by means of adverbial qualification*

The expansion of noun–epithet formulae by means of words in syntactical construction with the epithet, which may be

---

[1] The formation of such epithets is discussed by Witte, *Glotta* iii (1912) 125–7, their use by Parry, *ET* 80–84. On the 'rhopaloid' verses to which they lead see L. S. D. Richardson *Hermathena* lxv (1955) 50–65.

compendiously described as adverbial qualification, is a relatively minor technique. The poet's self-denial is not readily explained, since adverbs of weak force, such as μάλα, μέγα, and πολύ are very common in his general diction which at the same time is the greatest employer of the *graecus accusativus*, the accusative noun as a modifier of an adjective.[1] Typically the adverb is used to make an adverb–adjective formula, such as μάλα πολλά, μέγα νήπιος, νήπιος αὔτως, which is then constructed as a predicate.

(i) With an adverb

⟨πολὺ⟩ χείρονες ἄνδρες φ 325; ⟨μάλα⟩ πίονα δῆμον E 710; ⟨μάλα⟩ πολλοὶ ἑταῖροι θ 217; ⟨μάλα⟩ μέγα κῦδος I 303, X 435; ⟨μάλα⟩ λυγρὸς ὄλεθρος K 174; ⟨πολὺ⟩ χείρονι φωτί λ 621; and ⟨πολὺ⟩ μείζονα λᾶαν H 268, ι 537, which is not attested without the adverb.

All these (except for πολὺ μείζονα λᾶαν) are conflations, the adverb–adjective phrase being independently attested.

There seems to be no reason in principle why the adverbial increment should not follow rather than precede the formula, but clear examples are lacking.[2] One notes that the normal placings of most formulae are before major boundaries in the verse, so that the natural thing is to expand in front of them unless some strong verbal habit, such as continuation with epithets, pulls in the other direction.

(ii) With a constructed noun

Despite some obtrusive phraseology the construction of the accusative noun as modifier to an adjective is very ossified in Homer. Most expressions show a highly formulaic use; the rest are mostly clearly derivative. Note the series ⟨πόδας⟩ ταχὺς ἄγγελος, πόδας αἰόλος ἵππος, ⟨πόδας⟩ ταχὺν ἀμφ' Ἀχιλῆα, Ἀχιλῆα πόδας ταχύν, doubtless based on the πόδας ὠκὺς Ἀχιλλεύς formula. In this series we must place κύνες ⟨πόδας⟩ ἀργοί Σ 578,[3] the sole expression to concern us here. The dative noun is also found in

---

[1] Schwyzer, *Gr. Gr.* i. 84–85.

[2] ἕδος ἀσφαλὲς αἰεί ζ 42 has no simplex, καλὸν θρόνον ἄφθιτον αἰεί Ξ 238 contains an autonomous formula ἄφθιτον αἰεί 2× and once in neut. pl.

[3] With the sense 'swift of foot'. Thus πόδας ἀργός and its hypostases ἀργίπους and the names Πόδαργος (-η) are twice over revivals, since ἀργός is a gloss equated

construction with epithets, e.g. ποικίλα with χαλκῷ in various
τεύχεα- and ἄρματα-expressions. Our only instance has already
been noted. It is μῆλα . . . πίονα δημῷ ι 464.

(iii) With another adjective

Certain adjectives may perform the qualifying function where
the epithet is a numeral. These are πᾶς, οἷος, and μοῦνος. The
most extensively used is πᾶς. Like the true adverbs πᾶς shows
a tendency to make autonomous groupings separated from their
noun: ἐννέα πάντες (πᾶσαι), ἕνδεκα πάντα, δώδεκα πάντας (πᾶσαι).
This use of πᾶς may from time to time give rise to ambiguous
constructions. Thus at K 560, ἑτάρους δυοκαίδεκα πάντας ἀρίστους,
Ebeling takes πάντας with the numeral despite the fact that π.
ἄριστοι (-ους) 15 × is firmly entrenched as a formula. The use of
οἷος is similar but more restricted.

Seven expressions of the – ∪ ∪ – ≍ class are listed in this section
and two of the ∪ ∪ – ≍ class.

3. *Expansion by means of the article*

The Homeric article is of erratic use,[1] and its placing in noun–
epithet word-groups is not bound by the classical word-order.
Hence the motive for its employment, not being necessarily one
of sense, may sometimes be metrical, augmenting a phrase to
a more convenient length. Thus ⟨οἱ⟩ ἄλλοι πάντες Φ 371[2] (1st–3rd
feet); ⟨οἱ δ'⟩ ἄλλοι πάντες ρ 411 (πάντ̄ες, 1st–3rd feet), and Λ 693
(πάντ̄ες, 3rd–5th feet); σύμπαντες οἱ ἄλλοι Χ 380, cf. ἄλλοι
ἅπαντες; ⟨τὰ⟩ τεύχεα καλά Φ 317. Various expressions, all occurring once only, are not found without the article: τὸν δεξιὸν ἵππον
Ψ 336; αἱ κύνες αἵδε τ 372; τοῦ παιδὸς ἀγαυοῦ λ 492;[3] τὰ τείρεα

in the mature epic with ὠκύς. Carpenter has ingeniously taken the word as a noun
meaning 'hound', *AJA* liv (1950) 177 ff., while Delebècque, *Le Cheval dans l'Iliade*,
144–6, takes Πόδαργος as 'le rapide', but prefers 'qui tremble ou frémit sur les
jarrets' for πόδας αἰόλος. The Linear B *po-da-ko*, KN Ch 899 and 1029, (Πόδαργος,
the name of an ox), is presumably no gloss, and may be assigned the primitive
sense of ἀργός, whatever that was.

[1] Cf. Chantraine, *Gram. Hom.* ii. 158 ff.

[2] Chantraine, loc. cit., notes the 'tour en plein développement' of the article
with ἄλλος (and ἕτερος and αὐτός).

[3] The commonest παιδός-formula in this position is οὗ παιδός 8 ×. Thus the article
serves as a replacement, semantically not significant, for the possessive as in τοῖο
ἄνακτος 3 × beside οἷο ἄ.; cf. the use of φίλος in φίλην / ἑὴν εἰς πατρίδα γαῖαν.

καλά Σ 485; and the very elongated formula τὰ μῆλα ταναύποδα …ι 464.

Six expressions of the – ∪ ∪ – ⌣ class and one of the ∪ ∪ – ⌣ class are affected.

Considering its apparent usefulness in extending a formula at its head, a point where alternative formations in nouns and epithets are mostly lacking, the use made of the article seems very unenterprising. But this is to ignore the chronological factor. The poet cannot be said to neglect something that is not freely available to him, and we cannot assume that the article was so available.[1]

4. Expansion by means of a co-ordinated synonym

Synonyms sustain a role in epic diction both important and as yet unexplored. By the combination and interchange of both nouns and epithets which are wholly or partly synonymous a remarkable degree of elasticity is attained.[2] Thus at the appropriate points in the verse the poet has available (besides the unqualified nouns) the following phrases in the accusative singular giving the sense 'war': φύλοπιν αἰνήν, αἰνοτάτον πόλεμον, πόλεμον φθισήνορα, πόλεμον κακόν (or θρασύν), πόλεμον πολύδακρυν, κρατερὴν ὑσμίνην, πολύδακρυν Ἄρηα, οὖλον Ἄρηα. In some contexts the quasi-synonymous ἔρις and νεῖκος can be laid under contribution to give αἰνοτάτην ἔριδα, ἔριδα κρατερήν, and μέγα νεῖκος. μάχην (except for the functional μάχην ἀλίαστον) occurs in the prepositional formula μάχην ἐς (ἀνὰ) κυδιάνειραν, which complements πόλεμον κατὰ δακρυόεντα and κατὰ κρατερὴν ὑσμίνην in the second half of the verse. Synonyms moreover can be usefully co-ordinated, so that we have πόλεμον καὶ δηιότητα (the only formula of this sense to fill the whole second half without the aid of a preposition), πόλεμόν τε μάχην τε, ἔριδας καὶ νείκεα, and the lengthy πόλεμόν τε κακόν καὶ φύλοπιν αἰνήν.

Co-ordination with a second noun is a pattern of use exhibited by most shapes of noun–epithet formulae, but the usage

---

[1] Hoekstra, MFP passim, shows that developments in the vernacular penetrate deeply and apparently quickly into the epic diction. But the article has not (that is, not yet) become so organic as the movable -ν or the dropped ϝ-.

[2] First explored, like so many other matters now in prominence, by Düntzer, Hom. Abhandlungen, 535–48.

is especially common among the – ∪ ∪ – ∪ formulae located at the verse-end. The effect is to bring the whole phrase back to the main caesura. Should the co-ordinated noun be a synonym of the noun in the formula then the technique is a variety of expansion, for no meaningful content is added to the sentence. Eleven examples follow: ⟨μένος καὶ⟩ φαίδιμα γυῖα Z 27; ⟨μένος καὶ⟩ θυμὸς ἀγήνωρ Υ 174; ⟨κραδίη καὶ⟩ θυμὸς ἀγήνωρ I 635 etc. 6×; ⟨γόον καὶ⟩ κήδεα λυγρά E 156; ⟨θάνατον καὶ⟩ κῆρα μέλαιναν β 283 etc. 4×; ⟨φόνον καὶ⟩ κῆρα μέλαιναν E 652 = Λ 443; ⟨δόλους καὶ⟩ μήδεα πυκνά Γ 202; ⟨θάνατος καὶ⟩ μοῖρα κραταιή Π 853 etc. 6×; ⟨κορυφὰς καὶ⟩ πρώονας ἄκρους M 282; ⟨σκοπιαὶ καὶ⟩ πρώονες ἄκροι Θ 558 = Π 299; ⟨μένος καὶ⟩ χεῖρες (-ας) ἄαπτοι (-ους) Θ 450 etc. 6×.

Several of those listed are conflations, the two nouns being found independently co-ordinated: μένος καὶ θυμός 2× (acc. 11×); κραδίη καὶ θυμός 2× (acc. 6×); φόνον καὶ κῆρα 6×; θάνατον καὶ κῆρα 2×; θάνατος καὶ μοῖρα 4×; μένος καὶ χεῖρας 4×.

The distinction between the otiose synonym and the unrelated functional noun is too nice to be boldly drawn. Because powerful limbs are but the outward manifestation of the μένος within, the addition of that word is little more than a grace note on the γυῖα- and χείρ-formulae. Yet we must resist the danger of equating an 'empty' word, which tells us nothing that we did not know already, with a synonym. Exclude therefore such co-ordinations as πύλας καὶ μακρὸν ὀχῆα and χλαῖναι καὶ ῥήγεα καλά. But the construction of such phrases is only marginally different: the addition may not be a synonym even on the most liberal view, but it shares a similar area of meaning.

The co-ordinated synonym has a further potential. It can receive an epithet of its own, and carry the whole expression back into the first half of the verse:

⟨θάνατόν τε κακὸν καὶ⟩ κῆρα μέλαιναν Φ 66, χ 14;

⟨πορφύρεος θάνατος καὶ⟩ μοῖρα κραταιή E 83 etc. 3×;

⟨πόλεμός (-όν) τε κακὸς (-ὸν) καὶ⟩ φύλοπις (-ιν) αἰνή (-ήν) Δ 82, etc. 3×.

(The shorter πόλεμος καὶ φύλοπις αἰνή is not attested.) At this point, however, it must be clear that two co-ordinated formulae are in question and not an adjustment to a single one.

Eight formulae of the – ∪ ∪ – ⏒ class receive this kind of expansion.

5. *The contraction of extended and complex formulae*

It is evident that the expansion and continuation of formulae is a potent means by which the resources of a traditional poetic diction might be enriched and increased. The habit of adapting formulae by these devices provides a foot-hold for a new word-association to arise and develop unobtrusively, until it is secure enough to exist in its own right without the support of the primary formula at all. Some of the expressions which were for convenience labelled 'conflations' doubtless illustrate a point in this history, and are in fact the middle terms, A+B+C, through which a secondary association, A+C, grew out of a primary A+B: e.g. νηὶ μελαίνη tout court 13×, expanded to μεγακήτεϊ νηὶ μελαίνη 2×, contracted to μεγακήτεϊ νηὶ 1×. But here a difficulty is encountered, if the picture is presented in terms of the historical development of a poetic tradition. The evidence is only the regularities exhibited by a given poet's practice, and there is no necessity that what is most ancient will there be most regular. What can be inferred is only a sequence of suggestion: thus νηὶ μελαίνη is sufficiently popular to suggest itself in suitable contexts, μεγακήτεϊ νηὶ μελαίνη is suggested by it, and in its turn suggests μεγακήτεϊ νηί. In an accomplished performer, the mental processes that this implies may be, in the Homeric phrase, ὠκεῖαι ὡς εἰ . . . νόημα. Again, some extended phrases are quite frequent, e.g. εἰλίποδας ἕλικας βοῦς 6×, and may be more popular than their simple constituents. Whatever the real history, in the act of composition such a phrase, being itself established as a unit, may be analysed indifferently as (A+B)+C, or as (A+C)+B, according to whatever analogy the poet calls to mind.

That the resources of the Homeric diction included the apocope of formulaic sentences has been already noted in Homeric scholarship.[1] The phrase that suffers the apocope is regularly located between diaeresis and verse-end, e.g.

ἀμφὶ δὲ παιδὶ φίλῳ βάλε $\begin{cases} πήχεε\ δακρύσασα\quad ρ\ 38 \\ πήχεε·\ τὸν\ δὲ\ ποτὶ\ οἷ\quad ω\ 347 \end{cases}$

νῆα μὲν ἔνθ' ἐλθόντες $\begin{cases} ἐκέλσαμεν\ ἐν\ ψαμάθοισι\quad ι\ 546 = μ\ 5 \\ ἐκέλσαμεν,\ ἐκ\ δὲ\ τὰ\ μῆλα\quad λ\ 20. \end{cases}$

For the most part, however, the contraction of a formulaic

---

[1] Cf. Chantraine, 'Remarques sur l'emploi des formules dans le premier chant de l'Iliade', *REG* xlv (1932) 121–54, especially 138 ff.

phrase is a more complicated operation.[1] Often either the eliminated term is medial, or the words that survive the contraction are changed in position. It is rare that anything so simple as θάνατόν τε κακὸν καὶ κῆρα, without μέλαιναν Π 47, is encountered, nor are the frequencies generally sufficiently high to support an unimpeachable statistical argument. It is often necessary to be content with the point that the frequencies are compatible with, or are suggestive of, a certain origin.

Thus of the expansions noted above, εἰλίποδας ἕλικας βοῦς, φίλην ἐς πατρίδα γαῖαν, θάνατος καὶ μοῖρα κραταιή, σκοπίαι καὶ πρώονες ἄκροι, πορφύρεον μέγα φᾶρος, are more frequent in the extended form than in any other. It is therefore entirely probable that a given extended formula is more truly part of the basis of the poet's style than the simple member, which derives from it when the need arises by the process of contraction. However, it is not extended noun–epithet formulae that are the most fertile soil for the processes of contraction to flourish, but rather complex formulae. The complex formula arises through the repeated construction of the simple formula with the same governed or governing term. Every word that the poet uses (other than interjections and vocatives) must, of course, be construed. Construction, apart from the not infrequent whole formulaic sentences, implies the creation of a new sentence out of the words and phrases suggested by the context. With a regular need a regular complex formula develops, and at this stage the phrases used under a less regular need may be formed by the modification of the dominant complex formula. Thus, to take a frequent sentence-pattern, the – ∪ ∪ – ≏ noun–epithet formula lying at the verse-end is construed with a verb so as to bring the whole expression back to the main caesura. This has resulted in the emergence of several complex formulae, which may then be contracted: (σὴν/ἢν) πατρίδα γαῖαν ἱκέσθαι (-ηται etc.) 14× > ἢν γαῖαν ἱκέσθαι 2×, or πατρίδ' ἱκέσθαι 4× ; ἀκόντισε δουρὶ φαεινῷ 14× > ἀκόντισε δουρί 1× ; λίπε δ' (λίπ') ὀστέα θυμὸς ἀγήνωρ 3× > λίπε δ' ὀστέα θυμός 2× ; ἐμήσατο λυγρὸν ὄλεθρον 2× > μήσατ' (μήδετ') ὄλεθρον 2× ;(ἐπ-)ἤρκεσε λυγρὸν ὄλεθρον 4× > ἤρκεσ' (ἤρκει) ὄλεθρον 2× ; ἐδύσετο νώροπα χαλκόν 2× >

---

[1] Meister, *Hom. Kunstsprache*, 233 ff., has a section on the contraction of certain verbal formulae; otherwise only sporadic examples have been noticed, e.g. (δόμον) Ἄϊδος εἴσω, Witte, *Glotta* iii (1912) 105–6; ποικίλος (χαλκῷ), G. M. Bolling, *AJP* xxix (1958) 279.

δύσετο χαλκόν 1 ×. Quite different frequencies are also encountered within this group, e.g. ἐγείνατο πότνια μήτηρ 1 ×, cf. γείνατο
μήτηρ 8×, pointing in this instance to a genuine conflation. Ambiguous examples with low frequencies throughout are of course
very common, even when expressing ideas which would naturally
be considered quite regular, e.g. φύγαδ' ἔτραπε μώνυχας ἵππους
1 ×, cf. φύγαδ' ἔτραπεν ἵππους also once only. Nothing can be inferred from these, except that some process of adaptation is at
work.

Expansion, like modification, is not a technique for which the
evidence unequivocally exposes the poet's thought. It has also
some complications of its own. For the first (and only) time an
artifice is attested among unique expressions. This follows from
our selection of all noun–epithet phrases of certain shapes without
prejudging the nature of their formation, so that with δέρμα
βόειον ἐϋχροές in the text we list an expression δέρμα βόειον. Since
the – ∪ ∪ – ∪ shape is regularly a basic element in the poet's
diction it is likely enough that this really is an expansion: δέρμα
βόειον+ἐϋχροές. For there is no reason, if the poet is obliged to
create an expression, why he should not fit it into the verse by
means of any artifice at his disposal, although expansion is the
only one that is likely to reveal itself to us. The odd thing is that
he makes so very little use of it—only eight times for an assumed
basic expression of – ∪ ∪ – ⌣ shape and three times for the ∪ ∪ – ⌣
shape. I say 'odd' because we might be inclined to think that
a unique expression, which may well be an *ad hoc* creation, represents an awkward crisis in composition so that every artifice
must be called up in support. I prefer, however, to consider that
the rarity of expanded unique expressions tells us more about
regular formulae than about unique expressions, namely that
formulae can suggest themselves when there is no straightforward
way of using them. To express a non-formular idea, of course, the
poet does not necessarily have to create a phrase : the simple word
will usually do. Since we are here concerned with the manipulation of formulae these unique expansions do not figure in the
summary tables.

Maximum and minimum figures can be given for the extent of
expansion. The maximum figure assumes that all formulae of
the two inspected shapes which are involved in expansion are
the primary expressions in the extended phrases, and also that

the extended phrases are not unitary but are to be analysed. The latter clause at once points to the first class of extended phrases to be rejected in formulating the minimum figure. Whatever the previous history of a phrase its repetition means prima facie a formula. Second, in a conflation there is an expanded and an expanding member. The latter is simply the identified source of the term used and must be counted out. It is recognized by being less frequent and so less well-established in the poet's mind than the basic expanded formula. In the case of a tie the analogy of unambiguous conflations suggests that the formula placed in its normal position is most likely to be primary. The result is summarized as follows:

Shape	Total formulae	Expansions Maximum	Minimum	Proportion (%) Maximum	Minimum
$-\cup\cup-\underset{\smile}{}$	319	35	24	11	8
$\cup\cup-\underset{\smile}{}$	140	17	9	12	7

I have chosen to diagnose primary formulae by the numerical criterion because this is the only method that can be applied consistently to all types of formular adaptation. Yet from time to time other means of probing the poet's technique become available. Although these agree substantially with the results of the numerical method occasionally there is conflict. Thus the primary formula is typically located in one of the favoured positions for the shape in question. That arouses no surprise. But if we make a rule that a noun–epithet group which represents a formula of that shape in its normal position is the basic formula of the expansion then we find a small number of conflicts with the numerical evidence: αἴθοπα οἶνον ἐρυθρόν, where αἴθοπα οἶνον notches up eighteen further occurrences (and three more in the dative) against only five for οἶνον ἐρυθρόν. The clash is not so sharp in the case of μελιηδέα οἶνον ἐρυθρόν and ἕλικας βόας εὐρυμετώπους.[1] That the primary formula is normally in its natural position may tell us something about the motives for expansion, based on the stability of the formulaic kernel. But if this is stable we should not expect it to be split in order to accommodate the expanding

[1] Elsewhere μελιηδέα οἶνον 6×, 2× in gen. sing., and separated 3× in nom., acc. and gen. sing., a productive formula; οἶ. ἐρυθρός (-όν) 5× elsewhere, fixed both in shape and position. εὐρυμέτωπος is associated with βοῦς 6× elsewhere but only once juxtaposed, ἕλιξ has ten other occurrences, mostly very formulaic.

term. In Section 1 (i) there is only one[1] contravention of this rule, πάντας ἐϋκνήμιδας ἑταίρους,[2] against a dozen observances: in Section 1 (ii) and (iii) there are two, μῆλα ταναύποδα πίονα δήμῳ and ἄλλοι μάκαρες θεοί, against half a dozen clear observances. I believe, however, that the rule is tighter than the exceptions indicate. Two of them have functional epithets, always tricky material since the poet uses them under the compulsion of the context and not merely for their word-associations. In the third the expansion is complex and assimilates itself to the technique of paired compound epithets in the second half of the verse.[3] A clear case of a primary formula with decorative epithet being split for expansion seems not to occur among the common nouns.[4]

The expanded phrase with its heaped up epithets is so conspicuous that it may be overlooked that Homer does not use a discreeter artifice whereby the expanding term is detached a little in front of its primary formula: a line like ἡδέα δ' ἐκ κρητῆρος ἀφύσσατο οἶνον ἐρυθρόν is unhomeric. A functional epithet, however, may be so separated, e.g. πολλοὶ δ' ἐν τάφρῳ ἐρυσάρματες ὠκέες ἵπποι Π 370, and often is. The separation of an expanding word that follows the primary formula is attested, but only very rarely, e.g. πυκνοῖσιν λάεσσι κατεστόρεσαν μεγάλοισι Ω 798. I infer something about the purpose of expansion in the poet's technique. It is not a mere flourish or an Aeschylean display of *composita*, but derives from the usefulness of filling certain natural portions of the verse especially in the second half. The usefulness of such a device arises from the phrase-by-phrase construction of the Homeric sentence, the disadvantage of which is that the phrases which the context suggests may leave spaces between their natural positions. We have seen that formulae may be moved and this may close up the gap, but there is then

[1] In ἀμφιβρότην ... ἀσπίδα θοῦριν the new grammatical case requires that the regular ἀσπ. ἀμφιβρότης be adapted.

[2] ἐϋκνήμιδες (-ας) ἑταῖροι (-ους) occurs 5 × in all, in Odyssey only, and presumably derives from ἐϋκν. Ἀχαιοί (-ούς) 28 ×. Were πάντας ἐϋκν. Ἀχ. to occur, we should not wish, using the numerical criterion, to analyse it as an expansion, since π. Ἀχαιοί (-ούς) is not so frequent (23 ×) as the ornamental component.

[3] The paired epithet technique has several peculiar features, among which is the separation of the epithets from their noun, as in ποταμὸν ... βαθύρροον ἀγρυρο-δίνην Φ 8, which marks them as an autonomous unit. For the μῆλα-phrase the poet has drawn (rather unusually, be it said) on the regular associations of the word to fill the framework of the phrase-pattern.

[4] There are odd instances among the personal names, e.g. Τελαμώνιος ἄλκιμος Αἴας Μ 349 and 362.

the problem of continuing the sentence, and the formulae may not be readily movable. Expansion can thus be looked upon as in part an alternative or complement to mobility, an artifice whereby a formula may retain its natural place in the verse and be combined with other desirable words which might otherwise have to be abandoned.

Several ideas are latent in this inference. Formulaic associations are not only tenacious, as was shown both by their mobility and their modification, but are suggested also by contexts even when the metrical environment is not immediately suitable. This may not conform with formula-type theory but it does conform with most people's experience of clichés and formulae: they come into mind quite mysteriously and certainly with no respect for the grammar and structure of sentences. We must be on our guard against the notion that a formula is pure gain for the improviser even on the technical level. It is almost inevitable that a small price at least must be paid for the advantages. With formulae of various shapes and normal positions it is easy to see that part of the price is the hazard of the unfilled gap. Against it a device, expansion, must be developed. To operate it most dexterously, as the numerous conflated phrases make plain, what is needed is a fund of associations out of which the additional words can be provided.

VII

SEPARATION

U P to this point I have considered the formula as a word-group flexible in shape, word-order, and position, but (except in a few conflations as the secondary member) inseparable. In so doing I have been following received opinion about the nature and use of Homeric formulae. The formulaic group, it is said, necessarily has its constituent words in immediate physical contact because its very purpose is to fill a given portion of the hexameter beside other formulae that in their turn take up the adjacent natural portion of verse.[1] A certain amount of modification and expansion of formulae, even in fact a considerable amount, is not fatally disruptive of this picture: a modified or expanded formula is only filling a portion of the verse somewhat different or rather larger than that for which it is primarily designed. But let the formula be split apart and it is clear the effects of its dissolution are not confined only to that part of the hexameter where it is naturally at home: the arrangement of words in the portion into which the separated word is intruded is also thrown into confusion. Obviously our picture of the improvising method is both neater and simpler if the elements of a formula will be firmly cohesive, as in fact they usually are. The term 'organic' or 'organic unity' has been used to describe[2] the apparently indivisible juxtaposition of the members of a formula.

This way of looking at formulae goes back, of course, to Parry who, with the aid of some linguistic psychology, built it into his view of the non-significant nature of formulaic epithets:[3] if a

---

[1] e.g. Parry, *HSCP* xli (1930) 126; Kirk, *SoH* 60; Page, *HHI* 229–30 and note, a very forthright statement and made the basis of historical inferences.

[2] e.g. D. H. F. Gray, *CQ* xli (1947) 114.

[3] 'Il s'agit du fait que, s'il intervient entre le nom et son épithète un autre mot plus important qu'une simple conjonction ou particule, l'attention de l'auditeur doit momentanément abandonner le substantif et, lorsqu'elle y sera rappelée par l'épithète, l'union étroite entre l'idée de l'épithète et celle du nom aura été rompue. L'auditeur ne sera plus uniquement occupé de l'idée exprimée par le nom, comme il l'est d'un bout à l'autre d'une formule où l'épithète précède ou suit directement le

formula is divided, this was so grave an adjustment to its normal shape that it could not be regarded as a habitual, and so a formulaic use, of the epithet in question. But this is *a priori* argumentation from definitions, against which I have protested earlier. Parry had defined the formula in terms of an expression occupying a certain space, and consequently has no framework within which to discuss even modified word-groups, much less separated ones. Yet defined in such a way as to divorce its connotation from the manner in which it is supposed to be used, the association of one word with another need not, for an inflected language, imply the necessary juxtaposition of the words. The norm in Homer is certainly juxtaposition (especially among the proper names), and it is clear that the organic word-group, filling a section of the hexameter, lends itself easily to the additive manner of the Homeric λέξις εἰρομένη. Some discrete formulae nevertheless are attested,[1] e.g. ἐπιχθονίων ... ἀνδρῶν 2 × ; θεῶν ... (ἀ)πάντων 4 × ; νεῶν ... θοάων 2 × ; ξίφει ... κωπήεντι 2 ×, etc. None of these are complex formulae, as we should call a group in which the dividing term was always the same. This type of complex is relatively common, e.g. ἀδινοῦ ἐξῆρχε γόοιο 4 ×, χαλεποῖσιν ἀμείψασθαι ἐπέεσσιν 3 ×, ἔς ῥ' ἀσαμίνθους βάντες ἐϋξέστας 3 ×, νηῶν ἐπιβησέμεν ὠκειάων 2 ×, σάκος θέτο τετραθέλυμνον 2 ×, etc. Patterns by which normal formulae might actually be split therefore exist.[2] How extensive is this artifice?

The basic point that the use of formulae is intimately connected with the natural divisions of the hexameter is not contradicted by the principal examples of separated formulae: on the contrary it is strikingly confirmed. The most freely separable formulae

nom, et par conséquent il fera inévitablement plus attention à l'épithète, comme à un mot dont l'idée a sa propre importance. Nous voyons donc que l'épithète fixe n'est jamais séparée de son nom, sauf dans le cas des noms apparaissant si fréquemment dans la poésie qu'il était certain que l'indifférence de l'auditeur pour le sens particularisé possible se développerait rapidement.' *ET* 206. The exceptions referred to are such separations as κορυθαίολος ... Ἕκτωρ Χ 471, or πολύμητις ... Ὀδυσσεύς δ 763, noted at *ET* 100, where the placing is compared to that of certain generic epithets, such as δουρικλυτός, which have their fixed place in the verse without being necessarily juxtaposed with their nouns, cf. *ET* 80–84.

[1] These are settled expressions always divided by the same space. Other divided word-associations are found whose shape is more plastic, e.g. φύλλα ∪ − ∪ ∪ − τέρενα and τέρενα ∪ ∪ φύλλα; κρατερῷ ἐνὶ δεσμῷ, δεσμοῖο ∪ − κρατεροῦ, δεσμοῖς ∪ ∪ − κρατεροῖς, juxtaposed only at *H. Herm.* 409 καρτερὰ δεσμά.

[2] In addition non-traditional functional epithets are freely separated from their nouns: πυραὶ ... θαμειαί Α 52, ἐσθλὸν ... ἔπος Α 108, etc.

are those that contain a word that itself exactly fits a portion of the hexameter or has some affinity for a certain position, and these can be usefully sorted into three chief categories:

   (i) Those in which a word shaped $-\cup\cup-\underset{\smile}{-}$ is retained at, or brought to, the verse-end, or a phrase of that shape created there, with the intrusive words lying before it;

  (ii) Those in which a word shaped $(\cup)\cup-\cup\cup$ is retained at, or brought to, a position immediately after the caesura, or a phrase created there, with the intrusive words lying either before or after it;

 (iii) Those in which a word shaped $\cup\cup-\underset{\smile}{-}$, $\cup-\underset{\smile}{-}$ or $-\underset{\smile}{-}$, is retained at, or brought to, the verse-end, with the intrusive words lying before it.

The technique here pursued is evident. Words no less than formulae fall into their natural positions in the verse. Around this pivot the sentence is constructed, and its associated terms must fall where they can. There are various other separations whose origin is less evident.

1. *Separations based on a term scanned* $-\cup\cup-\underset{\smile}{-}$ *at the verse-end*

Even with the aid of additional adjustments the artifice is very feebly developed among the two classes of shorter formulae, for obvious reasons of physical size. Make the formulae a little longer, and the device will be found to enjoy a certain vogue. The un-shifted term will almost always be an epithet which, in order to achieve the dimensions of two whole feet, is usually compound and may present the appearance of being created for the verse-end position. With such an epithet a noun of pyrrhic scansion may be combined to give a formula of the useful shape $\cup\cup-\cup\cup$ $-\underset{\smile}{-}$, e.g. δέπας ἀμφικύπελλον, νέας ἀμφιελίσσας, etc. With all its advantages[1] the shape has one defect: it is impossible to con-strue a dactylic word with it without modification, unless the poet is willing to place the dactylic word at the beginning of the line and fill out the intervening space. The neatest modification is to split the formula and intrude the dactylic word into the fourth foot, e.g. δέπας ⟨οἴσεται⟩ ἀμφικύπελλον Ψ 663, 667; νέες

---

[1] *ET* 63–67 gives the sentence-patterns into which the personal name formulae of this shape enter (see p. 14 above). The common noun formulae are similarly used.

⟨ἤλυθον⟩ ἀμφιέλισσαι N 174 = O 549 etc.[1] Dactylic words are a hazard no poet of the Greek language could escape, but there are other pitfalls in the use of the longer formulae which are almost self-sought. The epic *likes* words of the measure (∪) ∪ – ∪ ∪ so useful in the 3rd–4th feet, and liking them must face their incompatibility with the longer formulae of the second half of the verse. Separation, if the word-divisions are right, is again an obvious artifice, but it must normally be combined with some sort of modification. A word displaced from the 4th foot will not immediately place itself before the caesura: hence νῆας ⟨ἅλαδ' ἑλκέμεν⟩ ἀμφιελίσσας B 165 = 181, or even νῆας ⟨ἐϋσσέλμους ἅλαδ' ἑλκέμεν⟩ ἀμφιελίσσας I 683 etc.[2] This pattern of use is like that of long epithets generally. Often they are fixed in position, sometimes under metrical necessity, while their noun falls where it can. N 614 κόρυθος φάλον ἤλασεν ἱπποδασείης is arranged very like B 165 above, but κόρυθος cannot be juxtaposed with its epithet. What then is surprising if a long epithet reverts to the convenient verse-end position when the formula in which it is incorporated is disrupted?[3] For instance, ἀθανάτοισι θεοῖσι 20 × in 1st–3rd or 4th–6th feet but θεοῖσι μετάγγελος ἀθανάτοισι O 144.[4]

I have introduced this additional formulaic material in order to establish the pattern of use into which a few of the shorter formulae have been attracted. All fill the 5th–6th feet by expanding their final component: τόδε ⟨δέξαι ἐμεῦ πάρα καλὸν⟩ ἄλεισον

---

[1] I count thirty formulae and possible formulae of the shape and word-division ∪ ∪ | – ∪ ∪ – ◡ of which nine are separated to admit a dactylic (or occasionally spondaic) word: βοὸς ... ἀγραύλοιο, δόμον ... εὐρώεντα, πτόλις ... εὐρυάγυια, χθονὶ ... πουλυβοτείρῃ, χροὸς ... ἀνδρομέοιο, besides the two examples quoted in the text, and with a change to the acc. sing. case βοῦν ... εὐρυμέτωπον, σῦν ... ἀργιόδοντα.

[2] Add seven examples of the shape and word-division – ∪ ∪ | – ∪ ∪ – ◡ (out of twenty-six formulae and possible formulae of that structure): ἀσπίδα ⟨μὲν⟩ ... πάντοσ' ἐΐσην, δένδρεα ⟨μακρὰ⟩ ... τηλεθόωντα, ἵππων ... ὠκειάων, πᾶσιν ⟨δὲ⟩ ... μνηστήρεσσι, οἰῶν ⟨μέγα πῶυ⟩ ... ἀργεννάων, οἴνοιο (for οἴνου) ... ἡδυπότοιο, υἱοῖσι (for υἱάσι) ... κυδαλίμοισι. An isolated example from a longer class is ποταμὸν (-οῦ) ... δινήεντα (-ος) cf. π. βαθυδινήεντα.

[3] Theoretically as many as eighty-five formulae and possible formulae of the shape – ∪ ∪ – ∪ ∪ – ◡ might fall victims to this accident. I count seven, the other six being μακρῇσι ... ἐγχείῃσι, ἐπέεσσι / ἔπεσσι ... μειλιχίοισι, ἵπποισι ... ὠκυπόδεσσι, νηυσὶ / νήεσσι ... ποντοπόροισι, νηυσὶ ... ὠκυπόροισι, χερσὶ ... ἀμφοτέρῃσι.

[4] ποσὶ ... ἀμφοτέροισι χ 87 cannot be quoted as a modification giving – ∪ ∪ – ∪. The expression attested in one of our shapes is πόδες ἄμφω which has no dative of the same shape. ἄμφω is found as genitive but not as dative and ἀμφοῖν is unknown.

Ω 429; σὸν ⟨δ' ἔκτανε πιστὸν⟩ ἑταῖρον P 589; ληΐδα ⟨δ' ἐκ πεδίου συνελάσσαμεν ἤλιθα⟩ πολλήν Λ 677; the expanded formula μῆλα ⟨ταναύποδα⟩ πίονα ⟨δημῷ⟩ ι 464 has the same structure. A fifth example has augmentation of more generous size at the verse-end: πᾶσιν ⟨ἐλέγχιστον θέμεναι μερόπεσσι⟩ βροτοῖσι B 285.[1]

2. *Separations based on a term scanned* (∪) ∪ – ∪ ∪ *in 3rd–4th feet*

The typical expression subjected to this kind of separation is located at the verse-end and consists of a long epithet scanned ∪∪ – ∪ ∪ with a trochaic or spondaic noun, e.g. περικαλλέα δίφρον, μεγαλήτορι θυμῷ, etc. The space between caesura and diaeresis, however, has a strong attraction for words of such dimensions, a position which they fill exactly. And if the epithet is drawn back to this position, dactylic words can be accommodated in the 5th foot between the epithet and noun, e.g. περικαλλέα ⟨βήσετο⟩ δίφρον γ 481.[2] The pattern of use has again attracted some of the short formulae, which must make use of modification or expansion to obtain the crucial (∪) ∪ – ∪ ∪ term: thus ποδώκεες ⟨ἔκφερον⟩ ἵπποι Ψ 376, and ποδώκεας ⟨ἤλασεν⟩ ἵππους P 614, cf. ὠκέες (-ας) ἵπποι (-ους); ἀεικέα ⟨μήδετο⟩ ἔργα X 395 = Ψ 24, cf. ἔργον ἀεικές;[3] ⟨μάλα⟩ μέρμερα ⟨μήσατο⟩ ἔργα K 289. An epithet scanned (∪) ∪ – – is undesirable in this position, but a few occur[4] and, as it happens, one provides a separated formula of one of our shapes: τάφρον ⟨δ' ἐκδιαβάντες⟩ ὀρυκτήν K 198, a much-separated formula with the noun itself this time shifted to the beginning of the verse.

The position between caesura and diaeresis is attractive to phrases as much as to words, and by lending one of their com-

---

[1] The only parallel to the length of the verse-end member appears to be ἀνδρῶν ... ὑπερηνορεόντων ψ 31.

[2] Fifty-two formulae and possible formulae of this structure might be affected, sixteen in fact are, the others being ναυσικλυτοὶ ... ἄνδρες, μεγαλήτορι ... θυμῷ, καλλίτριχε ... ἵππω (P 504, for acc. plur. but in the sense 'chariot'), χρυσάμπυκας ... ἵππους, διδυμάονε ... παῖδε, and the expanded formulae ἐρυσάρματες ⟨ὠκέες⟩ ἵπποι and Καπανήϊος ⟨ἀγλαὸς⟩ υἱός: and with the noun shifted into the first half of the verse: ἄγρον ... πολυδένδρεον, ἔγχος ... δολιχόσκιον, ἵππους ... κρατερώνυχας, πολλὰ ... κειμήλια, λώβην ... θυμαλγέα, νῆας ... δυώδεκα (for δυοκαίδεκα v.), οἶνον ... μελιηδέα, χαλκὸν ... ταμεσίχροα.

[3] A metrical equivalent is ἐμήσατο ἔργον ἀεικές λ 429. But the association of μήδεσθαι with ἔργον (-α) is very fluid: economy is a characteristic of *settled* formulaic phraseology.

[4] Only one other separated formula gives a comparable rhythm, πολυφόρβου ... χαίης Ξ 200, 301, cf. γαῖαν πολυφόρβην itself in the 2nd–4th feet, I 569.

ponents to the (◡) ◡ – ◡ ◡ phrase the short formulae may enter
the present pattern of separation. The additional word is usually
fully functional, but occasionally the key phrase is constructed
by the artifices of expansion. For the most part the second term
of the formula is then placed in the first half of the verse, thus:

⟨μάλα⟩ πολλὰ ⟨πάθ'⟩ ἄλγεα ν 90, and πολλὰ ⟨δ' ὅ γ' ἐν πόντῳ
    πάθεν⟩ ἄλγεα α 4, cf. ἄ. πολλά;
ἄνδρες ⟨νηῶν ἔνι⟩ τέκτονες ι 126, cf. τ. ἄνδρες;
πολλὰ ⟨βροτῶν ἐπὶ⟩ ἄστεα π 63, cf. ἄ. πολλά (the complex
    formula is mobile—2 × in 1st–3rd feet, 1 × in 3rd–5th feet—
    with elision);
ὀξὺ ⟨πάγη⟩ βέλος Δ 185, cf. β. ὀξύ;
δῶρα ⟨δ' ἄγ' ἀλλήλοισι⟩ περικλυτά Η 299, cf. κλυτὰ δ.;
ἕλκος ⟨μὲν γὰρ ἔχω τόδε⟩ καρτερόν Π 517, cf. (τόδε) κ. ἕ.;
⟨οἱ δ'⟩ ἄλλοι ⟨οὔ σφι πάρεσαν⟩ θεοί Λ 75, and ⟨οἱ δ'⟩ ἄλλοι
    ⟨πρὸς "Ολυμπον ἴσαν⟩ θεοί Φ 518, cf. θ. ἄλλοι;
ἱστὸν ⟨ἐποιχομένης⟩ μέγαν ⟨ἄμβροτον⟩ κ 222, cf. μ. ἱστόν;
πόλλ' ⟨ἐπὶ τοῖς πάθομεν⟩ κακά γ 113, cf. κ. πολλά;
μῆλα ⟨κατεκτάνομεν μάλα⟩ πίονα ω 66, cf. π. μῆλα;
ἡμετέρας ⟨ἰέναι⟩ νέας Ν 101, cf. ν. ἀμάς;
νὺξ ⟨φθῖτ'⟩ ἄμβροτος λ 330, cf. ἀμβροσίη νύξ;
εὐρὺ ⟨γὰρ ἀμφ' ὤμοισιν ἔχει⟩ σάκος Λ 527, cf. σ. εὐρύ;
τόξα ⟨λαβὼν φέρε⟩ καμπύλα φ 359, cf. κ. τόξα;
ὕπνος ⟨ἔχε⟩ γλυκύς ο 7, cf. γ. ὕπνος;
σῆσιν ⟨ἔχε⟩ φρεσίν Β 33, 70, cf. φρ. σῆσι;
πάντα ⟨δ' ἀπὸ πλευρῶν⟩ χρόα ⟨ἔργαθεν⟩ Λ 437, cf. χρ. πάντα.

The expanded formula ἄλλοι ⟨μάκαρες⟩ θεοί ε 7 etc. slips into
this pattern. The total is twenty-one formulae, eleven of the
– ◡ ◡ – ◡̲ and ten of the ◡ ◡ – ◡̲ class.

3. *Separations based on a term scanned* ◡ ◡ – ◡̲, ◡ – ◡̲, *or* – ◡̲ *at the verse-end*

The attraction felt towards the verse-end by words shorter than
those scanned – ◡ ◡ – ◡̲ is strictly related to the quantity of the
final syllable and the length of the word. A word ◡ ◡ – – is as
constricted as one – ◡ is emancipated.[1] In many cases therefore
the technique of anchoring one term in a favoured place while

---

[1] Using O'Neill's material from *Yale Classical Studies* viii (1942) we find that the
proportion of final placings for ◡ ◡ – – is *c.* 94 per cent., for ◡ – – 88 per cent., for
◡ ◡ – ◡ 30 per cent., for ◡ – ◡ 66 per cent., for – – 17 per cent., and for – ◡ only
12 per cent.

the other floats freely about the verse is not evident. Moreover many of the formulae that bring a short word to the verse-end are themselves of the shorter classes, and are freely movable, if need be, without adjustment. The separation of the words is therefore an alternative rather than a complementary technique to mobility.

I count only two of the shorter formulae divided on the basis of a final ∪ ∪ – ⌣: ἑοῦ ⟨περὶ σῆμ'⟩ ἑτάροιο Ω 755[1] cf. οὗ ἑτάροιο; and by the conflation of two ἔργα-formulae τάδε ⟨πευθόμενος κακὰ⟩ ἔργα ρ 158.

Formulae which have ∪ – ⌣ as their second term are naturally numerous in the – ∪ ∪ – ⌣ class. Thirteen are split. An obvious place for the first term is immediately before the caesura, hence:

δαιτὸς ⟨κεκορήμεθα θυμὸν⟩ ἐΐσης θ 98;
δαιτὶ ⟨συνήορός ἐστι⟩ θαλείη θ 99;
νηυσὶ . . . θοῇσι Ο 673, Ρ 708; (at Ο 673 ἠδ' ὅσσοι παρὰ νηυσὶ μάχην ἐμάχοντο θοῇσι the split is caused by the rearrangement of a complex formula caused in its turn by a change in the connective phrase, cf. ι 54 στησάμενοι δ' ἐμάχοντο μάχην παρὰ ν. θ.).
πᾶσι ⟨περιδείσασα⟩ θεοῖσι Ο 123; ἑῇ ⟨ἐπέδωκε⟩ θυγατρί Ι 148 = 290, a repeated passage, cf. θυγατέρα (-ος) ἥν (ἧς); τοῦτο ⟨θεῶν δείσειε⟩ νόημα Η 456; τάφρον (-ῳ) . . . ὀρυκτήν (-ῇ) Μ 72, Θ 179; and ταῦτα ⟨διεξερέεσθε⟩ ἕκαστα Κ 432; cf. the expanded formula πάντας ⟨ἐϋκνήμιδας⟩ ἑταίρους κ 203. The first term may even stand at the very beginning of the verse: πάντας . . . ἑταίρους γ 191; πολλὸς . . . ὅμιλος Σ 603, the juxtaposed form being πουλὺς ὅμ.; and τάφρῳ . . . ὀρυκτῇ Ο 344.[2]

If the first term remains in the second half of the verse it will require some sort of modification to evade the familiar difficulties of the fourth foot. This may be no more than to cancel the effects of elision or correption: hence ἀγλαὰ ⟨δέχθαι⟩ ἄποινα Α 23 = 377, a repeated passage; and πολλοὶ ⟨δ' ἀμφ' αὐτὸν⟩ ἑταῖροι λ 520; the *Iliad* has πολέες for πολλοί Β 417 etc. 3×, despite the juxtaposed πολλοὶ ἑταῖροι; and the conflated formula ἄλλοι ⟨πάντες⟩ ἑταῖροι

---

[1] One of a series of manipulations in Ω, cf. περὶ σῆμ' ἑτάροιο φίλοιο Ω 51 and περὶ σῆμα ἑοῦ ἑτάροιο φίλοιο Ω 416.

[2] The line is τάφρῳ καὶ σκολόπεσσιν ἐνιπλήξαντες ὀρυκτῇ, a harsh hyperbaton to be explained, like many grammatical questions in Homer, in terms of technique (the division of a formula) not of rhetoric (a hendiadys in the first half of the verse):

ι 367. Using a by-form are ἀνέρας ⟨εὗρον⟩ ἀρίστους M 127 and ἀνέρε ⟨δήμου⟩ ἀρίστω Λ 328, cf. ἄνδρας ἀρίστους. Formulae of the word-division ∪ | ∪ – ⌣ are rare, and separated I notice only τόδε ⟨φαίνετ'⟩ ἄεθλον φ 73 = 106.

Separation based on a word – ⌣ at the verse-end is a pattern into which the shorter formulae can naturally very freely enter. Most favoured is the ∪ ∪ | – ⌣ shape, between whose members a dactylic word may be intruded, filling the fifth foot and bringing the whole expression back to the fourth foot caesura, hence:

βροτὸς ⟨οὔτασεν⟩ ἀνήρ E 361;
ἄχος ⟨ἔσσεται⟩ αἰνόν π 87;
κακὰ ⟨μήσατο⟩ ἔργα ω 199;
μέγα – ∪ ∪ ἔργον γ 261, χ 408;
τάδε – ∪ ∪ ἔργα E 757 etc. 3×;
φίλον ⟨ἄϊον⟩ ἦτορ O 252;
μέγας ⟨ἔσσεται⟩ ὅρκος A 239;
μέγα ⟨βάλλετο⟩ φᾶρος B 43;
and φρεσὶ ⟨βάλλεο⟩ σῇσι A 297 etc. 13×.

That there are two intrusions of βάλλειν is fortuitous, one being metaphorical, but the three insertions of μήσατο (N.B. μέγα ⟨μήσατο⟩ ἔργον γ 261, and τάδε ⟨μήσατο⟩ ἔργα ω 444) form a related group and properly speaking are conflations of the nominal and verbal formulae. We note also the two intrusions of ἔσσεται, cf. κλέος ⟨ἔσσεται⟩ ἐσθλόν ω 94 in the 3rd–5th feet. The – ∪ ∪ – ⌣ class are brought back too close to the caesura by the separation to be so dexterously handled, but I count three examples: χαλκέῳ ⟨ἔστασαν⟩ οὐδῷ η 89; ἀγλαὸν ⟨οἰσέμεν⟩ ὕδωρ γ 429; and εὐρέας ⟨ἄμπεχεν⟩ ὤμους ζ 225.

The only other pattern to show any development shunts the first term as far back as the main caesura:

μέλαν ⟨δ' ἀνακήκιεν⟩ αἷμα H 262;
φίλον ∪ ∪ – ∪ ∪ ἦτορ Θ 437 etc. 8×;
θεοὶ ∪ ∪ – ∪ ∪ αὐτοί H 360 = M 234, ω 401;
πόλιν ∪ ∪ – ∪ ∪ αἰπήν γ 130 etc. 4×;
πόλιν ⟨κεραϊζέμεν⟩ ἀμήν Π 830, cf. π. ὑμήν;
κακὰ ⟨δὲ φρεσὶ μήδετο⟩ ἔργα Φ 19 = Ψ 176;

cf. Λ 241–3 πεσὼν κοιμήσατο χάλκεον ὕπνον | οἰκτρός, ἀπὸ μνηστῆς ἀλόχου, ἀστοῖσιν ἀρήγων, | κουριδίης, assisted or excused by the pattern of the runover word.

μέγα ⟨δὲ σφισὶ φαίνετο⟩ ἔργον M 416 and ⟨δ' αὐτῷ φ.⟩ χ 149;
πύρα ⟨δὲ σφισὶ καίετο⟩ πολλά Θ 554;
and with modifications, θεοῖς ⟨ἐνδέξια⟩ πᾶσι A 597, cf. π.
θεοῖσι;
and ἐμοῦ (ἐοῦ) ‿‿ – ‿ ‿ πατρός Χ 500, ο 459, cf. π. ἐμοῖο
(ἐοῖο). The conflated expression ἐμὸν ⟨δολιχόσκιον⟩ ἔγχος Ζ
126 has the same pattern, but is put into the 2nd–5th feet.

If convenience demands there is no reason why the first term
should not be drawn back still further: thus ἥδε (1st foot) . . .
βουλή B 5 etc. 6 ×, cf. ἥδε γε βουλή; and μέγα (2nd foot) . . . πῆμα
Ζ 282.

ὑψερεφὲς ⟨θέτο⟩ δῶμα ο 241 has no parallel at all, except in the
expanded formula ὑψερεφὲς μέγα δῶμα, from which it derives by
substitution of the verb.[1] Another unparalleled separation produced by expansion is εἰλίποδας ἕλικας βοῦς 5 ×, but εἰλίποδας is
there the secondary term.

Altogether in this section there are 35 split formulae, 18 of the
– ‿ ‿ – ⌣ shape and 17 of the ‿ ‿ – ⌣.

These patterns of separation include all those parts of the diction where there has been developed a technique of splitting
these noun–epithet formulae which correlates with recognizable
and familiar features in the distribution of words. There are
many other examples which seem to correlate only with the
convenience of the moment. Thus separation may occur when
a formula is partly displaced from the verse-end by a term
scanned ‿ – ⌣: hence πολλὰ ⟨τετεύξεται⟩ ἄλγε' ⟨ἐπ' αὐτῇ⟩
Φ 585, cf. ἄ. πολλά; οἱ δ' ἄλλοι ⟨φιλότητι νεώτεροι⟩ ἄνδρες ⟨ἕπονται⟩
γ 363, cf. ἀνέρες ἄλλοι; καλὰ ⟨περὶ χροΐ⟩ εἵματ' ⟨ἔχοντι⟩ π 210, cf.
εἵματα κ.; ταῦτα ⟨‿ – –⟩ πάντ' ⟨ἀγορεύω (-σαι)⟩ A 365, Μ 176, cf.
τ. γε π. It is no surprise that εἵματ' ἔχοντα and πάντ' ἀγορεύειν
are formulae in their own right. Other separated formulae that
locate a term in the 5th foot are τάδε ⟨γ' αἰὲν ἀεικέα⟩ ἔργα π 107
= υ 317; ἕνα ⟨φρεσὶ⟩ θυμόν Ν 487, an ingenious expansion of the
complex formula ἕνα θυμὸν ἔχοντες; πυκινὰ ⟨φρεσὶ⟩ μήδε' Ω 282

---

[1] Substitution is an important artifice in the handling of complex formulae, e.g.
κόρυθος φάλον (βάλεν) ἱπποδασείης, κεφαλὴν ἐπέθηκε (ἐφύπερθε) καλύπτρῃ, θοάων
ἔχματα (ἔκτοθι) νηῶν, ἄστυ μέγα (πέρι) Πριάμοιο. This must not be confused with
the formula-type systems as ordinarily presented, where the variables are of the
same grammatical category.

= 674, τ 353, cf. μήδεα πυκνά; κλέος ⟨ἔσσεται⟩ ἐσθλόν ω 94; τάδε ⟨δ᾽ αὐτοὶ⟩ πάντα β 368; and δύο ⟨δ᾽ οὔπω⟩ φῶτε P 377; cf. the two expanded formulae κύνες πόδας ἀργοί and ἐὸν φίλον υἱόν in this same position. Isolated, and with a pyrrhic term in the thesis of the fifth foot, is αἰνὸν ⟨ἀπὸ πραπίδων⟩ ἄχος X 43, cf. ἄ. αἰνόν.

The relatively frequent use made of the − ∪ ∪ − ∪ formulae in the first half of the verse leads to a number of separations in which the first term is placed at the beginning of the verse and the second kept at, or moved to, a point just before the feminine caesura: hence οἷς ⟨ἀγανοῖσι⟩ βέλεσσι Ω 759 etc. 6×, a firm complex, but cf. σοῖσι β.; δάκρυα ⟨δ᾽ ἔκβαλε⟩ θερμά τ 362; κτήμαθ᾽ ⟨ἑλὼν εὖ⟩ πάντα Γ 72 = 93, a repeated passage; νῆα ⟨μὲν οἵγε⟩ μέλαιναν A 485 etc. 3×; πῦρ ⟨ἐθέλεις⟩ ἀΐδηλον I 436; and ταῦτα ∪ −∪∪ πάντα I 135 etc. 3×. Modification naturally appears also, if necessary or convenient: τῷδ᾽ ⟨ἔφες⟩ ἀνδρί E 174 (2nd–3rd feet), cf. ἀνέρι τῷδε; γαστέρα ⟨τύψε⟩ μέσην Δ 531 (2nd–4th feet), a variant of a regular complex formula, cf. γ. μέσσην; and πάντας ⟨ἰὼν⟩ ἑτάρους γ 424, for ἑταίρους. For the ∪ ∪ − ∪ class inversion or modification is de rigueur: ἀνδρὶ ⟨δέμας ἐϊκυῖα⟩ νέῳ ν 222; ἄλλο ⟨δέ τοί τι⟩ ἔπος ο 27; πᾶν ⟨δ᾽ ἐξηράνθη⟩ πεδίον Φ 345; ὕπνος ∪ − γλυκερός τ 511 and (2nd–4th feet) K 4. δόλον ⟨τόνδ᾽⟩ ἄλλον β 93 retains its word-order because it is not brought to the very beginning of the first foot.

Counting all varieties of separation there are forty-five divided formulae in the − ∪ ∪ − ∪ class and thirty-eight in the ∪ ∪ − ∪ class. These are separations made to accommodate a major functional term in the formula's immediate vicinity. The separation is thus physically fairly wide, sometimes indeed very wide. I pass on now to consider less disruptive separations of formulae caused by minor functional words, the enclitic connectives and infixed prepositions.

The adaptation of formulae to receive connectives and prepositions

No small number of divided formulae, both in the second and first half of the verse, receive a connective between their members along with the words of weightier import, e.g. κακὰ δὲ φρεσὶ μήδετο ἔργα, δάκρυα δ᾽ ἔκβαλε θερμά, etc. At the point of discussion this was of no great consequence. Yet it signals one of the improviser's gravest problems. A formula is not made to exist in isolation but to be used in conjunction with other words.

Unhappily for our understanding of the art of the formula the most
obvious formulae are verse-end phrases, whose position makes
it unlikely they will often be the first phrases of new sentences. Consequently the problem of fitting the formulae together was seen as a matter of the poet's 'hitting, as he composed,
upon the type of formula and the particular formula, which,
at any point in his poem, he needed'. A special class of connective formulae would, it is presumed, be the type he would hit
upon for beginning a sentence. Let us concede at once that there
are such connective formulae—ἀλλ' ὅτε δή, αὐτὰρ ἐπεί (ῥα, δή),
ἦμος δ' ... τῆμος (ἄρ'), οἱ δ' ἐπεὶ οὖν, ἀλλ' οὐδ' ὥς, αὐτὰρ ἐγώ (γε),
αὐτὰρ ἔπειτα.[1] But we have seen that the rigidity of the Homeric
formulaic systems is not exempt from a certain looseness. The
noun–epithet formula and the connective will not for ever be
kept apart. What happens when they come face to face? Very
often there is no reason why anything should happen at all:
ἀλλά, αὐτάρ, καί, and the adverbial conjunctions simply lie outside
the formula, and unless the formula is very long there need be
no difficulty in accommodating them. But the enclitic connectives are quite a different matter. Unless they can be elided away
the length of the formula is necessarily increased, and such an
increment may bring no end of further mutations in its train.

There are in fact some types of formula where a short connective can be inserted with every facility, e.g. κουριδίην ⟨δ'⟩ ἄλοχον,
ἀγροτέρας ⟨τ'⟩ ἐλάφους, νηῶν ⟨τ'⟩ ὠκυπόρων, etc., which are first-
half formulae, and at the verse-end θαλερούς ⟨τ'⟩ αἰζηούς, προτέρων
⟨τ'⟩ ἀνθρώπων, κλειτῶν ⟨τ'⟩ ἐπικούρων. The conditions that permit
this intrusion are, of course, extremely limited: the first word of
the formula must end in a long syllable and be followed by a
word with initial vowel. That a member of the ∪ ∪ – ◡ class
should fulfill these conditions is almost inconceivable. (How
many monosyllabic nouns with vocalic initial have regular
Homeric employment? There are no adjectives, for ὅς has a most
persistent digamma.) A member of the – ∪ ∪ – ◡ class would
have to follow the pattern of βοῦς ἀγελαίας, but although half
a dozen regular formulae do conform to this structure not one
suffers the intrusion of a connective. Very occasionally a for-
tunate accident makes it possible to modify the formula, take in

[1] For a detailed study of the particles αὐτάρ, ἰδέ, and νυ in formulaic usage see
C. J. Ruijgh, *L'Élément achéen dans la langue épique*, Assen 1957, 29–67.

the connective, and not disturb the over-all shape. Thus for χερσὶν ἐμῇσι we have χερσί ⟨τ'⟩ ἐμῇσι θ 181, for δῆμον ἅπαντα, πάντα τε δῆμον θ 157, cf. Γ 50, Ω 706, and for ταῦτά γε πάντα, ταῦτά ⟨τε⟩ πάντ' or τ. ⟨δὲ⟩ π. I 35 etc. 3×, cf. ταῦτά ⟨κε⟩ π. K 211. The shorter class shows δύο ⟨δ'⟩ ἄνδρες N 499, Σ 498, for δύο γ' ἄνδρε; and κρέα ⟨τ'⟩ ὀπτά χ 21, for κρέας ὀπτόν.

Such convenience is not generally at hand. However, the intruded connective need not be violently disruptive, though it might require the elongated formula to change its position. Thus φίλον ⟨δέ οἱ⟩ ἦτορ[1] δ 840, and θεὸς ⟨δέ οἱ⟩ αὐτός τ 396 move back to the caesura; δαιτὸς ⟨μὲν⟩ ἐΐσης I 225 straddles the caesura; and οὗτος ⟨μὲν δὴ⟩ ἄεθλος χ 5, cf. τοῦτον ἄ.; ἄλλοι ⟨μὲν γὰρ⟩ πάντες E 877 et sim. 11×, cf. ἄ. ἅπαντες. ἠέρι ⟨γὰρ⟩ πολλῇ Π 790, and κτήματα ⟨γάρ κεν⟩ πάντα β 335 move to the beginning of the verse.

The initial position, one of obvious importance for beginning sentences, is impossible for the ∪∪–⊻ shape, and the intrusion of an enclitic does nothing to improve it. Inversion may give a perfect shape: thus ἥδε ⟨δ'⟩ ὁδός ο 198; αἰπὺ ⟨δ'⟩ ὄρος τ 431; and σῆμα ⟨δέ μοι⟩ τόδ' ψ 273. ἄλλοι ⟨τε⟩ θεοί Z 476 begins in the thesis of the first foot. πᾶν δ' ἦμαρ A 592, Σ 453, cf. πρόπαν ἦμαρ, falls back on modification. Inversion is neither so necessary nor so neat for the –∪∪–⊻ class, but inevitably the odd example occurs: πολλὰ ⟨γὰρ⟩ ἄλγε' δ 164; and with strong modification δώματά ⟨θ'⟩ ὑψερεφέα δ 757, cf. ὑψερεφὲς δῶ.

One small advantage that the enclitic connective gives is that its attachment to a word scanned ∪–∪, by abolishing the danger of a weak caesura in the 4th foot, enables the word to be used after the main caesura. Since the word-division –∪ | ∪–∪ is not unusual, by inverting the components of the formula a neat connective phrase can be created: βίηφί ⟨τε⟩ ἦφι φ 315; θεοῖσι ⟨δὲ⟩ πᾶσι Ξ 334; and λοετρά ⟨τε⟩ θερμά θ 249. Similarly constructed is φίλῃσι ⟨δὲ⟩ χερσί Σ 27 which is placed before the caesura. The ∪∪–∪ class needs no adjustments to secure this shape with connectives, but to begin the phrase at the masculine caesura requires some ingenuity and good luck in the alternatives available: one example only, γλυκερὸς ⟨δέ μοι⟩ ὕπνος ε 472, cf. γλυκὺς ὕ.

Formulae with an infixed connective at the verse-end are rare, the reason being that sentences do not regularly begin at

---

[1] I count the groups δέ οἱ, δέ σε, etc., among connectives; their use is often parallel to that of the compound connective δέ τε.

the 4th foot caesura while the space after the diaeresis, where sentences do often begin, is insufficient for an augmented noun–epithet formula. I count only one formula in each of our two classes νῆάς ⟨τε⟩ προπάσας B 493, cf. v. ἁπάσας; and ταχέες ⟨δέ μιν⟩ ἵπποι X 464, cf. ταχέ᾽ ἵππω.

Finally there are two odd examples that lie before the 4th foot caesura: ἄλλοι ⟨δὲ⟩ θεοί I 535; and ἡμετέρην ⟨τε⟩ πόλιν ζ 191, cf. π. ὑμήν.

Since the modification of formulae in these circumstances is by no means an extensive technique, it is natural to ask how the enclitic connectives are normally introduced into the formulaic phraseology. In many cases the answer is that they are not; they are embodied in phrases that are in no way formulaic at all, e.g. ἔκλαγξαν δ᾽ ἄρ᾽ ὀϊστοί . . . A 46. Or they are arranged to be outside the formulae and placed with one of the functional words of the sentence, e.g. εὖ δ᾽ οἴκαδ᾽ ἱκέσθαι A 19. Some functional words indeed seem to have a special affinity for connectives, e.g. πολλὰ δέ A 35, which appears no less than thirty-eight times in the first foot. There are also many quasi-formulaic phrases such as ὁ γάρ A 9, ὁ δέ A 47, or σὺ δέ A 76, which are by no means confined to hexameter writing. Whole-sentence formulae, often quite short, are common, which being whole sentences necessarily incorporate the connective, e.g. κρατερὸν δ᾽ ἐπὶ μῦθον ἔτελλε A 25 etc. 4×. But we also find phrases that are not regular themselves with the connective, but that use and adapt formulaic material, e.g. Ἀτρείδης τε ἄναξ ἀνδρῶν A 7.[1]

Construction with the prepositions presents nothing like the same problems, because in the normal way the preposition may be expected to fall beside the formula, not in it. The problem, if any, is one of space. In the second half of the verse, except for the very longest formulae, all is easy: κατ᾽ ἀσπίδα πάντοσ᾽ ἐΐσην, ἐπὶ χθονὶ πουλυβοτείρῃ, παρὰ νηὶ μελαίνῃ, εἰς ἅλα δῖαν. Notoriously the preposition at this point may become a regular adjunct to the formula, effectively increasing its length and restricting its capacity for movement. Expansion may take place before it, and

---

[1] There is no developed technique for connectives that we should want to call improvisatory. The connectives are naturally the most formulaic part of any language by reason of sheer frequency, so that repetition in Homer of similar connective phrases (e.g. ἐξ οὗ δή A 6 and ξ 379) is without significance unless correlated with extension and economy (e.g. αὐτὰρ ἐπεί [ῥα, δή, δή ῥ᾽]), or very high frequency (e.g. αὐτὰρ ἔπειτα 52×, the hallmark of run-of-the-mill epic versifying, Anth. Pal. xi. 130).

it may play an intimate part in some modifications.[1] Generally the shorter formulae leave the poet with adequate space for prepositional constructions and figure only to a small extent among the modifications made to formulae for this purpose.

It is in the first half of the verse that difficulties are most likely to arise, since the natural thing is to place the preposition *in front* of the formula. Some first-half formulae are forced into a medial position by the need for a prepositional construction, e.g. μετ' ἀγροτέρας ἐλάφους ζ 133 (1st–4th feet), but initially and without preposition at Φ 486. Indeed the disyllabic prepositions are a special problem at the beginning of the verse, a problem that is met very largely by postponing the preposition, so that expressions of the structure exemplified by νηὸς ἄπο πρύμνης, πέτρης πρὸς μεγάλῃσι, and τύμβῳ ἐπ' ἀκροτάτῳ are frequent.[2] Into this pattern are fitted four highly modified members of the – ∪ ∪ – ⌣ class: ἀσκῷ ἐν αἰγείῳ Γ 247, ζ 78, cf. αἴγεον ἀσκόν; ἡμέτερον πρὸς δῶμα υ 192, cf. ἡμέτερον δῶ; δῶμα καθ' ὑψερεφές δ 46, η 85, cf. ὑψερεφὲς δῶ; and δεξιτερὸν δ' ὑπὲρ ὦμον Κ 373, cf. δεξιὸν ὦμον.

The remainder fall into no marked pattern of prepositional construction, but conform to shapes which it is evidently desirable to obtain by modification: ᾗσιν ἐνὶ φρεσί in 3rd–4th feet Α 333 etc. 4×, cf. φ. ᾗσι; after the caesura we have μέγα προτὶ ἄστυ Ο 681, cf. μ. ἄστυ; μέσην κατὰ γαστέρα Ρ 313, and in dative (with δ' ἐν) Ν 372, 398, cf. γ. μέσσην; πολὺν καθ' ὅμιλον Ρ 462, cf. πουλὺν ὅμ.; and ἐμῆς ἐν χερσί aut sim. Φ 104 etc. 5×, cf. χ. ἐμῇσι.

In the – ∪ ∪ – ⌣ class are 14 formulae separated by connectives and 7 by prepositions, and in the ∪ ∪ – ⌣ class 11 by connectives but only two by prepositions.

The poet's willingness to use separated formulae can be sum-

[1] Notably in prepositional formulae that alternate between the second and first half of the verse, the preposition being infixed in the first half, e.g. ἐν εἰλιπόδεσσι βόεσσι—βουσὶν ἐπ' εἰλιπόδεσσι, ἀπὸ κράατος ἀθανάτοιο—κρατὸς ἀπ' ἀθανάτοιο, ἐνὶ τρητοῖσι λέχεσσι—τρητοῖς ἐν λεχέεσσι, ἐνὶ μεγάροισι τεοῖσι (ἑοῖσι)—σοῖσιν (οἷσιν) ἐνὶ μεγάροισι. The alternation παραὶ / πὰρ Διὸς αἰγιόχοιο points to an unexploited artifice. There are also shifts between the initial and a medial position, e.g. ἀνδρὸς ἐς ἀφνειοῦ—ἐν ἀφνειοῦ ἀνδρός, πόντον ἐπ' ἀτρύγετον—ἐπ' ἀτρύγετον πόντον, πυργῷ ἐφ' ὑψηλῷ—ἀφ' ὑψηλοῦ πυργοῦ. For expansions made outside the preposition see p. 78.

[2] The three examples quoted are all regular without the preposition (πρύμνης νεός, πέτρῃσιν μεγάλῃσι, ἀκροτάτῳ τύμβῳ) but the infixing artifice cannot be relied on. The numerous first-half formulae which regularly have the infixed preposition tend to be an independent class using material peculiar to themselves, e.g. ἀσπίδ' ἐνὶ κρατερῇ, δηΐῳ ἐν πολέμῳ, etc., and not the normally juxtaposed epithets.

marized with more precision than his willingness to modify or expand. Separations normally occur but once and show very little tendency to become regular, so that more obviously than other kinds of adaptation separation is an adjustment in the face of a particular exigency. Since, however, discrete formulae do exist it must be allowed that a separated word-group might become regular in that form or might even be the primary form of a formula, so I make the usual allowance in calculation.

Shape	Total formulae	Separations		Proportion (%)	
		Maximum	Minimum	Maximum	Minimum
$- \cup \cup - \underline{\cup}$	319	57	43	18	14
$\cup \cup - \underline{\cup}$	140	46	38	40	27

A separation is hardly ever likely to be opportunist in the way that a modification might be used to fill a space that happened to be available. The formula is split by pressure of the intruding word, which the poet needs to use equally with the formula. It is very rare to encounter a gratuitous separation, one that necessity has not enforced upon the poet.[1] But as with modification, up to a point the poet's difficulty is of his technique's own making. Consider such groups of phrases as the following:

$$\nu\acute{\epsilon}\alpha\varsigma \ \dot{\alpha}\mu\phi\iota\epsilon\lambda\acute{\iota}\sigma\sigma\alpha\varsigma \quad 5 \times$$
$$\nu\hat{\eta}\alpha\varsigma \ \ddot{\alpha}\lambda\alpha\delta' \ \dot{\epsilon}\lambda\kappa\acute{\epsilon}\mu\epsilon\nu \ \dot{\alpha}\mu\phi\iota\epsilon\lambda\acute{\iota}\sigma\sigma\alpha\varsigma \quad 2 \times$$
$$\nu\hat{\eta}\alpha\varsigma \ \dot{\epsilon}\ddot{\upsilon}\sigma\sigma\acute{\epsilon}\lambda\mu\upsilon\varsigma \ \ddot{\alpha}\lambda\alpha\delta' \ \dot{\epsilon}\lambda\kappa\acute{\epsilon}\mu\epsilon\nu \ \dot{\alpha}\mu\phi\iota\epsilon\lambda\acute{\iota}\sigma\sigma\alpha\varsigma \quad 1 \times$$
$$\nu\hat{\eta}\alpha\varsigma \ \dot{\epsilon}\ddot{\upsilon}\sigma\sigma\acute{\epsilon}\lambda\mu\upsilon\varsigma \ \ddot{\alpha}\lambda\alpha\delta' \ \dot{\epsilon}\lambda\kappa\acute{\epsilon}\mu\epsilon\nu \quad 2 \times$$

$$\kappa\alpha\kappa\grave{\alpha} \ \ddot{\epsilon}\rho\gamma\alpha \quad 11 \times$$
$$\kappa\alpha\kappa\grave{\alpha} \ \mu\acute{\eta}\sigma\alpha\tau\upsilon \ \ddot{\epsilon}\rho\gamma\alpha \quad 1 \times$$
$$\kappa\alpha\kappa\grave{\alpha} - \cup \cup \ \mu\acute{\eta}\delta\epsilon\tau\upsilon \ \ddot{\epsilon}\rho\gamma\alpha \quad 2 \times$$
$$\kappa\alpha\kappa\grave{\alpha} \ \mu\acute{\eta}\sigma\alpha\tau\upsilon \quad 3 \times$$
$$\kappa\alpha\kappa\grave{\alpha} \ \mu\acute{\eta}\delta\epsilon\tau\upsilon \quad 4 \times$$

$$\pi\upsilon\nu\tau\upsilon\pi\acute{\upsilon}\rho\upsilon\iota\sigma\iota \ \nu\acute{\epsilon}\epsilon\sigma\sigma\iota \quad 2 \times$$
$$\nu\eta\upsilon\sigma\grave{\iota} \ \nu\epsilon\acute{\omega}\mu\epsilon\theta\alpha \ \pi\upsilon\nu\tau\upsilon\pi\acute{\upsilon}\rho\upsilon\iota\sigma\iota \quad 1 \times$$
$$\nu\eta\upsilon\sigma\grave{\iota} \ \nu\epsilon\acute{\omega}\mu\epsilon\theta\alpha \quad 2 \times$$
$$\nu\eta\upsilon\sigma\grave{\iota}\nu \ \dot{\epsilon}\pi\grave{\iota} \ \gamma\lambda\alpha\phi\upsilon\rho\hat{\eta}\sigma\iota \ \nu\epsilon\acute{\omega}\mu\epsilon\theta\alpha \quad 1 \times$$

[1] There is one point where the artifices of separation and continuation overlap, the complex formulae of the structure 'noun+third term+epithet' shaped $\cup - | \cup \cup | - \cup \cup - \underline{\cup}$. The long epithet is omissible and the first element of the complex follows the word-order normal for words of that shape in that position, viz. noun+verb or dependent genitive+noun. So we have $\Delta\iota\grave{\upsilon}\varsigma$ with $\delta\acute{\upsilon}\mu\upsilon\nu$, $\nu\acute{\upsilon}\upsilon\nu$, $\pi\acute{\alpha}\ddot{\iota}\varsigma$, $\tau\acute{\epsilon}\kappa\upsilon\varsigma$, and $\tau\acute{\epsilon}\rho\alpha\varsigma$, both with and without a following $\alpha\dot{\iota}\gamma\iota\acute{\upsilon}\chi\upsilon\iota\upsilon$.

The filiation is obvious. Here the separation of noun and epithet arises through the multiplicity of word-associations that the poet employs, so that much of his phraseology is a conflation of two or even three formulae. Naturally such conflations must often mean the disruption and adjustment of some of the components.

APPENDIX

The Division of Formulae by the Verse-end

A SPECIAL case of separation is that of a noun–epithet formula divided, with or without the intrusion of other words, by the verse-end itself. The case is special because if, as is usually the case, the term in the second verse is the epithet, then the usage falls under a prominent and well-defined sentence-pattern: the prolongation of a sentence by means of one (or sometimes two or three) 'runover' epithets, which in their turn may be followed by a relative clause or its equivalent, e.g. A 1–2. There is no comparable pattern of separated noun and epithet within the verse in Homer, the so-called Leonine verse being alien to his art. The runover epithet, as a noteworthy case of enjambement, has been extensively studied,[1] and its function elucidated.[2] However, as usual, little attention has been paid to the source of the vocabulary in the runover phrases. Using the same arguments as he did for separation within the verse, Parry himself insisted that an epithet placed in such a position by being thrown into relief had to be functional, and so fell outside his investigations.[3] But there are a few normal-looking formulae straddling the verse-end, e.g. ἀχλὺν | θεσπεσίην 2×,[4] φαρέτρη (-ην) | ἰοδόκος (-ον) 3×.

Divided as it is, the over-all shape of a runover phrase is different from that of most normal groups, and the vocabulary is consequently often quite distinct, e.g. ἔγχος ... βριθὺ μέγα στιβαρόν 6×, where the epithets make a runover phrase regularly associated with the noun

---

[1] La Roche, *Wiener Stud.* xix (1897) 169–75; H. W. Prescott, *CP* vii (1912) 35–58; S. E. Bassett, *TAPA* lvii (1926) 116–48.

[2] The function according to Bassett is 'to add a new idea, either to be expanded by what follows, or to act in some other way as a bond between this and the preceding idea' (op. cit. 122).

[3] *ET* 207, with an exception made for the 'quasi-independent' epithets like διΐφιλος. But what, for example, are we to say of the special epithet in Χίμαιραν | – ∪ ἀμαιμακέτην Π 329, juxtaposed within the verse at Ζ 179?

[4] The epithet, being formulaic in our sense, persists even when the construction of the noun is changed: νέφος ἀχλύος ... θεσπέσιον Ο 668–9.

but unused outside this sentence-pattern. But when the poet's thought is cast into any marked verse-pattern the choice of vocabulary may reflect any of his established word-associations, so that in the runover pattern one repeatedly encounters such phraseology as ἄρουραι | πυρο-φόροι Ξ 122–3, cf. ἀρούρης πυροφόροιο; βροτῶν . . . | δειλῶν Φ 463–4, cf. δειλοῖσι βροτοῖσι etc. When the grammatical cases of the juxtaposed and separated word-groups are different the use of the same epithets illustrates only (but forcibly) the persistence of formulaic groups once they have been formed. I am concerned here rather with those instances of separation where the compulsion of a new grammatical case is lacking and the poet has chosen to split a formula which he could perfectly well have juxtaposed within the verse but for the pressure of other words that he required to use.

The clearest instances of such separation are those where the noun (or epithet) terminates one verse and the epithet (or noun) begins the next. Without modification this requires very precise conditions of over-all shape and word-division, e.g. ἀνδρῶν | ἡρώων E 746–7, juxtaposed in the 1st–3rd feet. The verse-end formulae of any length have no alternative but to modify themselves, since a word – ⌣ cannot be passed into the following verse without leaving an impossible – ⌣ ⌣, ⌣ ⌣ – ⌣ ⌣, etc., to be drawn to the verse-end. Thus we have δοῦρα| μακρά χ 148–9 and δοῦρε | μάκρ' μ 228–9, modified from δούρατα μακρά, an isolated piece of versatility. However, the shape – ⌣ ⌣ | – ⌣ is ideal for splitting across the verse-end if the elements are reversed: hence ἦτορ | ἄλκιμον Φ 571–2; θυμῷ | πρόφρονι Θ 39–40 = X 183–4; ἵππους | ὠκέας N 535–6, Ξ 429–30 (and ἵπποι | ὠκύποδες E 295–6 etc. 4×, or ἵπποι (-ους) | – ⌣ ⌣ ὠκύποδες (-ας) K 568–9 etc. 4×); and ὦμον | δεξιόν E 188–9. The shape – ⌣ | ⌣ – ⌣ would be equally amenable to inversion, but I find only ἀρίστην (predicative) | μῆτιν ψ 124–5.

These expressions are like simple modifications in that the words are not physically separate. But we have seen that there is no reason why they should be juxtaposed in the flexible style. Such physical separation has almost limitless possibilities, even if the runover word conforms to the usual pattern and is first word of its verse. All that is necessary is that the formula contain a dactylic or trochaic word (a true monosyllable not elided is very rare as a runover). Almost all members of the – ⌣ ⌣ – ⌣ class fulfil this condition, and many accordingly are split. The ⌣ ⌣ – ⌣ class ought to be well enough represented also. (Why not a κλέος οὐρανὸν ἵκει | ἐσθλόν . . .?) Its handicap is that the – ⌣ element is normally the noun, whereas the runover word is regularly an epithet.[1] Examples thus are rare.

[1] La Roche (op. cit., p. 105, n. 1) calculated that in noun–epithet combinations

Split formulae (all of the – ᴗ ᴗ – ᷒ class) passing their second term into the next verse are as follows. I omit to specify some minor and obvious modifications.

ἄλγεα... | πολλὰ μάλ' *T* 264–5, λ 279–80;
ἀνέρες... | ἄλλοι α 176–7;
δάκρυα... | θερμά *P* 437–8;
δώματ'... | καλά *Z* 313–4;
εἵματ'... | καλά η 234–5;
ἔντεα... | καλά *K* 471–2 etc. 3×;
κτήματα... | πάντ' *H* 363–4, *H* 389–91 (κτήματα in 1st foot);
  κτήμαθ'... | πάντα μάλ' *X* 114–15; and πάντα... | κτήματα
  γ 315–16 = ο 12–13;
τεύχεα... | ... | καλά *Σ* 82–4.

The following formulae pass their first term into the next verse, inverting the word-order. The original second term is then normally drawn back into the body of the first verse.

αἶγες... | ἄγριαι ι 118–19;
ἄνδρ'... | ἄγριον ι 214–15, and ἄνδρες... | ἄγριοι α 198–9;
γυναῖκας... | ἕπτ' *T* 245–6;
δῶρα... | καλά ο 75–6, cf. κάλλιμα δ.
ἔγχος... | χάλκεον *O* 126–7, *X* 285–6;
ἑταῖρος... | ἐσθλός θ 584–5;
ἵπποι... | θηλεῖαι *Y* 221–2;
πολλὰ... | κτήματα *Σ* 291–2;
πάσας | ... νῆας *Ξ* 33–4, cf. ν. ἁπάσας;
νὺξ... | ἀμβροσίη *Σ* 267–8;
ὅρμον... | χρύσεον σ 295–6;
ὕπνου... | ἡδέος ψ 16–17;
πολλὰ... | χρήματ' ξ 285–6.

The intervening words are of all parts of speech, following no obvious patterns, and the position of the first term of the formula is also extremely variable. In some instances it may even stand at the very beginning of its verse. The prevalence of certain words will be noted: the mildly cohesive πολύς 3× and the established runover word καλός 6×.

The use of the runover word is compatible with the presence of a normal juxtaposed noun–epithet group in the first verse. This produces a sort of expansion:

the noun was deferred less than 100 times, the epithet more than 430 times. (At σ 308–9 ξύλα... | αὖα is a true plural, not a modification of ξύλον αὖον.)

ἰξάλου αἰγὸς | ἀγρίου Δ 105–6;
ἄλκιμα δοῦρε δύω . . . | ὀξέα Λ 43–4;
χαλκοβατὲς δῶ | ὑψερεφές ν 4–5;
ἐϋκνήμιδας ἑταίρους | πάντας ψ 319–20; and ἐσθλοὶ ἑταῖροι | πάντες
    Ψ 331–2;
πιστὸν ἑταῖρον | ἐσθλόν P 589–90;
ἀθανάτοισι θεοῖσι . . . | πᾶσι μάλ’ λ 133–4;
ἄρσενες ἵπποι | Τρώϊοι Ψ 377–8;
μέλανος οἴνοιο | ἡδέος ι 196–7;
θεσπιδαὲς πῦρ | . . . ἀκάματον O 597–8;
χάλκεα τεύχεα | καλά X 322–3,[1] and κλυτὰ τεύχεα . . . | καλά T 10–11.

A curious and isolated instance in which the runover repeats the
juxtaposed epithet in the next verse but one occurs at δ 724–6 =
814–16, πόσιν ἐσθλὸν . . . | . . . | ἐσθλόν. Since the runover technique
is an artifice of continuation, not of anticipation, it is very unusual to
find the noun–epithet group in the second verse. One example only,
πᾶσαι | νῆες ἐΰσσελμοι ι 554–5.

Another kind of expansion is that applied to the runover word itself.
The pattern is common, and from time to time vocabulary is drawn
from the regular juxtaposed formulae to put in it.

δέρμα . . . | . . . μέγα καὶ δασύ ξ 50–1, cf. μέγα δ.;
δούρατ’ . . . | ὀξέα παμφανόωντα E 618–19, cf. ὀ. δοῦρα;
ἵππους . . . | πάσας θηλείας Λ 680–1, cf. θηλέας ἵ.;
and κῦμα . . . | πορφύρεον μέγα ν 84–5, cf. μέγα κ.

The runover technique marks one of the limits of formular composition. Within the verse, it seems to me, it is normally fair to say
that the formula is the basic element in composition. It is the formula
which is present to the poet's mind and which he will use even if he
must avail himself of various artifices. But the runover is a very strong
pattern, although it is an optional pattern in that the sense could be
stopped instead of continued. (Many plus-verses in the manuscript
tradition fall into this pattern.) Consequently it seems that the structure is here the basic element and that for the content the poet draws
on words associated with the pattern (like καλός) or on his general
resources of vocabulary, rather than on formulae. Thus στιβαρός is
a regular epithet of χείρ, and χερσὶ στιβαρῇσι 7 × is a very well-estab-

---

[1] 'The formulaic τεύχεα καλά is broken up to allow of the addition of the mention
of Achilles' armour in X 323 (= P 187) and the obvious χάλκεα added to complete
the verse: G. P. Shipp, *Studies in the Language of Homer*, Cambridge 1953, 130.

lished formula, yet at δ 287–8 the old poetical epithet is replaced by a commonplace vernacular word χερσὶ πίεζε | νωλεμέως κρατερῇσι.

If these formulae are counted in with the formulae split within the verse the $- \cup \cup - \underset{\smile}{\smile}$ class has considerably augmented numbers of split formulae (78 maximum and 62 minimum, giving a range of 20–25 per cent. of the total), but the $\cup \cup - \underset{\smile}{\smile}$ class is hardly affected.

VIII

THE FLEXIBLE FORMULA

To what part of the diction should we turn to see Homeric craftsmanship in its most typical form? Since Homer's is a broad genius the question has no obvious answer. However, if it is need with time that hammers out the poetical craftsman's tools then it will be the routine scenes that show the poet's skill least obscured by his art. In the *Iliad* at least the staple is battle. In its barest form an adequate fight can be put together out of a few whole-line and half-line formulae eked out by some associated ideas. Take for example the series of scenes at the beginning of *E*:

45   ἔγχεϊ μακρῷ

νύξ' ἵππων ἐπιβησόμενον κατὰ δεξιὸν ὦμον·

ἤριπε δ' ἐξ ὀχέων, στυγερὸς δ' ἄρα μιν σκότος εἶλε.

56 πρόσθεν ἔθεν φεύγοντα μετάφρενον οὖτασε δουρὶ

ὤμων μεσσηγύς, διὰ δὲ στήθεσφιν ἔλασσεν,

ἤριπε δὲ πρηνής, ἀράβησε δὲ τεύχε' ἐπ' αὐτῷ.

65   ὅτε δὴ κατέμαρπτε διώκων,

βεβλήκει γλουτὸν κατὰ δεξιόν· ἡ δὲ διαπρὸ

ἀντικρὺ κατὰ κύστιν ὑπ' ὀστέον ἤλυθ' ἀκωκή·

γνὺξ δ' ἔριπ' οἰμώξας, θάνατος δέ μιν ἀμφικάλυψε.

I underline the formulae, i.e. the phrases that are verbally repeated elsewhere. But the identification of the formulae does not exhaust the poet's resources. There are also the mutual similarities of the formulae, their generative capacity, or whatever we care to call it. The model customarily used to relate these interconnections to the formular art is that of the phrase-pattern. Accordingly we should mention together the two first-half participial formulae (νύξ') ἵππων ἐπιβησόμενον and πρόσθεν ἔθεν φεύγοντα, and quote such patterns of substitution as

$$\ddot{\eta}\rho\iota\pi\epsilon\ \delta'\begin{cases}\grave{\epsilon}\xi\ \grave{o}\chi\acute{\epsilon}\omega\nu\\ \grave{\epsilon}\nu\ \kappa o\nu\acute{\iota}\eta\sigma\iota\end{cases}\qquad\ddot{\eta}\rho\iota\pi\epsilon\ \delta\grave{\epsilon}/\delta'\begin{cases}\pi\rho\eta\nu\acute{\eta}s\\ \grave{\epsilon}\xi o\pi\acute{\iota}\sigma\omega\end{cases}$$

$$\delta\iota\grave{a}\begin{cases}\sigma\tau\acute{\eta}\theta\epsilon\sigma\phi\iota\nu\\ \zeta\omega\sigma\tau\hat{\eta}\rho os\end{cases}\ddot{\epsilon}\lambda a\sigma\sigma\epsilon\quad\grave{a}\nu\tau\iota\kappa\rho\grave{\upsilon}\begin{cases}\kappa a\tau\grave{a}\ \kappa\acute{\upsilon}\sigma\tau\iota\nu\ \acute{\upsilon}\pi'\ \grave{o}\sigma\tau\acute{\epsilon}o\nu\\ \delta'\ \grave{a}\pi a\lambda o\hat{\iota}o\ \delta\iota'\ a\mathring{\upsilon}\chi\acute{\epsilon}\nu os.\end{cases}$$

There can be no quarrel with drawing attention to such realities, but we should not be too easily satisfied. For these patternings are too much like the substitution-patterns of ordinary speech, and without much refinement cannot tell us much about the *poetical* art, still less the *oral poetical* art. Let us, however, not overlook the point that the battle scenes incorporate many formulae that are not related by pattern but by idea, e.g.

56 cf. οὔτασε δουρί (2nd–3rd feet) . . . ὀξυόεντι Ξ 443; οὔτησε . . . ἔγχεϊ μακρῷ Φ 402.

58 cf. ἀμφὶ δέ οἱ βράχε τεύχεα ποικίλα χαλκῷ Μ 396.

66 cf. καί ῥ' ἔβαλε γλουτόν . . . Ν 651.

66–7 cf. ἀντικρὺς δὲ διῆλθε φαεινοῦ δουρὸς ἀκωκή τ 453; ἀντικρὺ . . . ἔγχος | ἦλθε Δ 481–2; αἰχμὴ δὲ διαμπερὲς ἦλθ' ἀλεγεινή Ε 658.

68a cf. κάππεσεν οἰμώξας Π 290.

68b cf. θανάτου δὲ μέλαν νέφος ἀμφικάλυψε Π 350; τέλος θανάτοιο κάλυψε Ε 553.

We see here some familiar points. Formulae are shifted in position, expanded, split, adapted to take connectives, modified, and transformed by the use of synonyms. Nor can I see that there is any less adaptation than there is phrase patterning.

Now let us turn to a passage of an entirely different quality, the Lament of Helen over the body of Hector, Ω 762–75:

"Εκτορ, ἐμῷ θυμῷ δαέρων πολὺ φίλτατε πάντων,

ἦ μέν μοι πόσις ἐστὶν Ἀλέξανδρος θεοειδής,

ὅς μ' ἄγαγε Τροίηνδ'· ὡς πρὶν ὤφελλον ὀλέσθαι.

ἤδη γὰρ νῦν μοι τόδ' ἐεικοστὸν ἔτος ἐστὶν   765

ἐξ οὗ κεῖθεν ἔβην καὶ ἐμῆς ἀπελήλυθα πάτρης·

ἀλλ' οὔ πω σεῦ ἄκουσα κακὸν ἔπος οὐδ' ἀσύφηλον·

ἀλλ' εἴ τίς με καὶ ἄλλος ἐνὶ μεγάροισιν ἐνίπτοι

δαέρων ἢ γαλόων ἢ εἰνατέρων εὐπέπλων,

ἢ ἑκυρή—ἑκυρὸς δὲ πατὴρ ὡς ἤπιος αἰεί—,   770

ἀλλὰ σὺ τὸν ἐπέεσσι παραιφάμενος κατέρυκες,

σῆ τ' ἀγανοφροσύνῃ καὶ σοῖς ἀγανοῖς ἐπέεσσι.

τῶ σέ θ' ἅμα κλαίω καὶ ἔμ' ἄμμορον ἀχνυμένη κῆρ·

οὐ γάρ τίς μοι ἔτ' ἄλλος ἐνὶ Τροίῃ εὐρείῃ

ἤπιος οὐδὲ φίλος, πάντες δέ με πεφρίκασιν.   775

The formulaic density, at least as it can be demonstrated by exact repetition, is sharply reduced in comparison with the battle scenes. As for the phraseology apparently not available from stock a great deal echoes familiar word-associations, e.g.

762. ἐμῷ θυμῷ is formulaic cf. X 53, but usually (11 ×) the disyllabic personal adjectives (ἐμῷ, ἐῷ) are separated from θυμῷ.

762b. cf. 748 πάντων πολὺ φίλτατε παιδῶν, the parallel verse in Hecuba's Lament. The structure is reproduced by ω 517 πάντων πολύ φίλταθ' ἑταίρων. But it would be hasty to set up a substitution-pattern on the strength of it. ω 517 itself looks derivative: πολὺ φίλτατος is well entrenched (11 ×), φίλταθ' ἑταίρων is formulaic (3 ×), πάντων πολὺ φίλτατος is attested at E 378. ω 517 is thus a conflation. As for Ω 748, though the superlative φίλτατος is prevented by metre from being a regular adjunct of παῖς, the positive φίλος is frequent (παῖδα φίλον 5 × in various cases, φίλον π. 3 ×, π. φίλοι 1 ×, παῖδα ... φίλην 1 ×, φίλῳ περὶ παιδί 1 ×). Thus the construction of Ω 748 would not present undue difficulties in content, and Ω 762 follows naturally from it.

764. The line is adapted from H 390 ἠγάγετο Τροίηνδ' —ὡς πρὶν ὤφελλ' ἀπολέσθαι. For the thought cf. § 68. 764a may be related to ἠγάγετο πρὸς δῶματ' 2 × by substitution.

765b–766. The lines are evidently formulaic in toto, cf. τ 222–3, with a variant (πεμπτόν for ἐεικοστόν) ω 309–10.

767–8. cf. ἔπεσσίν τε κακοῖσιν ἐνίσσομεν ω 161.

768a and 774a. The first half-verses utilize forms of the fluid connective formula with ἄλλος cf. οὐ μὲν γάρ τίς σ' ἄλλος Υ 339.

769. Expanded from the usual collocation of γαλόοι and εἰνατέρες; cf. ἠὲ ... γαλόων ἢ εἰνατέρων εὐπέπλων Ζ 378.

770. The position and order of πατὴρ ὥς suggest the analogy of θεὸς ὥς or λέων ὥς.

771. cf. παρφάμενος ἐπέεσσι 1st–3rd feet at M 249.

Although these interrelationships do not escape the close

reader they have never been exploited properly. The reason is
that at this level the tradition of scholarship descending from
L'Épithète traditionnelle has been preoccupied with structure and
pattern at the expense of content. I have stressed already the
limited area over which the formula-types and sentence-patterns
provide a satisfactory model of the poet's technique. It is only by
an analogy, whose weaknesses we inspected, that this model is
extended further. Yet it is obvious that a poet of Homer's verbal
power is not confined to one basic artifice of composition to whose
requirements the whole diction must conform. Consequently
when less than perfectly schematized usages are called 'untraditional' it is important that this stigma should not be made to
bear an implication for the poet's craft. He is not close to breakdown, or incompetent, or manipulating a degenerate diction,
or aspiring to new heights of literate fancy, when his phraseology
is unschematic. My own instinct is to invert the direction of the
analogical reasoning and to regard as typical of the poet's technical equipment the sort of diction that is built around the most
frequent common nouns. This consists of a few regular formulae
(not always used in their regular place), a few derivatives of
these, and a few uniquely occurring phrases (which will surely
include some *ad hoc* creations). Highly schematized formula-types
are then the consequence of ossification of more flexible systems
at points of frequent use.

This direction of argument has certain merits. One is that we
have a more plausible historical perspective. Naturally enough
no one supposes that the formulaic diction came into being with
a sudden perfection: it developed. But I do not know that this is
ever spelt out in terms of the basic character of the diction.
Yet clearly the dictions for various topics have various upper
chronological limits and broadly speaking will therefore be at
different stages of evolution. There is no independent means of
telling which themes or stories are older than which others, but
we do know that the epic, though laggard and archaistic, keeps
pace with changes in the technology and practice of its principal
subject, warfare. It is enough to mention the invaluable paper of
Miss Gray on the epithets of the Homeric helmet and shield.[1] The
diction for the two artefacts is far from settled, less regular for the

[1] *CQ* lxi (1947) 109–21, now reprinted in *Language and Background of Homer*, ed.
G. S. Kirk, Cambridge 1964.

helmet than for the shield, and least settled where the sense of the description refers to an object for a more recent archaeological period. In contrast the diction for the unchanging sea is very settled indeed.

The consolidation of a system of formulae is the result of time and repetition, by which the most useful elements are sifted out. But utility for verse-making is not the same as necessity. There was never any objective reason for saying that the poet had to be possessed of formulaic systems in order to be able to compose. The poet can talk about helmets as easily as he can talk about waves, and just as frequently, though we may permit ourselves to think that he would reach a point of mental exhaustion rather sooner in handling a relatively unschematized part of his diction than in putting together a routine passage. I see no reason why the progressive consolidation of a set of formulae should ever be complete or why grave conclusions should be drawn from 'non-traditional' usages in Homer, as if his predecessors had not worked in a similar way.

There are indeed some treatments of formulae which must be Homeric, or at any rate very close in time to the great epics, because they take advantage of linguistic developments which are not characteristic of the more schematized parts of the diction. Hoekstra has accomplished valuable work in this field, and although his broad conclusion is that 'from a date not much anterior to Homer up to the creation of our poems epic diction as a whole took on a much suppler form and a different colour-ing',[1] yet he recognizes that the process is essentially continuous. Each linguistic development gives the poets scope for new and for the moment unschematized usages, and indeed encourages innovation by making parts of the settled diction obsolete.[2] Thus the Hesiodic corpus and the Homeric Hymns show the epic diction at a more evolved stage than the Homeric epics.[3] Earlier stages would show the impact of, perhaps, the decline of the dual number, the rise of the -σαν third plural, the

---

[1] *MFP* 137, cf. 147 and 26–9.

[2] Cf. Parry, *HSCP* xliii (1932) 20 ff.

[3] Cf. Hoekstra, *MFP* 28. I see no need to view this as degeneracy. A breakdown in the Greek improvising technique is not proved by the contrast with Homer in respect of particular usages, but by the decline of the technique's charac-teristic effects on the diction, i.e. by the absence of extension and economy at points where they are to be expected. To show this, of course, a certain bulk of the poet's work is required. For the 'anti-traditional' usage see p. 116.

-οο genitive singular, certain contractions,[1] and, I dare say, the fashion for Wernicke's prosodical law.[2] Most unschematized uses, however, bear no such chronological tags. Separation and change of position might be used at any stage, and doubtless were. A certain degree of flexibility is as traditional as a certain degree of rigidity.

Repetition is the result not only of time but also of need. A frequent formula tends to be more stabilized than a less frequent one regardless of its period of origin. This fact is especially visible in the case of mobile formulae. An even distribution of occurrences among the possible positions usually means low frequencies in each. Really common formulae tend to show a high concentration at one point and no great increase (or none at all) elsewhere, e.g. δολιχόσκιον ἔγχος medially 1 ×, finally 24 × ; ἀθανάτοισι θεοῖσι initially 1 ×, finally 16 ×. Many instances of similar distribution will be found in Tables VII and XV. The regular placing generally results from the development of complex formulae. If the complex formulae are themselves interrelated a schematization of great elaboration may emerge. The introductory lines to speeches are the prime example of this sort of high stabilization, both in their content and in their structure. At this point the formulae (the celebrated personal names in the nominative singular) are grouped into highly economical sets, but their economy is not fully echoed by the sentence-patterns. To select part of a rather complex situation, there are three important and related patterns in which the sense 'X said in reply' may be expressed:

(i) τὸν δ' αὖτε προσέειπε ∪ − ∪ ∪ − ∪ ∪ − ⏒
(ii) τὸν δ' ἀπαμειβόμενος προσέφη ∪ ∪ − ∪ ∪ − ⏒
(iii) τὸν δ' ἀπαμειβόμενος προσεφώνεε − ∪ ∪ − ⏒.

The three sentence frames are necessary to take care of gaps in the

[1] See Hoekstra, MFP 131 ff., and T. B. L. Webster, 'Early and Late in Homeric Diction', Eranos liv (1956) 34–48.

[2] The positional lengthening βοῶπις πότνια ˝Ηρη is unique; the formula is most antique: but the original quantity of −ις is doubtful, cf. Schwyzer, GG. 463. Surallongement is more extensive: Parry, ET 52 and 237, noted in the ∪ − ⏗ − ∪ ∪ − ⏒ class Ἀχαιῶν χαλκοχιτώνων, ποδάρκης δῖος Ἀχιλλεύς and περίφρων Πηνελόπεια, to which add πολύτλας δῖος 'Οδυσσεύς, ἐχέφρων Πηνελόπεια, ἱερὴ ἴς Τηλεμάχοιο, and δαΐφρων Τυδέος υἱός. Some of these are unavoidable if the name must be used, but that the formulae for the two main heroes, who are as old as the epic stories themselves, unnecessarily violate the rule (ἐσθλός may replace δῖος) suggests that it was not observed so strictly at an earlier period.

personal name systems.[1] We should expect one to be dominant, the others to be called in if the first choice is impossible. This is the way in which the system, roughly, works. In frame (i) there are 30 expressions, in (ii) 11, and in (iii) only 4. But of the 11 expressions in frame (ii) only one personage (actually εἴδωλον ἀμαυρόν) has no formula which could enter frame (i), the other 10 both have the formula and in fact enter frame (i).[2] It may be that the economical use of the diction is upset by the analogy of other participial supplements in the προσέφη frame, but the fact is that it is upset. The economy of the system is still further diluted by the existence of a competitor for frame (i), viz. τὸν δ' ἠμείβετ' ἔπειτα . . . and by various idiosyncratic lines, e.g. τὸν δ' ἄρ' ὑποβλήδην ἠμείβετο δῖος Ἀχιλλεύς A 292, or τὸν δ' αὖ διογενὴς Ὀδυσεὺς ἠμείβετο μύθῳ o 485.[3] If this is what we find in an area of high schematization we have no reason to demand as good oral craftsmanship an equal degree of schematization elsewhere and no reason to condemn harshly abnormal phrases and usages.

Up till this point I have avoided the distinction which has recently been drawn between the 'occasional untraditional' usage and the 'anti-traditional' usage.[4] The latter means mistreatment of the traditional language in a way that would be inconceivable on the lips of an oral poet of normal competence. The anti-traditional is thus diagnostic of the inroads which it is reasonable to suppose were made upon the traditional form of the poems during the period when their performance, and perhaps their transmission, were in the hands of the rhapsodes. I should be content to have it so, for no one wishes to burden the great poet with unnecessary blemishes. But a wish is no argument, and since the distinction between untraditional and anti-traditional is blurred in many a particular instance the more we regard the circumstances that call for adaptable diction as of normal occur-

---

[1] A few other verbs can cope with the inadequacies of their subject formulae, e.g. ἀπέβη—ἀπεβήσατο, ἦρχε—ἡγήσατο, but by no means all: hence κρήδεμνόν θ', ὅ ῥά οἱ δῶκε χρυσέη Ἀφροδίτη X 470; χρ. Ἀφ. is modelled on the oblique cases and its internal hiatus is abnormal in a formula. Generally it is the names that help out the verbs.

[2] Od. is more tidy than Il., with only four formulae in the προσέφη-frame—which are used very intensively.

[3] There are other signs of reconstruction in these systems demanded by the increasing popularity of choriambic names (Ἀντίνοος, Εὐρύμαχος, etc.), see MFP 137.

[4] Page, HHI 267 ff., Kirk, SoH 204 ff.

rence the smaller the amount of anti-traditional diction we must be willing to recognize.[1] In this way we shall be confronted again with the old Unitarian dilemma, that if the poems are what they seem to be, artistic unities, then Homer seems by our standards to be at once a very good poet and a very bad one. If the issue is faced, one must abandon either the unity (even if only to a slight degree) or one's standards. I suspect the latter rather than the former, if the canons of the Lower Criticism of Homer are reappraised in the same way as the judgements of the analytical Higher Criticism. At present we know little enough of the craftsmanship of Greek oral art, its standards and tolerances, so that it is easy to transfer our own prejudices and, for want of any alternative, to fault the transmission. But the character of the early transmission is *obscurius* to the poems' *obscurum*, and it is only as we clarify the latter that we see what may permissibly be blamed on the former.

Irregular phraseology comes into being because some kind of generative mechanisms are necessary in a formulaic diction designed for the dactylic hexameter and the Greek language. Within the verse the number of shapes word-groups may take we saw to be much higher than the four or five usually discussed. But to provide ten or a dozen formulae in several grammatical cases for every common idea would be a heavy burden even on the illiterate memory, and it is obvious that the Homeric technique makes no attempt to do so. All formula-systems have gaps. The hazard that this involves may be for long concealed by the fact that the poet's needs are concentrated on a few frequent formulae. Moreover the gaps in one system may be complemented by the filled shapes in others. Sooner or later, however, the poet must want a phrase with which his memory does not provide him. At δ 172–3 the poet has said νόστον ἔδωκε | νηυσὶ θοῇσι γενέσθαι and requires to express the subject, which happens to be Zeus.

---

[1] Thus it appears to me that Page is somewhat too free with the attribution, if indeed he uses the term in Kirk's strongly pejorative sense: e.g. μελιηδέος οἴνου, *HHI* 269, is exactly what would arise when (i) -ου became available, (ii) ϝ- fell (in μέλανος ϝοίνοιο), and (iii) μελιηδέα (-έϊ) οἶνον (-ῳ) existed. Neither of the first two conditions is post-Homeric. Kirk, *SoH* 206, condemns the *conflation* πολλὴν ἐπ' ἀπείρονα γαῖαν ο 79, cf. πολλοὶ ἀπειρέσιοι τ 174: and κούρητες Ἀχαιῶν Τ 248, which as a 'Leumannism' (cf. the tribal name Κουρῆτες Ι 529 etc.) is not clearly worse than many another transfer. It encroaches on a digammated formula, ϝελίκωπες Ἀχαιοί, and so is part of the same trend as μελιηδέος οἴνου. Kirk's other examples do not concern the creation of formulae.

The system provides no regular formula for the god of the shape needed beginning with a vowel. Hence a conflation Ὀλύμπιος εὐρύοπα Ζεύς. Many unforeseen requirements arise in this way purely by chance. The displacements of many mobile and separated formulae are of this sort. Other needs arise out of the poet's own habit-forming propensities. I have stressed that the common-noun formulae especially are prone to form complex formulae with their associated words, usually verbs. Such complex formulae are manifestly helpful—until the verb must be conjugated. Often this is well within normal formulaic resources, e.g. ἔχε μώνυχας ἵππους 8 × but ἔχον ὠκέας ἵππους 4 ×, or λυώμεθα μώνυχας ἵππους Ψ 7 but λύον δ᾽ ὑψηχέας ἵππους Ψ 27. But the persistence of a formulaic association in conjugation may force a formula out of its normal position, e.g. φέροι δ᾽ ἔναρα βροτόεντα Ζ 480 but ἔναρα βροτόεντα φέρωμαι Θ 534; or induce some sort of adaptation, e.g. ἐλαύνετε μώνυχας ἵππους Λ 289, ἐλαύνομεν ὠκέας ἵππους Μ 62 etc. 4 × but ποδώκεας ἤλασεν ἵππους Ρ 614. We saw too that without any inflexional changes the crowding in of a word's associations may require the modification of a regular shape if all are to be realized.

It is high time to estimate the demand made upon this productive capacity. The proportion of adapted formulae can be estimated in the same way as that of modified formulae or expanded formulae. We thus obtain a maximum, which counts all expressions in any way involved in adaptation, and a minimum, from which are excluded those whose 'adaptations' may always be autonomous formulae themselves or are best derivable from such word-groups. The totals of the preceding chapters cannot be simply added together, for many formulae are adapted in several ways and there is also some duplication in that a modification, for example, may turn out to be part of an expanded expression and be noted under both heads. The consolidated totals, including separation over the verse-end, give a maximum of 123 (39 per cent.) out of 319 formulae shaped – ∪ ∪ – ⊻ and 88 (63 per cent.) out of 140 shaped ∪ ∪ – ⊻ the minimum figures are 99 (31 per cent.) and 63 (45 per cent.) respectively.[1] The estimate is based as before on the assumption that the expressions

---

[1] The extent of adaptation decreases as the formulae increase in length. The ∪ ∪ – ∪ ∪ – ⊻ class has a range of 27 to 32 per cent. of formulae adapted, the (∪) ∪ – ∪ ∪ – ∪ ∪ – ⊻ 17 to 20 per cent.

of the two shapes are primary. This is plainly true generally, but equally obviously there are a few exceptions and a rather greater number of expressions of ambiguous status. An obvious and easy adjustment to our estimate is therefore to eject the whole category of doubtful formulae (those of single occurrence in our shapes) and make the calculation from the regular formulae only. The range is then 81–96 adapted formulae (29–34 per cent.) out of 281 in the $- \cup \cup - \underline{\cup}$ class, and 49–66 (43–58 per cent.) out of 114 in the $\cup \cup - \underline{\cup}$ class. Any further attempt to refine the material in my view would mean adopting assumptions of a problematical nature, or passing subjective judgements on individual formulae. The result would be a doubtful as well as a marginal improvement.

Proportions of a third or a half are not at all negligible, and it is apparent that many more formulae are mutable than is commonly stated, perhaps than is commonly suspected. The gross figure that I have given is useful as a signpost to further questions. How often is this flexibility in demand? What sort of formulae are most flexible? I touch on the second question first. Adaptation is by no means evenly applied throughout a class of formulae. A very great many adapted formulae are adapted in more than one way. Thus we have ἄλγεα πολλά adapted in five different ways, ὑψερεφὲς δῶ in five ways, πάντες (-ας) ἑταῖροι (-ους) in six ways, and so on, in contrast with such monolithic formulae as πότνια μήτηρ 32 ×, θούριδος ἀλκῆς 21 ×, αἰπὺς (-ὺν) ὄλεθρος (-ον) 24 ×, etc. Since the three latter examples have decorative epithets while two of the former have functional qualifiers one naturally asks if the distinction 'decorative *versus* functional' does not correspond to 'fixed *versus* flexible'. In some measure it does, but the contrast is wrongly labelled. A check on those adjectives that combine most function with least decoration shows that 10 πολύς-formulae out of 17 of our two shapes are adapted, 14 πᾶς-formulae out of 26, and 22 formulae with the personal adjectives out of 36. But among the decorative epithets are some that are equally prominent in adaptations, e.g. μέγας with 13 adapted formulae out of 18, or καλός with 7 out of 17. We must therefore ask rather what it is that πολύς-, πᾶς-, ὅς-, μέγας-, and καλός-formulae have in common against such types as the μακρός-formulae (2 adapted out of 9) or the πίων-formulae (2 adapted out of 7). The opportunity for adaptation is certainly higher in the former class, since most of the epithets offer some convenient alternating forms. The same contrast is visible between the ἀνήρ-formulae (12 adapted out of 22) where an alternating stem is available and the ἦμαρ-formulae (1 out of 17) where all modification must be applied to the epithet. But opportunity is not more than a sufficient condition of adaptation. What we seek is an explanation in terms of technique why the poet finds it necessary to adapt certain kinds of formula, or unnecessary to adapt certain others. For artefacts it is the most recent phraseology that is least stable. The emergence of set formulae is a function of time and the instability reflects the creation and re-creation of the phraseology. The history of expressions made with the common functional adjectives and with weak and widely used generic words cannot be so comparatively simple. Such expressions are at once very old and very new, since even with well-formed word-associations the level of re-creation is bound to be high, in the one case because the context demands the functional words, in the other because the point of the generic apparatus is to provide the means for the creation (and, of course, re-creation) of suitable phrases. Consequently this part of the diction is slower to consolidate further associations with other terms by which it may be kept in shape and position.[1]

Where there is no argument from the character of the epithet it is doubtful if a formulaic association in the fluid state can be identified by any faculty but intuition. We may not, of course, at this point argue from flexibility, since it is a correlation between flexibility and re-creation that we are seeking to draw. Low frequency is far too treacherous a criterion, nor does it appear that there is any connexion between low frequencies in general and adaptability. There are, however, a certain number of cases where mutation seems to follow less portentous operations on the basic formula. The datives κηρὶ μελαίνῃ and χειρὶ βαρείῃ, declined from the accusative, are unique in that grammatical case: both are inverted. The dative δαιτὶ θαλείῃ 1 × (acc. sing. 2 ×) is also found separated. The accusative ἠέρα πολλήν 1 × (dat. sing. 5 ×) provides several adaptations. I infer that the unfamiliar case-

---

[1] Note that the very stable ἤματα πάντα 30 ×, presumably an old formula (ἦμαρ is an 'Achaean' word), owes much of its immutability to use in complex formulae: ἀγήραος (-ον) ἤ. π. 5 × ; ἐέλδομαι ἤ. π. 5 × (and ἔλπομαι 1 ×) ; μεμνημένος ἤ. π. 3 × (and μιμνήσκομαι 1 ×).

form disturbs the flow of the poet's words and upsets the pattern of the formula's further associations. I should explain in a similar way the use of the untraditional θέσπιν ἀοιδόν at ρ 385. It falls in the 2nd–3rd feet, and the shift from the normal position at the verse-end has caused the poet to hesitate between θεῖον ἀοιδόν and θέσπιν ἀοιδήν.[1]

What is the proportion over the two formular classes as a whole of regular to adapted diction? We can estimate this crudely by contrasting the number of adapted occurrences with the number of regular occurrences and calculating maxima and minima as was done for the formulae themselves. This will give us in the – ∪ ∪ – ⌣ class more than 370 adapted occurrences (16 per cent. of all occurrences of the formulae) as a maximum and less than 160 (8 per cent.) as a minimum against more than 1,930 normal occurrences: and in the ∪ ∪ – ⌣ class a maximum of 320 adapted occurrences (30 per cent.) but only 80 plus (10 per cent.) as a minimum against around 780 normal occurrences. In comparison with any subsequent poetry the Homeric poems are very formulaic, and the use of the noun–epithet phraseology very formulaic indeed. Yet the phrases are not all regular formulae, if this implies drawn from stock ready made and needing no change. Nor have we taken into account (it would be almost impossible to do so) the very considerable number of unique expressions of all shapes and sizes. Some of them were doubtless used rather than a common formula which the problems of a particular verse had made impossible. Moreover a calculation such as this must be viewed in the light of all the factors that make up the technical side of the poet's art. One that deserves attention at this point is what I shall call the self-inducing property of well-established formulae. In the – ∪ ∪ – ⌣ class there are 28 formulae appearing 15 times or more, and 7 more than 30 times. With these very high frequencies it seems implausible to say that in every case the sense-context has determined the choice of noun and the metrical context the choice of formula. Rather the dominant formula has steered the poet into a particular train of thought. Once a certain threshold is passed we must reckon with some formulae becoming active factors in the composition of their immediate contexts and not passive tools in

[1] The predicative use πάντες ἄριστοι ἐόντες Ν 117 in the 1st–2nd feet might be a further example, but ἄριστος is rather common as a predicate.

the hands of the poet. It would be arbitrary to specify the threshold, but clearly if we were to put on one side those parts of the diction where the poet is as it were freewheeling and concentrate on those parts where he is actively working at the composition then the proportion of data to creation and adaptation will be much diminished. How much diminished can only be guessed at. The stock will certainly be providing less than two-thirds of requirements, but usually, I should think, not less than one half. An estimate of greater precision would conceal assumptions about the extent of re-creation in the formulae themselves and in repeated 'adapted' uses as well as about the self-induction of frequent formulae. Such assumptions could only be made plausible, if at all, by an evaluation in favourable circumstances of each particular formula.

The point of these calculations was to impugn the idea that the regularities of the Homeric diction, though vastly greater than those of any subsequent Greek poetry, are so regular that any departure from the norm is an insignificant exception. This does not mean that the part of the diction which is not composed of regular formulae is sheer extemporization. Our examination of the Homeric diction was bound to begin in terms of concepts already familiar. Hence the juxtaposed words of the familiar formula were taken as a datum. This has its justification in the fact that such formulae do play a cardinal role in the poet's craft. But the role has limits. Now the more flexible the formula appears the more striking is the persistence of the word-association that survives such vicissitudes. Recognizing this we ask if word-association is not exemplified in other directions. The declension of a formula is an obvious point, but worth a moment's thought. Even if the over-all shape of the formula is unchanged, as is very often the case, a new case-form means a different sentence-pattern and some rearrangement of complex formulae. It is thus not so easy as may be thought.[1] The only metrical advantage to the poet is that the new case-form retains whatever inherent usefulness the first may have possessed. Formulae of course change case in much more dramatic circumstances. Declension is permitted to overrule bad metre, e.g. μέροπες ἄνθρωποι (normally genitive plural); to pervert morphology, e.g. εὐρέα πόντον (after the dative); very commonly to separate a formula,

[1] Cf. Parry at *HSCP* xli (1930) 83-4.

e.g. βοῶν ∪ ∪ εὐρυμετώπων (juxtaposed in accusative plural); to receive a connective, e.g. κλειτοί τ' ἐπίκουροι (normally accusative or genitive plural); and very commonly indeed to change the over-all shape of a formula, e.g. χρύσεον δέπας—χρυσέῳ δέπαϊ —χρυσέοις δεπάεσσι.

Except for the faults in metrics and morphology declension of the same word-group has not attracted much attention. On the other hand certain amplified declensions which change their constituents while preserving the same shape, e.g.

πατρὶς ἄρουρα	περικλυτὸς Ἀμφιγυήεις	μοῖρ' ὀλοή
πατρίδα γαῖαν	περικλυτοῦ Ἡφαίστοιο	κῆρ' ὀλοήν
πατρίδος αἴης		
πατρίδι γαίῃ		

have long figured in the handbooks, without any clear conclusions being drawn from them. It is possible that there are no profound conclusions to draw. From the standpoint of the composing poet, which it is necessary always to assume so far as it can be imagined, πατρὶς ἄρουρα is distant from πατρίδα γαῖαν by several steps and analogies. They share no complex formulae together, much less with the mainly prepositional (ἀπὸ) πατρίδος αἴης. But the associated context must be *the* factor in the suggestion of diction, which is to say that it is the series of formulae of the same grammatical case that are associated with each other. The homoeomorphic declension has no utility in itself, and arises only because certain shapes have an inherent convenience.[1] On the other hand the value of a declined formula where the different case-forms result in different shapes or in the separation of the terms cannot be metrical. The economy of the diction as a whole is served, but I prefer to see declension as a generative mechanism whereby a basic stock of formulae can be generously amplified as the occasion demands.

The persistence of a word-association in declension is itself only a case of the persistence of the same association of ideas throughout a formula-series. This would be part of the study of

---

[1] This is not to say that the cases of an amplified declension have no impact on each other. The declensions obey the law of economy, generalizing the same epithet where possible. The economy is practical rather than absolute and must be understood in terms of a dominant case. Thus ἀσπίδας εὐκύκλους 4× as the type form requires (until -ου became available) a different genitive, ἀσπίδος ἀμφιβρότης 3×. This explains why we have πατρίδα γαῖαν, the dominant case, but never *πατρίδ' ἄρουραν after πατρὶς ἄρουρα.

synonymy in Homer, a large subject. Synonymous adjectives qualify the same noun[1] (ἐρεβεννὴ / κελαινὴ νύξ, νὺξ . . . μέλαινα); synonymous nouns are qualified by the same epithet (ἄορ / ξίφος / φάσγανον ὀξύ); synonymous adjectives and synonymous nouns can give a fine series (δούρατα / ἔγχεα μακρά, δολίχ᾽ ἔγχεα, δολιχὸν δόρυ, δολιχόσκιον ἔγχος. It is probably correct to think of these as spreading from a central term, in some cases doubtless with re-creation of the derivative phrases. The association of ideas must thus be vital. An ossified phrase spawns no progeny; there is no *ὄβριμα δοῦρα after ὄβριμον ἔγχος, only ἄλκιμα δοῦρα with the weak generic epithet. When an association is strongly felt it need not always be realized in phrases of the same syntactical structure. Thus 'heart' and 'hope' go together: we have both ἔλπετο θυμός and ἔλπετο θυμῷ; similarly ἤθελε θυμός and ἤθελε θυμῷ, cf. λάμπετο χαλκός and λάμπετο χαλκῷ, ἔντεα μαρμαίροντα and ἔντεσι μαρμαίροντα. An alternation of the noun between subject and object of a verbal form is seen in θυμὸν ὄρινε (-ω etc.) and ὀρίνθη θυμός and ὠρίνετο θυμός, κῦμα κύλινδον (nom.) and κῦμα κυλίνδων. The construction of an epithet may shift to words outside the phrase: χλωρὸν δέος and χλωρὸς ὑπαὶ δείους, τανύφυλλος ἐλαίη and (θάμνος) τανύφυλλος ἐλαίης. φρένες ἐσθλῶν has a substantivized adjective, cf. φρένες ἐσθλαί. There is also from time to time some interchange between verbal and nominal or adjectival expressions of the same thought. The phrase εὔρυναν ἀγῶνα θ 260 owes something to εὐρὺν ἀγῶνα Ψ 258; nor should we wish to separate μενοεικέα δαῖτα I 90 from τάφον μενοεικέα δαίνυ Ψ 29 or μενοεικέα πολλὰ | δαίνυσθ᾽ I 227–8. The noun ἔργα and verb ῥέζειν alternate in their αἴσυλα-,[2] κακά-, and μέρμερα-formulae. Sometimes the varying syntax may look more mechanical in origin: ἄγγελος ὠκύς π 468 only, is perhaps formulaic (also at H. Dem. 407, derivative from ταχὺς (-ὺν) ἄγγελος (-ον) 4×), but at ω 413 we have ἄγγελος ὦκα κατὰ πτόλιν ᾤχετο, as if the following consonant disarranged the poet's formula. Other lines reveal a mechanical linkage of words even more clearly. At I 360 Ἑλλήσποντον ἐπ᾽ ἰχθυόεντα celebrates a quality of the deep sea, cf. πόντον ἐπ᾽ ἰχθυόεντα 5×, rather than the Dardanelles. The Homeric bird (οἰωνός) as a scavenger has normally no ornamentation, but at ξ 133 the

---

[1] See W. Whallon, 'The Homeric Epithets', *Yale Classical Studies* xvii (1961) 97–142, for this feature in the ornamentation of personal names.

[2] The nominal formula has the by-form ἀήσυλα ἔργα E 876.

vultures become swift, yet only because the pariahs precede, κύνες ταχέες τ' οἰωνοί cf. κύνες ταχέες, ταχέες κύνες, etc. 6× : similarly δώροισίν τ' ἀγανοῖσιν ἔπεσσί τε *I* 113, cf. ἀγανοῖς ἐπέεσσι 3×. A special case of this kind of verbal suggestion is to be seen in such lines as Σάτνιον οὔτασε, δουρὶ μετάλμενος ὀξυόεντι *Ξ* 443, where in view of οὔτασε δουρί 11 ×, δουρί might almost be taken ἀπὸ κοινοῦ with both phrases. This is by no means an isolated instance.[1]

Association must be incorporated into our picture of Greek heroic improvisation alongside the formula. The Homeric text requires it as part of the solution, and it is on the evidence of the text alone that our model of the improvising method must first be contructed. Perhaps then in the hands of a skilful and prudent practitioner of the comparative method it may shed light on the craftsmanship of other heroic traditions and receive in its turn illumination. But the first step has to be the understanding of the Greek on its own terms.

I have spoken often of the 'further associations' of formulae, with an implication that the association of, say, a noun–epithet formula with a verb was looser or in some way subordinate to the association of the members of the formula. This is generally true as an analysis of the typical epic sentence, and will serve as a model for the poet's synthesis of the sentence, always assuming that the sentence is not hardening into a complex formula and is produced as a unit. The grammar, form, and position of the secondary term are very variable, e.g. φάνη μέγα ἔργον Ἄρηος *Λ* 733, but νῦν δὲ πέφανται | φυλόπιδος μέγα ἔργον *Π* 207–8; or γήθησε δέ μοι φίλον ἦτορ *η* 269, but ἐγέλασσε δέ οἱ φίλον ἦτορ | γηθοσύνῃ *Φ* 389–90. This is precisely what we should expect, for this is how word-association works generally. There is no need at this point to bring in the sentence-pattern, if this is to play a role in the poet's craft. For the location of the formula is determined, in so far as it is determined by technique at all, by the

---

[1] Cf. Τρωσὶ φέρειν ποτὶ ἄστυ, μέγα κλέος *P* 131 ; προτὶ ἄστυ, μέγα φρονέων *X* 21 ; παθὼν κακά, πολλὰ δ' ἀληθείς *π* 205 ; ὦ φίλοι, ἀνέρες ἔστε *E* 529 etc. ; ἐξαιρεύμην μενοεικέα, πολλὰ δ' ὀπίσσω *ξ* 232 ; ἵππους, ἡμίονοι δὲ *Ω* 697, cf. ἵππους θ' ἡμίονους τε *Ψ* 260 etc. With the usual punctuation Ἀρχεπτόλεμον, θρασὺν Ἕκτορος ἡνιοχῆα *Θ* 312 is similar, but we may take this as a conflation, cf. Ἀρχ. θρασὺν *Θ* 128 and θρασὺν ἡνίοχον *Θ* 89: likewise Πάνθου υἱὸν ἐϋμμελίην Εὔφορβον *P* 59, where ἐϋμμ. Εὔφορβον looks like a second-half phrase, but cf. Πάνθου υἱὸς ἐϋμμελίης *P* 9 (and nom. pl. *P* 23) ; ἄγριον αἰχμητήν, κρατερὸν μήστωρα φόβοιο *Z* 97 = 278, cf. κρατερός (-ῷ) τ' αἰχμητής (-ῇ) *Γ* 179 etc., and as a runover δεξιὸς ὄρνις, | αἰετός *N* 821–2, *o* 160–1.

shape of the complex word-group into which it is incorporated. Of course the sentences are patterned, but only in the sense that all speech is patterned and all hexameter speech patterned in certain ways. There is nothing to show that the poet is working within abnormal limits in this respect in what I feel to be the typical situation. There are indeed special contexts in which the sentence-pattern is important, but there is no basis for our generalization of their technique. Can we say that the poet's looser thought-associations show any limitations or other features that entitle them to a special place in our model of his improvising craft? Provisionally it appears to me that the status of the further associations is like that of the theme, of which after all it may be regarded as the very minimal form. The theme has its place in oral poetry because certain themes are more frequent and certain set thematic sequences are more regular than one would expect them to be other things being equal. Nor must we overlook the negative side of this frequency. Each use of a theme implies the lack of any wish or ability to channel the thought into any less familiar mode. It seems to me that a quantitative argument in parallel terms could be used of the looser word-associations. However, an association of any kind, no matter how loose it may be, is a formula in the making; and the more regular the association is, the more effective are the pressures for economy in diction and the extension of the formula-series. We can sometimes witness the results of these processes. Thus the association of 'tears' with 'eyes' is inevitable. But why is ὀφθαλμός so rare in association with δάκρυ and the very precise βλέφαρον so common? Moreover the βλέφαρον-phrases arrange themselves into a related group:

$$\beta\lambda\epsilon\phi\acute{a}\rho\omega\nu \begin{cases} \delta' \ \mathring{a}\pi\grave{o} \ \delta\acute{a}\kappa\rho\upsilon o\nu \ \mathring{\eta}\kappa\epsilon \quad \psi \ 33 \\ \mathring{a}\pi o \ \delta\acute{a}\kappa\rho\upsilon a \ \pi\acute{\iota}\pi\tau\epsilon\iota \quad \xi \ 129, \end{cases}$$

and with a note of the tear's destination:

δάκρυ δ' ἀπὸ βλεφάρων χαμάδις βάλε   δ 114
δάκρυ χαμαὶ βάλεν ἐκ βλεφάροιϊν   ρ 490
δάκρυα δέ σφι | θερμὰ κατὰ βλεφάρων χαμάδις ῥέε   P 437–8.

This is too amorphous for us to speak yet of extension and economy, but we may certainly do so of the association of λύω and γυῖα. We have in the active

$$\lambda \hat{v} \sigma \epsilon \; \delta \grave{\epsilon} \; \gamma v \hat{\iota} a \quad \varDelta \; 469 \; \text{etc.}$$
$$\hat{v} \pi \acute{\epsilon} \lambda v \sigma \epsilon \; \delta \grave{\epsilon} \; \gamma v \hat{\iota} a \quad O \; 581 \; \text{etc.}$$
$$\hat{v} \pi \acute{\epsilon} \lambda v \sigma \epsilon \; \mu \acute{\epsilon} v o \varsigma \; \kappa a \grave{\iota} \; \phi a \acute{\iota} \delta \iota \mu a \; \gamma v \hat{\iota} a \quad Z \; 27;$$

and correspondingly in the passive

$$\lambda \acute{v} v \tau o \; \delta \grave{\epsilon} \; \gamma v \hat{\iota} a \quad H \; 16 \; \text{etc.}$$
$$\hat{v} \pi \acute{\epsilon} \lambda v v \tau o \; \delta \grave{\epsilon} \; \gamma v \hat{\iota} a \quad \varPi \; 341$$
$$\lambda \acute{v} \theta \epsilon v \; \delta' \; \hat{v} \pi \grave{o} \; \phi a \acute{\iota} \delta \iota \mu a \; \gamma v \hat{\iota} a \quad \varPi \; 805.$$

As we have seen, the adaptability of the formula is already needed at this level if its further associations are always to be given expression. This is the level of the manipulation of data, and it is a level to which Homeric technique cannot by any means be reduced completely. The economy of the technique as a whole, not to mention the free ranging of the poet's thought, requires the existence of generative devices. It is at this point that the substitution-systems or phrase-patterns, properly controlled, have validity. The control and validity mean the degree to which we can establish a contrast between the Homeric diction and a hexameter diction which does not belong to an oral tradition. Consequently it will not usually suffice to list nouns of every class used with a given verb, or such like. The nouns must have something in common with each other on the strength of which we may posit a filiation between the phrases, otherwise the phrase-pattern will be indistinguishable from normal speech versified. If this requirement is fulfilled the substitution-technique provides the poet in this field of limited creativity with the equivalent of the complex formulae among his stock expressions. There can be nothing corresponding to the further associations of the formulae, because a word- or idea-association is not transferable, or at least not transferable in a casual way.[1] But as soon as thoughts harden into a stable verbal form then substitution is easy. In this way a central concept, as Ἀργεῖοι, lends some phraseology to a peri-

---

[1] To take an imaginary case, if a Θησηΐς were to be modelled on a Ἡρακληΐς, the name Θησεύς might come to mean as much to the poet as did Ἡρακλέης, but not quickly. It may even be the case, if the Iliadic plot is of relatively recent emergence in the heroic tradition and owes something to a Μελεαγρίς or an early Αἰθιοπίς, that such transference actually happened. But this is very different from the situation of a poet accustomed to thinking of, say, Ἀργεῖοι and Τρῶες who finds himself for a short space and in a single incident wishing to tell of Θρήϊκες (in K), Κύκλωπες, or Φαίηκες.

pheral one, such as *Φαίηκες*.[1] Besides this there is required some
means of making formula-like short phrases around which the
sentence may be constructed. The role of free creation cannot be
ignored, but the talent for free creation is, of course, God-given
and is not part of technical craftsmanship. In that sphere are
several productive artifices: the generic epithet, most prominent
among the personal names but by no means absent elsewhere;
synonyms, a usual aid among common noun systems; and the
adaptation of existing material, besides minor and incidental
devices. At this point we must now stop. Beyond lie the techniques of elaborating themes and building incidents and stories,
at which the genius of the poet must be most obvious. Yet even
at the humbler level of the traditional diction there is ample room
for virtuosity and skill or their opposites. The language may
be flat or vigorous, dextrous or cumbersome. In *ἀοιδή* there are
necessarily already planted the seeds of *ποίησις*.

[1] Thus: *Φαιήκεσσι φιληρέτμοισι* ⎫ *μεταύδα*
       Ἀργείοισι φιλοπτολέμοισι ⎭

       Φαιήκων ⎫ *ἡγήτορες ἠδὲ μέδοντες*
       Ἀργείων ⎭

       Φαιήκων ⎫ *οἱ ἄριστοι.*
       Ἀργείων ⎭

NOTE TO THE TABLES

QUANTITATIVE allegations about Homeric diction are not useful without precise definition of the field considered, otherwise the different totals will be as many as the counting scholars. The following lists are therefore in the nature of an ostensive definition of the material used in the present study. The aim in their compilation is to bring together a mass of material of which one could reasonably assume that the problems presented to the poet by its use would be uniform.

The basic criterion of selection is that the expressions are made up of a noun, other than a proper name or ethnic term, with a juxtaposed attributive epithet whether decorative or functional. This leaves one many decisions of inclusion and exclusion to make. I include:

(i) Expressions with substantivized adjectives. There is no fluctuation between nominal and adjectival uses in our two classes, but this does sometimes occur, e.g. μενοεικέα πολλά nominal at I 227, adjectival ε 267.

(ii) All apparent constituents of complex noun–epithet phrases. Thus αἴθοπα οἶνον ἐρυθρόν provides an instance of αἴθοπα οἶνον and οἶνον ἐρυθρόν.

(iii) Expressions which sometimes suffer elision in medial positions. Such elision is fairly common without being in any way typical.

(iv) Expressions which without changing their shape occasionally change their adjective to a predicative use.

I exclude:

(i) Personifications.

(ii) Complex groups, e.g. αἷμ᾿ ἔτι θερμόν, ὃν φίλον υἱόν.

(iii) Participial phrases.

(iv) Expressions which invariably suffer elision, e.g. αἴσχεα πόλλ᾿.

(v) Expressions of dubious metrics, e.g. ἱδρῶ πολλόν.

(vi) Expressions incorporating an enclitic connective, e.g. δύο δ᾿ ἄνδρες, χερσί τ᾿ ἐμῇσι.

The lists are supplemented, I hope not excessively, with certain symbols. The ciphers in the lists of regular formulae indicate the gross total of occurrences in the shape and cases quoted. In the tables of mobile formulae the four ciphers indicate the totals in the 1st–2nd, 2nd–3rd, 4th–5th, and 5th–6th feet respectively (two ciphers for 3rd–4th and 5th–6th feet in Table X). The prefixed letters M, E, and S indicate that the expression is involved in modification, expansion, or separation and is noted in the appropriate chapter.

Each principal table is divided into three parts. In the section A are put unique expressions, i.e. those phrases which have no immediate antecedents extant in the diction. I ignore here remoter possibilities of derivation which may be indicated by the play of synonymy, the generic epithet, association of ideas or the handling of substitution systems. In the section B are put expressions that appear only once in the shape quoted but whose word-association is otherwise attested. The classification of these depends on the value ascribed to relative frequency. If the attestation is once in the quoted form and once in another form we may speak of a 'possible formula', since expressions of the quoted shapes are usually clearly primary. Otherwise the phrase in its uniquely occurring shape is likely to be derivative. Declension is a common source of this class of expression. In the section C are placed the repeated formulae attested only in that position. Some of the mobile formulae will, of course, be found there also.

Given in the sections A and B are a small number of phrases which appear twice in the text, but as a result of fortuitous not formulaic repetition, that is, in circumstances of ring-composition, repetition of messages, execution of commands, or the like. These are κλίμακα μακρήν, ἄλλος ὁδίτης, φαιδίμῳ ὤμῳ (II. A); υἱέας ἐσθλούς (II. B); δήμιον ἄλλο (IV. A); ἑπτὰ γυναῖκες (IV. B); and ἄντιτα ἔργα (V.B) I have interpreted strictly this fortuitous repetition. One could go further, for the repetition of blocks of lines is common apart from these conventions: again the echoing of a line or passage within a short distance is very common, I suppose simply because the thought remains in the poet's mind. I prefer, mainly for the descriptive convenience rather than out of any conviction, to regard the repeated blocks as put together on each occasion and not as fixed (and therefore *recited*) passages. Repetition at a short interval is not easily classified, but I do not see why we should not look upon the stock of formulae as fluid enough to admit temporary members rather than devise rules for their exclusion.

Since the primary sorting of the material is in terms of the quantity of the final syllable, some expressions appear in more than one Table as a result of being declined or modified. There are thirty of these duplicates in the $- \cup \cup - \smile$ class and eight in the $\cup \cup - \smile$ class. The consolidation of the Tables would reduce the number of derivative formulae (since many dative singulars, for example, now join their nominatives and accusatives) and increase slightly the number of mobile formulae (see pp. 53 and 55), and also the number of formulae in general, since a few formulae (αἰπόλος and βουκόλος ἀνήρ,

ἀργέτι and δίπλακι δημῷ, ἕλκεϊ λυγρῷ, and πίονι νηῷ with their nominative and accusative forms) occur twice only but in different and diver-
sifying cases. I group ἀνδρὶ χέρηϊ (VI. B) with χείρονος ἀνδρός (IV. C),
and πατέρι ᾧ (IX. B) with πατέρα σφόν (XIV. B). In summary form
the consolidation gives the following results:

Position	1st–2nd	2nd–3rd	3rd–4th	4th–5th	5th–6th	Mobile	Total
– ∪ ∪ – ∪							
Unique expressions	14	36	4	20	119	..	193
Possible formulae	1	8	..	6	23	..	38
Regular formulae	3	16	1	12	147	102	281
∪ ∪ – ∪							
Unique expressions	4	33	..	13	23	..	73
Possible formulae	..	8	1	3	14	..	26
Regular formulae	1	20	1	6	18	68	114

TABLE I

Expressions shaped – ∪ ∪ – – in initial or medial positions

A. In 1st–2nd feet.

    Unique expression: γρηῒ καμινοῖ

    Positionally lengthened formulae: ἐννέα νῆας
                                   νηυσὶ θοῇσιν

B. In 3rd–4th feet.

    Unique expressions: μακρὸν ἐέλδωρ   E παιδὸς ἀγαυοῦ
                            λιμὸς ἀτερπής   παιδὸς ἀφαυροῦ

    Regular formulae: τούτου ἀέθλου 3
               M S τάφρον ὀρυκτήν 2

TABLE II

Expressions shaped – ⌣ ⌣ – – in 5th–6th feet

A. Unique expressions

θέσφατος ἀήρ νηλέϊ δεσμῷ μητέρι κεδνῇ
δεινὸς ἀήτης δῆμος ἀπείρων νηὶ ἑκάστῃ
αἰετὸς αἴθων ἔνδεκα δίφροι ἔνδεκα νηῶν
αἰετὸς ὄρνις πᾶσαν ἐδωδήν νόστος ἀπήμων
ἄσπετος ἀλκή θῆλυς ἐέρση ἀμφιλύκη νύξ
ἄνδρες ἀλῆται ἄφρονι θυμῷ ὀξέες ὄγκοι
ἀνδρὶ δικαίῳ ἥσσονας ἵππους ἄλλος ὁδίτης
ἀνδρὶ προΐκτῃ ἰχθύες ἄλλοι παῖδ' ἐρατεινήν
ἄνθεϊ λευκῷ ἱερὸν ἰχθύν ἐννέα ταύρους
φήγινος ἄξων εἰναλίη κήξ χάλκεα τεύχεα
χάλκεος ἄξων ἠπύτα κῆρυξ ὄβριμον ὕδωρ
ἀσπίδος αὐτῆς κλίμακα μακρήν νηλέϊ ὕπνῳ
οὔλιος ἀστήρ ἄφρονα κούρην φάρεϊ λευκῷ
ἄγριον ἄτην κρατὶ ἑκάστῳ χεῖρα ἀραιήν
θηλὺς ἀϋτή κύματι κωφῷ φαιδίμῳ ὤμῳ
ἡδὺς ἀϋτμή μητέρα χηρήν
γαστέρι μάργῃ

B. Possible formulae and derivative expressions

αἰπόλος ἀνήρ πίονι δημῷ μῆτις ἀμύμων
βουκόλος ἀνήρ ἕλκεϊ λυγρῷ S νῆας ἁπάσας
ἀστέρι καλῷ E S πολλοὶ ἑταῖροι πίονι νηῷ
βοῦς ἐριμύκους S πρόφρονι θυμῷ M πότνια νύμφη
S γαστέρα μέσσην S θήλεας ἵππους οὖρος ἀπήμων
S δαιτὶ θαλείῃ M κηρὶ μελαίνῃ υἱέας ἐσθλούς
ἀργέτι δημῷ S ληΐδα πολλήν M χειρὶ βαρείῃ
δίπλακι δημῷ

C. Regular formulae confined to 5th–6th feet

πίονες (-ας) ἄγροι (-ους) 3 S ἀνέρες (-ας) ἄλλοι (-ους) 2
πᾶσαι ἀγυιαί 7 ἀνδρὶ ἑκάστῳ 3
E πατρίδος αἴης 16 καρτερὸς ἀνήρ 3
ἄσπετος αἰθήρ 2 θέσπιν ἀοιδήν 2
αἵματι πολλῷ 2 M πάντες (-ας) ἄριστοι (-ους) 16
θούριδος ἀλκῆς 22 S ἤδε γε βουλή 2
ἄνδρα κορυστήν 3 βοῦν (-ς) ἀγελαίην (-ας) 5
S ἄνδρας ἀρίστους 2

TABLE II 133

E S εἰλίποδας βοῦς 2
E πατρίδι γαίῃ 7
  γήραϊ λυγρῷ 4
  δαῖτ' ἐρατεινήν 2
S δαιτὸς (-ας) ἐΐσης (-ας) 11
  πίονι δήμῳ 8
  δουρὶ φαεινῷ 22
M S ἡμέτερον (ὑμ-) δῶ 7
E S ὑψερεφὲς δῶ 3
  χαλκοβατὲς δῶ 6
  ἔγχεϊ μακρῷ 7
S ἄλλοι ἑταῖροι 3
  δῖοι ἑταῖροι 2
  ἐσθλοὶ ἑταῖροι 7
E S πάντες (-ας)
    ἑταῖροι (-ους) 16
  εἴκοσ' ἑταίρους 2
M S ἠέρα (-ι) πολλήν (-ῇ) 6
  ἤματι κείνῳ 5
S θυγατέρα (-ος) ἥν (ἧς) 6
E θυμὸς ἀγήνωρ 24
  νηλέϊ θυμῷ 3
  ταρφέες (-ας) ἰοί (-ούς) 3
  ἄρσενες ἵπποι 2
  μώνυχες (-ας) ἵπποι
    (-ους) 34
M E S ὠκέες (-ας) ἵπποι (-ους)
    31
  χαλκόποδ' ἵππω 2
  κυδάλιμον κῆρ 4
M κίονα μακρήν 2
  κύματι πηγῷ 2
  λᾶας ἀναιδής 2
  λαίλαπα (-ι) πολλήν (-ῇ) 2
  μάντις ἀμύμων 3
  παντὶ μετώπῳ 2
  πότνια μήτηρ 33
M μῆτιν ἀρίστην (ἀμείνω) 3
E μοῖρα κραταιή 9
  μῦθος ἀπήμων 2
E νηὸς (-ες, -ας, -υσὶν)
    ἐΐσης (-αι, -ας -ης) 19
E νηῒ μελαίνῃ 29
  νῆσον (-ῳ) ἐρήμην (-η⸍ 2

νηῦς εὐεργής 3
ποντοπόρος νηῦς 4
ὠκύαλος νηῦς 2
νυκτὶ μελαίνῃ 5
M S ἀμβροσίη νύξ 3
M νὺξ ἐρεβεννή 2
S ἡδέος (-εϊ) οἴνου (-ῳ) 4
  αἴθοπι οἴνῳ 3
  δεξιὸς ὄρνις 4
M ὄσσε φαεινώ 6
  παρθένος ἄδμης 2
  πένθεϊ λυγρῷ 2
  πήχεε λευκώ 2
  εὐρέϊ πόντῳ 6
  οἴνοπι πόντῳ 7
E πρώονες (-ας) ἄκροι (-ους)
    3
S ἀκάματον πῦρ 9
  θεσπιδαὲς πῦρ 8
  ὕδατι λευκῷ 2
S ἀγλαὸν ὕδωρ 3
  ἁλμυρὸν ὕδωρ 8
  υἷε κραταιώ 2
  υἷες (-ας) ἄριστοι (-ους)
    and υἱὸς ἀμείνων 4
  υἱὸς ἀμύμων 2
  ἄσπετον ὕλην 3
  δάσκιος (-ον) ὕλη (-ην) 2
  φύλοπις (-ιν) αἰνή (-ήν) 12
  ἀλλότριος φώς 3
  ἰσόθεος φώς 14
  φῶτες (-ας) ἄριστοι (-ους)
    4
M φωτὶ ἑκάστῳ 3
  χαλκὸς ἀτειρής 3
  αἴθοπι χαλκῷ 11
  ἤνοπι χαλκῷ 3
  νηλέϊ χαλκῷ 19
  νώροπι χαλκῷ 3
  ὀξέϊ χαλκῷ 37
M E χεῖρες (-ας) ἄαπτοι (-ους)
    13
  χειρὶ παχείῃ 18
S εὐῑεές (-ας) ὦμοι (-ους) 6

TABLE III

Expressions shaped – ᴗ ᴗ – ᴗ in 1st–2nd feet

A. Unique expressions

ἄμβροτα δῶρα	τλήμονα θυμόν	
ἄξια δῶρα	κῆρ ἀτέραμνον	
ἄφρονα τοῦτον	κρημνὸν ἅπαντα	Corrected:
μυρία δῶρα	λύματα πάντα	αἰόλαι εὖλαι
νηλέες ἦτορ	μύελον οἷον	
θάρσος ἄητον	φάσγανον οἷον	

B. Possible formulae and derivative expressions

νηλέα θυμόν

S χρύσεον ὅρμον

Corrected:

πάντες ἄριστοι

C. Regular formulae confined to 1st–2nd feet

ἄνδρα γέροντα 2

S δάκρυα θερμά 2

τέτρατον ἦμαρ 2

TABLE IV

Expressions shaped – ᴗ ᴗ – ᴗ in 2nd–3rd feet

A. Unique expressions

ἄγρια πάντα	τοῦτον ἱμάντα	τοῦτό γε τόξον
παντὸς ἀγῶνος	κέρδεα πολλά	τεῖχος ἄρειον
ἄνδρα φέριστον	λαὸν ἄριστον	τείρεα πάντα
θέσπιν ἀοιδόν	τόνδε μολοβρόν	φάσγανα καλά
ἄρματα καλά	μῦθον ἅπαντα	μυρία φῦλα
ἄσπετα πολλά	νείκεα πολλά	χώρον ἐρῆμον
δήμιον ἄλλο	οἶκον ἄτιμον	ψεύδεα πολλά
δέρμα βόειον	τόνδε γ’ ὄλεθρον	
χρύσεα δῶρα	αἰόλος οἶστρος	Corrected:
εἴρια καλά	σφοῖς ὀχέεσσι	τέσσαρες ἀρχοί
ἀνσχετὰ ἔργα	δώδεκα παῖδες	ἀσπέτῳ ὄμβρῳ
ἔργα βίαια	σὺν ἀκάμαντα	μείλανι πόντῳ
ἔργα γελαστά	δοιὰ τάλαντα	

TABLE IV   135

B. Possible formulae and derivative expressions

M φίλτατοι ἄνδρες	S ἑπτὰ γυναῖκες	Correpted:
S αἴγεον ἀσκόν	ἐννέα νῆας	ἀνδρὶ ἑκάστῳ
S ἄστεα πολλά	M ὄσσε φαεινά	πρόφρονι θυμῷ
S ἧφι βίηφι	δεινὰ πέλωρα	
γούνασιν οἷσι	M σοῖσι πόδεσσι	

C. Regular formulae confined to 2nd–3rd feet

M ἄλκιμον ἄνδρα 2	ἕβδομον ἦμαρ 2	S πῦρ ἀΐδηλον 2
E χείρονος (-ας)	ἡμέρη ἥδε 3	S ταῦτά γε πάντα 8
ἀνδρός (-ας) 2	ἄλλον ὀϊστόν 3	φάρεα καλά 2
E ἄττα γεραιέ 2	ὅπλα ἕκαστα 2	M S χρήματα πολλά 2
δάκρυσ' ἐμοῖσι 2	παῖς (παῖδ')	ἄξιον ὦνον 2
ἄλκιμα δοῦρε 3	ἀγαπητός (-όν)	Correpted:
λοίγια ἔργα 2	3	M S Τρώϊοι ἵπποι 2

TABLE V

Expressions shaped – ◡ ◡ – ◡ in 4th–5th feet

A. Unique expressions

ἄλσεα καλά	ἔντεσιν οἷσι	ἄργυφα μῆλα
E ἄλφιτα πολλά	ἕρκεα καλά	τοῦτό γε νεῖκος
ἔξοχον ἄνδρα	ἕρματα μακρά	οὔρεα μακρά
ἤμονες ἄνδρες	ἀγλαὸν εὖχος	πάννυχον ὕπνον
γλήνεα πολλά	ἡγέμον' ἐσθλόν	φρείατα μακρά
ἄνθινον εἶδαρ	ἄξιον ἦμαρ	ἄσπετον ὦνον
ἕλκεα πάντα	ἔξοχα λυγρά	

B. Possible formulae and derivative expressions

αἰθέρα δῖαν	S καρτερὸν ἕλκος	Correpted:
MS ἀνέρι τῷδε	M ἄντιτα ἔργα	S ἡδέος ὕπνου
ἔγχεα μακρά	M E εἴκοσι φῶτες	

C. Regular formulae confined to 4th–5th feet

ἀθρόα πάντα 3	ἤματα μακρά 3	ὄμματα καλά 2
M ἄλφιτα λευκά 4	ἤματα πολλά 2	ἄφρονι φωτί 2
ἄρμασιν οἷσι 3	M κίονα μακρόν 3	νείατον ὦμον 2
ἀγλαὰ ἔργα 4	E μείζονα λᾶαν 2	
M ἠέρα πουλύν 2	εὐρέα νῶτα 10	Correpted:
		ἀνέρες ἐσθλοί 2

TABLE VI

Expressions shaped – ⌣ ⌣ – ⌣ in 5th–6th feet

A. Unique expressions

ἄγγεα πάντα	ἔχθεα λυγρά	πίονα οἶκον
ἄγγελος ὠκύς	ζῶμα φαεινόν	αἰνὸν ὄνειρον
εὐρὺν ἀγῶνα	δείελον ἦμαρ	νείατον ὄρχον
ἀγλά᾽ ἄεθλα	πᾶσα θάλασσα	κάλλιμος οὖρος
μεῖζον ἄεθλον	δεξιὸν ἵππον	αἰόλον ὄφιν
τόνδε γ᾽ ἄεθλον	αἰόλος ἵππος	παῖδ᾽ ἀίδηλον
χεῖρον ἄεθλον	ἱστία πάντα	παῖδα συφορβόν
αἰγίδα θοῦριν	αἴθοπα καπνόν	παιδὸς ἑῆος
ἰξάλου αἰγός	λευκὰ κάρηνα	αἰνὰ πέλωρα
φοίνιον αἷμα	ξανθὰ κάρηνα	δεινὰ ῥέεθρα
ὀλβίου ἀνδρός	μήλοπα καρπόν	σήματα λυγρά
ἀγκύλον ἅρμα	αὐτὰ κέλευθα	σῖτον ἅπαντα
καμπύλον ἅρμα	κῆπον ἅπαντα	στείνεϊ τῷδε
ὄβριμον ἄχθος	ἄκρα κόρυμβα	ἱρὰ τάλαντα
πικρὰ βέλεμνα	καμπύλα κύκλα	τεύχε᾽ ἄριστα
ᾗσι βόεσσι	κῦμα κελαινόν	υἷε δαΐφρον
βρῶσιν ἅπασαν	πτῶκα λαγωόν	χάλκεον ὕπνον
δῖε γεραιέ	ὀξέϊ λᾶϊ	φάρμακον ἄλλο
ἀγλαὰ γυῖα	εἴκοσι μέτρα	σοῖο φονῆος
δέρμα κελαινόν	χίλια μέτρα	φωτὸς ἑῆος
εἴδεϊ τῷδε	ἄρσενα μῆλα	χαλκὸν ἐρυθρόν
ποικίλον ἐλλόν	μοῦσα λίγεια	μυρίον ὦνον
πᾶσιν ἔπεσσι	νεῦρα βόεια	ὥρια πάντα
σοῖσιν ἔτῃσι	πάντας ὀδόντας	

B. Possible formulae and derivative expressions

M S τοῦτον ἄεθλον	S σοῖσι βέλεσσι	ἕλκεα λυγρά
M E S ἄλλοι ἅπαντες	βουσὶν ἕλιξι	κεστὸν ἱμάντα
αἰπόλοι	M S πᾶσι βροτοῖσι	πότνια μῆτερ
ἄνδρες	S δῆμον ἅπαντα	πίονα νηόν
βουκόλοι	ἀργέτα δημόν	M ἄρσενος οἰός
ἄνδρες	δίπλακα δημόν	M πῆμα μέγιστον
ἀνδρὶ χέρηϊ	M πᾶσι δόλοισι	τοίσδεσι πᾶσι
S ἀγλά᾽ ἄποινα	νήϊα δοῦρα	

TABLE VI 137

C. Regular formulae confined to 5th–6th feet

μέσσον ἀγῶνα 2
E S ἄγριον (-ου)
αἶγα (-ός) 3
μηκάδες (-ας)
αἶγες (-ας) 5
πίονος (-ας)
αἰγός (-ας) 6
ἄλγεα λυγρά 2
πλησίον ἄλλον 9
M ἧς ἀλόχοιο 3
S ἄγριον ἄνδρα 3
βώτορες (-ας)
ἄνδρες (-ας) 3
S τέκτονες ἄνδρες 3
πηκτὸν ἄροτρον 3
πατρὶς ἄρουρα 3
E ἀσπίδα θοῦριν 2
ἄψεα πάντα 2
γαστέρ᾽ ἄναλτον 2
E φαίδιμα γυῖα 7
δαίδαλα πάντα 2
δαῖτα θάλειαν 2
πίονα δημόν 2
ὄνδε δόμονδε 8
μείλινα δοῦρα 2
S κάλλιμα δῶρα 3
μείλινον ἔγχος 6

ὄβριμον ἔγχος 13
μυρία ἔδνα 3
S εἵματα καλά 6
ὑγρὸν ἔλαιον 4
καρτερὰ ἔργα 2
S μέρμερα ἔργα 2
πίονα ἔργα 2
S ἐσθλὸν ἑταῖρον 5
πιστὸς (-ὸν)
ἑταῖρος (-ον) 8
ἱερὸν ἦμαρ 3
νηλέες ἦμαρ 9
ἀγλαὸν ἱστόν 2
ὑγρὰ κέλευθα 5
E κήδεα λυγρά 3
E κῆρα μέλαιναν 17
εὐρέα κόλπον 3
λαὸν ἅπαντα 5
E S μήδεα πυκνά 2
E S πίονα μῆλα 6
νέκταρ ἐρυθρόν 2
S τοῦτο νόημα 2
οἶκον ἅπαντα 2
E οἶνος (-ον)
ἐρυθρός (-όν) 7
πικρὸς (-ὸν)
ὀϊστός (-όν) 11
καρτερὸν ὅρκον 6

ἄσπετον οὖδας 4
μακρὸν ὀχῆα 3
M E παιδὸς ἑοῖο
(ἐμοῖο) 3
πατρὶ γέροντι 3
σῇ (ἦν) παρά-
κοιτις (-ιν) 2
καλὰ πέδιλα 12
M καλὰ πρόσωπα 3
πώεα καλά 4
αἰπὰ ῥέεθρα 2
ῥήγεα καλά 5
ἑπτὰ τάλαντα 2
τείχεα μακρά 3
M σοῖσι (οἷσι)
τέκεσσι 5
νήπια τέκνα 14
νήπιον υἱόν 3
ἄλκιμος (-ον)
υἱός (-όν) 15
υἱὸς ἑῆος 3
φάεα καλά 3
M φῶτα ἕκαστον 4
νώροπα χαλκόν 5
χεῖρα βαρεῖαν 2
S χερσὶν ἐμῇσι
(ἑῇσι) 4
χῶρον ἅπαντα 2

TABLE VII

Formulae shaped – ∪ ∪ – ∪ mobile between 1st–2nd, 2nd–3rd, 4th–5th, and 5th–6th feet

M αἷμα κελαινόν –:4:–:6
ἄμβροτον αἷμα –:1:1:–
αἴσιμα πάντα –:1:–:2
ὀξὺν ἄκοντα –:3:–:1
M S ἄλγεα πολλά –:2:5:–
καλὸν ἄλεισον –:2:–:1

ἀγλαὸν ἄλσος –:1:–:1
σοῖο (οἷο) ἄνακτος
–:1:–:1
ἄνδρα ἕκαστον –:1:–:9
δήϊον ἄνδρα –:1:–:1
ἀνδρὸς ἑῆος –:1:–:1

ἀνέρα τοῦτον −:1:−:1
θεῖος (-ον) ἀοιδός (-όν)
 −:1:−:11
αὐχένα μέσσον 1:−:3:1
γαῖα μέλαινα 1:1:−:5
E πατρίδα γαῖαν −:1:15:62
δαίδαλα πολλά −:1:−:2
δένδρεα μακρά −:2:3:1
E πίονα δῆμον −:−:1:2
σοῖο (οἷο, οἷσι, σφοῖσι)
 δόμοιο (-οισι) −:2:−:6
S ὀξέϊ (-έα) δουρί (-α)
 −:3:1:13
S δούρατα μακρά −:2:−:2
δώμασι σοῖσι (οἷσι,
 ἐμοῖσι) −:−:2:2
S δώματα καλά 1:−:3:8
ἀγλαὰ δῶρα −:−:7:13
ἄσπετα δῶρα −:−:1:1
ἔγκατα πάντα −:−:2:1
ἄλκιμον ἔγχος −:8:2:−
S χάλκεον ἔγχος 1:−:−:22
ἔθνεα πολλά −:2:−:2
S ἔντεα καλά −:1:1:3
θέσκελα ἔργα −:−:2:1
σχέτλια ἔργα 1:1:−:1
M S ἔργον ἀεικές 1:−:−:5
M E S οὗ (σοῖς, οἷς)
 ἑτάροιο (-οισι) −:4:−:8
ἤϊα πάντα −:1:−:1
δούλιον ἦμαρ −:1:1:1
αἴσιμον ἦμαρ −:−:1:3
μόρσιμον ἦμαρ −:−:1:1
νόστιμον ἦμαρ −:−:4:7
ἤματα πάντα −:4:−:26
ἤματι τῷδε 3:2:−:1
S ἄλκιμον ἦτορ −:1:2:2
M S πᾶσι θεοῖσι −:2:−:12
σὸν (ᾧ) θεράποντ᾽ (-ι)
 −:1:1:−
καλὰ θύρετρα −:1:−:1
M ἱερὰ καλά −:4:−:3
ἵν᾽ ἀπέλεθρον 1:−:−:2
ἱστία λευκά −:2:6:−

S κτήματα (-σι)
 πάντα (-σι) −:−:4:1
M S κτήματα πολλά −:1:1:1
κύματα μακρά −:1:1:2
κύντερον ἄλλο −:−:2:2
S θερμὰ λοετρά 1:2:−:−
 ἴφια μῆλα −:3:−:10
S νῆα μέλαιναν −:4:−:14
M S νηυσὶ θοῇσι 1:5:−:4
E νύκτα μέλαιναν −:1:−:5
λευκὸν (-ῷ, -οὶ) ὀδόντα
 (-ι, -ες) −:1:−:6
E αἴθοπα οἶνον −:3:2:16
ὠκὺς (-ὺν) ὀϊστός (-όν)
 −:1:−:2
αἰπὺς (-ὺν) ὄλεθρος (-ον)
 −:2:−:23
E λυγρὸς (-ὸν) ὄλεθρος (-ον)
 −:4:−:12
S πουλὺς (-ὺν, πλεῖστον)
 ὅμιλος (-ον) −:1:−:3
ὅρκια πιστά 3:−:7:4
M ὀστέα λευκά 1:−:−:2
λάϊνος (-ον) οὐδός (-όν)
 −:1:−:5
S χάλκεος (-ον) οὐδός (-όν)
 −:−:1:1
οὐρανὸν εὐρύν −:1:25:7
ἴκμενον οὖρον 2:3:−:−
M E S πατρὸς ἐμοῖο (ἑοῖο)
 3:3:−:7
πένθος ἄλαστον 1:−:−:1
εὐρέα πόντον −:−:1:2
οἴνοπα πόντον −:1:−:9
καλὰ ῥέεθρα −:3:−:5
S ταῦτα ἕκαστα 2:2:−:−
ἀγλαὰ τέκνα −:3:−:3
E S τεύχεα καλά 2:7:−:10
ἀγκύλα τόξα −:−:1:2
S καμπύλα τόξα −:2:−:5
ἀγλαὸς (-ὸν) υἱός (-όν)
 −:1:−:26
φαίδιμος (-ον) υἱός (-όν)
 −:2:−:14

TABLE VII   139

M υἱός (-άσι) ἑοῖο (οἷσι)
   1 :—: 1 : 2
νήδυμος (-ον) ὕπνος (-ον)
   —: 2 :—: 8
δῖος (-ον) ὑφορβός (-όν)
   —: 1 :—: 17
φάρμακον ἐσθλόν 1 : 1 :—:—
φάσγανον ὀξύ —: 1 :—: 6
οἷσι φίλοισι —: 1 :—: 3
ἄγρια φῦλα —:—: 1 : 1

E χείρονα (-ι) φῶτα (-ί)
   1 : 1 :—: 1
M S χερσὶ φίλῃσι —: 1 :—: 2
  S δεξιὸν ὦμον —: 2 :—: 10

Correpted:

  πάντες ἄριστοι 1 :—:—: 5
  ἀνδρὶ ἑκάστῳ —: 1 :—: 3
  πρόφρονι θυμῷ —: 1 :—: 1

TABLE VIII

Expressions shaped ◡ ◡ – – in medial positions

A. In 1st–2nd feet
  Unique expression: ἕκατον βοῦς

B. In 2nd–3rd feet
  Derivative expression: M ἀρετὴν σήν

C. In 3rd–4th feet
  Derivative expressions: S βροτὸς ἀνήρ
                   M S πεδίον πᾶν

  Regular formula: ἱερὴ ἴς 7

TABLE IX

Expressions shaped ◡ ◡ – – in 5th–6th feet

A. Unique expressions

γλυκὺς αἰών	πάϊς ἄφρων	σθένεϊ ᾧ
βόας αὖας	ἴα πάτρη	στρατοῦ ἄλλου
μεγάλη ἴς	πόδας ἄκρους	τρίχες ἄκραι
ὀλοὸν κῆρ	πόλιν αὐτήν	φλόγα πολλήν
δέκα μηλέας		

TABLE IX

B. Possible formulae and derivative expressions

M πυκινὸν δῶ   γλαφυρὴ νηῦς   πόδες ἄμφω
κύνας ἀργούς   M ὁδὸν αὐτήν   S πόλιν αἰπήν
S νέας ἁμάς   M πατέρι ᾧ   M ὀλοὸν πῦρ

C. Regular formulae confined to 5th–6th feet

βροτοὶ ἄλλοι 3	ἀδινὸν κῆρ 2	δήϊον πῦρ 4
δαῒ λυγρῇ 2	λάσιον κῆρ 2	πυρὶ πολλῷ 2
E S θεοὶ ἄλλοι 19	μένεῖ σφῷ 3	τέκεϊ ᾧ 2
S θεοὶ αὐτοί 6	M ὀπὶ καλῇ 4	M μέλαν ὕδωρ 6
S ταχέ᾽ ἵππω 2	M S πόλις (-ιν)	φρένες (-ας)
τεῷ ἵππω 2	ὑμή (-ήν) 2	ἐσθλαί (-άς) 4

TABLE X

Formulae shaped ⌣ ⌣ – – mobile between 3rd–4th and 5th–6th feet

M E ἕλικας βοῦς 1:8   E πόσιος (-εϊ) οὗ (ᾧ) 1:1
M πόλιν (-ει) ἄκρην (-η)   M πυρὶ κηλέῳ 1:6
1:4

TABLE XI

Expressions shaped ⌣ ⌣ – ⌣ in 1st–2nd feet

A. Unique expressions

ἐμὸν αἷμα   μένος ἐσθλόν   ἕνα παῖδα

B. Regular formula confined to 1st–2nd feet

Correpted: ἐνὶ δίφρῳ 4

TABLE XII

Expressions shaped ⌣ ⌣ – ⌣ in 2nd–3rd feet

A. Unique expressions

μέγ' ἄγαλμα	τρόφι κῦμα	στόμα μακρόν
τρί' ἄλεισα	Ε κύνες αἵδε	κακὰ τέκνα
μέγ' ἀναιδές	Ε λόφον αὐτόν	τρία τέκνα
βρόχον αἰπύν	ἕνα μῆνα	θρασὺν υἱόν
γέρας ἐσθλόν	γλυκὺ νέκταρ	ὕπαρ ἐσθλόν
γέρας οἷον	Ε πολὺν ὄμβρον	φλέβα πᾶσαν
μέγα δόρπον	μέγαν οὐδόν	ἕνα φῶτα
μέγ' ἔρισμα	πατέρ' ἀμόν	μέγα χάρμα
νέον ἔρνος	μέγα πεῖραρ	
ζυγὸν οἷον	πρόμον ἄλλον	Correpted:
μέγαν ἵππον	σθένος ἐσθλόν	βόες ἀργοί
τόδε κῦδος	σκοπὸν ἄλλον	δέκα οἷμοι

B. Possible formulae and derivative expressions

Μ ἐὸν ἄνδρα	S ἔπος ἄλλο	Μ μέγα πῶυ
S τόδ' ἄλεισον	ταχὺν ἵππον	Μ Ε σπέος εὐρύ
S μέγα δέρμα	ξύλον αὖον	

C. Regular formulae confined to 2nd–3rd feet

ἄορ ὀξύ 3	δύο κῆρε 2	Μ τόδε πῆμα 2
Μ θοὸν ἅρμα 2	κλέος εὐρύ 7	S πόσιν ἐσθλόν 2
ἄχος ὀξύ 3	τόδε λαῖτμα 2	S πύρα πολλά 4
φίλα δῶρα 2	ὅδε μῦθος 2	Ε ῥάκος ἄλλο 2
S πρόπαν ἦμαρ	S ὁδὸς ἥδε 2	Μ μέγα τεῖχος 5
10	λιγὺς οὖρος 2	Μ Ε S μέγα φᾶρος 3
τρίτον ἦμαρ 3	πατέρ' ἐσθλόν	S δύο φῶτε 2
στατὸς ἵππος	6	
2		

TABLE XIII

Expressions shaped ⌣ ⌣ – ⌣ in 4th–5th feet

A. Unique expressions

κλυτὸν ἄλσος	πολὺ κάλλος	τέρας ἄλλο
γόνον ἠΰν	μένος ἀμόν	χρόα λευκόν
μέγα ἔθνος	μόρος αἰνός	
μέσον ἧπαρ	ξύλα δανά	Correpted:
κακὸν ἄλλο	στόνον οἷον	δέκα πύργοι

B. Possible formulae and derivative expressions

M S ἄχος αἰνόν χθόνα δῖαν
M τιτὰ ἔργα

C. Regular formulae confined to 4th–5th feet

M βροτὸν(-ῷ, -οὶ)	δρυμὰ πυκνά 3	Correpted:
ἄνδρα(-ί,-ες) 5	M πόλις (πτ-)	E S κύνες ἀργοί
M S δύο γ᾽ ἄνδρε 2	ἤδε 2	4
M E S βέλος ὀξύ 2	κότον αἰνόν 2	
φίλα γυῖα 3		

TABLE XIV

Expressions shaped ⌣ ⌣ – ⌣ in 5th–6th feet

A. Unique expressions

πρόμον ἄνδρα	μέσα νῶτα	πολὺς ὕπνος
ἴα γῆρυς	ὅδε οἶνος	χόλος αἰνός
ταχὺν ἰόν	μέγ᾽ ὄνειαρ	
κλυτὰ μῆλα	ῥύπα πάντα	

B. Possible formulae and derivative expressions

M τόδε ἄστυ	M μέλι χλωρόν	πατέρα σφόν
μέγα δῶρον	M δύο νύκτας	M ποσὶν οἷσι
M S κρέας ὀπτόν	M ἐὸν οἶκον	

C. Regular formulae confined to 5th–6th feet

M S μέγα ἄστυ 2	μέσον ἦμαρ 2	S ὄρος αἰπύ 4
κακὸν ἦμαρ 7	μένος ἠΰ 6	ταχὺς υἱός 2

TABLE XV

Formulae shaped ‿ ‿ – ‿ mobile between 1st–2nd, 2nd–3rd, 4th–5th, and 5th–6th feet

S τόδ' (τάδ') ἄεθλον (-α)
  —:2:—:1
M μέλαν αἷμα —:3:1:3
  ἅλα δῖαν —:1:—:11
M S νέον (-ου, -οι) ἄνδρα (-ός,
  -ες) —:2:—:1
M φίλον (-ου, -ῳ, -οι) ἄνδρα
  (-ός, -ί, -ες) 1:3:—:—
M βέλος ὠκύ —:5:1:2
E βροτὸς (-ὸν) ἄλλος (-ον)
  —:—:1:6
  γάλα λευκόν —:1:—:1
E S δόλον ἄλλον —:1:1:—
  δόρυ μακρόν —:4:—:5
M E δύο δοῦρε —:2:1:5
E μέγα δῶμα —:3:—:8
M E τόδε δῶμα —:—:1:7
M S κλυτὰ δῶρα —:1:1:—
M E S ἐμὸν ἔγχος —:—:1:1
  ἐμὰ ἔργα 1:—:1:—
M S κακὰ ἔργα —:2:—:9
S μέγα ἔργον 2:11:2:1
M S τόδε (τάδε) ἔργον (-α)
  —:7:2:13
M S σὸν (ὸν) ἑταῖρον —:2:—:1
S φίλον ἦτορ —:4:4:32
M S θεὸς ἄλλος —:—:1:1
S θεὸς αὐτός
  —:—:2:3
S ἕνα θυμόν 1:—:4:—
S μέγαν ἱστόν —:4:1:5
M S κακὰ πολλά 3:3:14:2
S κλέος ἐσθλόν —:5:4:2
  κρέα πολλά —:2:1:1
E μέγα κῦδος —:4:13:—
M S μέγα κῦμα —:11:6:1
M μέγα λαῖτμα —:—:3:2

μέθυ ἡδύ —:3:—:6
μέγα νεῖκος —:1:5:—
ξίφος ὀξύ —:7:4:6
ξύλα πολλά —:1:2:—
κακὸν οἶτον —:4:3:—
S μέγαν ὅρκον —:1:7:1
δύο παῖδε —:4:—:1
μέγα πένθος —:4:1:—
M S μέγα πῆμα —:4:1:—
πόνον αἰπύν —:1:—:1
πόνος ἄλλος —:1:1:—
M πτερὰ πυκνά —:—:2:1
S σάκος εὐρύ —:3:1:—
μέγα σῆμα —:2:1:—
S τόδε σῆμα —:2:1:—
στρατὸν εὐρύν —:1:8:—
M S τάδε πάντα —:11:1:1
M φίλε (-α) τέκνον (-α)
  —:5:—:1
μέγα τόξον —:2:2:2
M E τόδε (τάδε) τόξον (-α)
  —:4:1:—
τρόμος αἰνός —:2:1:—
M E S ἐμὸν (ἐὸν)
  υἱόν —:1:1:2
νόθος (-ον) υἱός (-όν)
  —:4:—:1
M φίλος (-ον, -οι) υἱός (-όν, -α,
  -ες) —:31:7:27
S γλυκὺς (-ὺν) ὕπνος (-ον)
  —:4:9:2
φόνον αἰπύν —:2:—:1
M S φρεσὶ σῇσι (ᾗσι)
  —:11:17:3
M χρόα καλόν —:6:5:3
S χρόα πάντα —:1:1:—

INDEX

PRINTED IN GREAT BRITAIN
AT THE UNIVERSITY PRESS, OXFORD
BY VIVIAN RIDLER
PRINTER TO THE UNIVERSITY